D0215487

JOURNEY TO XIBALBA

Journey to Xibalba

A Life in Archaeology

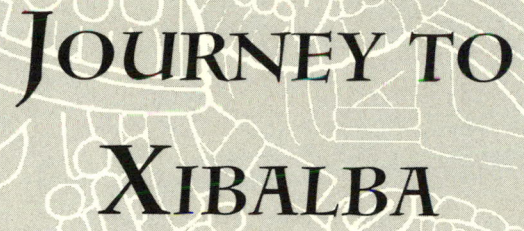

Don Patterson

University of New Mexico Press

Albuquerque

12 11 10 09 08 07   1 2 3 4 5 6

Library of Congress Cataloging-in-Publication Data

Patterson, Don, 1942–
Journey to Xibalba : a life in archaeology / Don Patterson.
p. cm.
Includes index.
ISBN 978-0-8263-4292-8 (cloth : alk. paper)
1. Mayas—Antiquities.
2. Maya mythology.
3. Excavations (Archaeology)—Central America.
4. Excavations (Archaeology)—Mexico.
5. Central America—Antiquities.
6. Mexico—Antiquities.
7. Patterson, Don, 1942–
8. Archaeologists—Mexico—San Miguel de Allende—Biography.
I. Title.
F1435.P38 2007
972'.01092—dc22
2007015080

DESIGN AND COMPOSITION: *Mina Yamashita*

CONTENTS

ACKNOWLEDGMENTS

There are several persons that need to be acknowledged for their participation in this endeavor. First and foremost is my wife, Marisela Garcia de La Sota, without whose support and patience the book could not have been written. In addition to her, there are a number of people who believed in the project and encouraged me to write the manuscript in the first place.

In this regard, words are not enough to express the gratitude I owe to my editor, the late Sareda Miloz. Even while struggling with the final stages of her melanoma, she took the time to edit the text and advise me. My only regret is that she did not live to see the manuscript in print. She did everything from turning my "Spanglish" rambles into readable English to motivating me to write when I looked for pretexts to quit.

Next, my thanks go to Davíd Carrasco and Luther Wilson. Aside from Sareda, they were the first to read the manuscript and astonished me by verifying that the manuscript had some merit.

Other friends who read the manuscript in one or more of its stages and offered advice and suggestions are: Ruth Cretcher, Jorge Hernandez, Don Knowles, Bob Haas, and César Arias. Many of their suggestions are found in the final draft.

Last, but not least, are the myriad Mesoamerican scholars and technicians who have taken this journey long before I did.

Opening Letter to Jessica

You cannot create experience.

You must undergo it.

—*Alberto Camus*

Dear Jessica,

One day my *tocayo* (same name), Don Knoles, a painter and free-lance reporter in San Miguel, encouraged me to write something about Mesoamerican archaeology for the public. He only requested that I not write about archaeological field methods and techniques, which he finds boring, and hinted that I might try to be a little philosophical.

So I began to reflect upon the possibilities. In the process, I asked myself if the sum or even portions of my life's journey would be interesting for others. This book began to take shape in my head, and you, Jessica, gave the book purpose.

You asked my advice about your education and professional life. You were at a crossroads and tormented by indecision. I understood this, having faced the same situation many times in my life. Indeed, I am tormented with indecision even as I write, because the fear of making a bad decision in my professional life is surpassed by my fear of giving you bad advice.

Although our lives have taken different paths, we have experienced some similar patterns. I have watched you traveling down the road of your life for twenty-seven years. You have migrated north to New York. This is the same age I was when I crossed the border south and came to Mexico. It was the beginning of something new and strange for me. While I did not end up doing what I thought I had prepared for, everything I had previously studied, when correctly applied, turned out to be useful. Like the person in Robert Frost's poem who stands in an autumn wood before a fork in the trail, you seem to have reached diverging paths in your life just as I did, as many of us do, at your age.

You recently expressed a desire to change your life, your dilemma being that you really like your boss but feel your job activities utilize neither your studies nor your potential. In all fairness, you do admit that you have learned something of human relationships and diplomacy as the Trade Representative to the U.S. Mexican Chamber of Commerce in New York.

I guarantee that you will be able to use these experiences in the future so that your time at the chamber has not been wasted. Just make sure that you utilize those social qualities and graces that you picked up there with your boss and fellow employees when you decide to leave. Unfortunately, I didn't always do this.

You have to make your own decision about what path you will take, but I have written the following tale so that you can examine a portion of the journey I took, the people and institutions that made it possible, and the decisions both good and bad that I made. So it is, each time I have sat in front of the computer to write, you have been present. You are the reason for the form and content that the text takes.

If there are any lessons to be learned from my life, it is important that I be truthful. Dr. Paul Kirchoff said, "If history is to be written, what really count are the events to which date and locality can be assigned—the rest are mere mythology." Hence, the people, places, institutions, and conversations in this journey are real, as my memory recorded them. If, on the other hand, I ascribe motives to any of the people in the tale, and I am correct, it is merely coincidental. Your mother says that I am not a good judge of character of anything that is Mexican. There you have it.

The Mesoamerican experience and my journey on the road to the world of Xibalba began in a book, the *Popol Vuh*.

Early on my adventure, I came across a reference in Coe's *The Maya* to an ancient sixteenth-century manuscript called the *Popol Vuh*. Miraculously, I found a copy of the first English translation of the manuscript a week later at a book sale at the public library in San Miguel. I paid eighty cents for the hardback copy of what the author of the edition referred to as the "Sacred Book of the Quiche Maya." It was difficult reading because of my complete lack of knowledge of the subject, and I was forced to consult all of the copious footnotes. This distracted me from the storyline so often that I had to immediately reread almost every page in order to make heads or tails of it. In spite of this, I couldn't put the book down. While I found the creation myths fascinating, I was particularly impressed by the story of the twins Hunahpu and Xbalanque, and their journey and experiences in the ancient Maya underworld known as Xibalba.

From the moment these young twins stood indecisively at the crossroads, to the end of the game they were destined to play, the twins were subjected to the deceptive trickery and punishments of dark lords that ruled the underworld with menacing, plaguelike names (Blood Gatherer, Demon of Pus, Demon of Jaundice, Skull Scepter, Bloody Teeth, and Bloody Claws). As one writer explained, "Even today their names bring to mind images of sickness, disease and death." Looking back with some amusement, I have probably encountered all of these archetypes during my journey and believe you will, too. That is why I have used their story as an analogy to our own journey through life. The mythical tale provides us with clues for the daily challenge of winning the end game.

There are eight chapters to this journey. I have named each chapter after the houses of testing in Xibalba. They are about the people, the environment, the financing, and the politics of the different archaeological projects I worked on over most of a thirty-year period of my life. Since only six houses are mentioned by name in the *Popol Vuh*, and keeping in mind Mesoamerican preoccupations, I have taken the liberty of creating two more. The Epilogue, titled "The Nine Lords of the Night," is about the vehicle I most often used on my journey, the National Institute of Anthropology and History of Mexico. It is known to Mesoamerican scholars everywhere simply as INAH.

▣ ▣ ▣

Prologue

The Messenger from Xibalba

"Shake the cobwebs outta your head, boy."

I was expecting Lady Xoc of Yaxchilan, but instead it was the voice of my father.

Funny isn't it? But almost every bit of advice and instruction that I recall from my father either started or ended with the word "boy." He never called me son. He never called me Don, even though we shared the same name. He always referred to me as "boy." As a teenager I hated it.

We were never close. We never had any of those father-to-son talks. Instead he enjoyed a singular vocabulary that consisted of the word "chores." All of our communication focused on these activities, which, as I grew older, he added to and accented their definition by his direct manner, stern expressions, and the pronoun "boy." "Shake the cobwebs outta your head, boy," he would say each time he caught me daydreaming. He must have done some dreaming of his own because he left my mother when I was fifteen. A few months later, so did I.

My great life adventure began in the train station in Pueblo, Colorado. I can't say there were any "great expectations" when I found myself on my own. I can still picture the Redstone railroad station where I awaited the Colorado Eagle coming down the track from Denver. (Although I know it was impossible in 1957, the music of Simon and Garfunkel's "The Boxer" wafts softly in

*the background.) I can still see, in the sweaty and trembling palm
of my hand, the eight dollars and change that remained after I
purchased a ticket to Lindsborg, Kansas.*

*I had no idea where Lindsborg was, but then it didn't matter.
I did not have enough money for recognizable places like Wichita
or Kansas City.*

*I didn't see my dad again until I was twenty-seven. I did not
know what to expect after twelve years without communicating,
but I soon found out nothing had changed. My father's first words
to me were, "I might a known you'd a had a mustache, boy." Then
he shook my extended hand and, grabbing me around the shoulder (he never hugged), ushered me into his house and presented
me to my stepmother.*

*Ten months later I left Colorado again, this time on my way
to Mesoamerica. Of course I didn't know it was Mesoamerica.
I thought I was just going to Mexico. Nevertheless, here I was
on the banks of the Usumacinta River kneeling in the eerie,
bat-filled darkness below a candlelit lintel in the ancient Maya
city Yaxchilan.*

"Shake the cobwebs outta your head, boy."

Damn it, Dad!

I must have answered the voice in my head because Thorrun, the
Icelander, motioned me quiet. I tried once again to focus on the burning
candles and to meditate. It wasn't going to be easy to bring Lady Xoc
back. I was skeptical. I suspected that I would just keep bringing back
my own ancestors.

*Reflecting on the last thirty-six years living in Mexico, I have come
to the conclusion that my journey to Xibalba began much earlier,
in some childhood portal of my mind. There, in the dim recesses
of my past, I picture the five-year-old boy sitting on the floor in
front of the Zenith radio, frustrated as he tries to adjust the dial to
make sure that he didn't miss a single word of another adventure*

of Jack, Doc, and Reggie in "I Love a Mystery." The episode that spurred his youthful imagination took place in some vampire-infested temple in the jungles of Central America.

I will probably never know if that was the moment that I was sucked into a portal and down the road to Xibalba. But the journey has certainly been more fantastic than I could have imagined, even in my wildest childhood dreams.

I hadn't been in Mexico more than a few weeks when the Lords of the Xibalba sent me a messenger with an invitation.

It was 1970. I was standing near the edge of the lake just west of San Miguel de Allende when the messenger suddenly appeared. He seemed to materialize out of the thorny huizaches, mesquites, and cactus.

His complexion matched the color of the dirt where he stood. He spoke a few words in a language that I did not understand and extended his closed fist. The gesture was not aggressive. It suggested the game of "guess which hand contains . . ." but I wasn't sure, and, seeing my hesitation, he took hold of my hand and motioned me to receive what was in his.

He placed a string of beads and a pendant-sized ceramic snakehead in my hand. As I examined the string of beads, I saw they were hand-drilled pieces of shells, bones, and small stones. The string was new but the beads were old. The ceramic head of the reptile bore long, narrow scales that retreated from the eyes toward the neck and fanned out above it like feathers. It also had two drilled holes, and I wondered why it was not strung along with the beads. I lifted my eyes, smiled, and focused my attention on the man.

My impression was that he was poor, and his clothing indicated he was a farmer. He returned my smile and his yellow teeth showed years of neglect. Because of the bright sunlight, his wide-brimmed hat cast a dark shadow across his forehead, cutting a contrasting horizontal line at the level of his bushy eyebrows. The many lines on his face were like arroyos created by millennia of erosion. The rest of his features—eyes, mouth, and nose—were comically pinched together in the lower

Figure 1 The Messenger (photo by Henry Miller)

portion of his face like a baby. He must have had some kind of nervous twitch because he frequently squinted his eyes closed. It wasn't a blink, because they closed completely and very slowly. But it was his tiny nose, curved and pointed like that of a barn owl, that tempted me to laugh. A strange odor emanated from him that reminded me of the smell of clothes after spending the night around a campfire. I was surprised that his feet, shod in the typical leather huaraches of the region, were without scars or calluses. "How does he avoid cutting his feet in all those thorns?" I remember wondering to myself. He was the earth itself. His dark eyes penetrated through my own shallow urban facade, making me feel uneasy.

Without speaking, he slowly turned his head, looking over his shoulders to the right and then to the left. As I followed his gaze I saw mounds of dirt and rocks behind him. Somehow, without any past experience, I knew that they were not part of the natural topography, but rather some ancient, man-made structures that were buried beneath the dirt and vegetation. When he caught my eyes anew he seemed satisfied with my puzzled expression and extended his hand outward once again, this time with his palm up. Without a word I returned the items to him. He smiled and turned to walk away into the *matorrales* (bushes) in the direction of the mounds.

I supposed that he wanted me to follow him in order to show me the mounds, so I started after him. But as I picked my way carefully through the thorny bushes my eye fastened on something black and shining on the ground near my right foot. I stooped to pick it up, and when I lifted my head again the man had disappeared. I took a closer look at the black, shiny object in my hand. I held it up to the sky and decided that I had picked up a small flake of obsidian. But when my focus returned to the earth below my feet, the magic occurred. It was as if a veil had been lifted from my eyes. Everything on the ground had taken on the characteristics of humanity. There were more obsidian flakes, pottery shards, and other broken fragments of the past lying at my feet. Ten minutes earlier I had walked over this past with no awareness of it. Something told me that I would never let that happen again.

In hindsight, this amazing moment brought together all of the elements for an equally amazing myth. Was it just one of those outrageously improbable coincidences that I had held in my hand the face of *Quetzalcoatl* (feathered serpent) and the power of *Tezcatlipoca* (smoking mirror) that day?

After describing the incident to my gringo friends in San Miguel, they suggested that the man was trying to sell me the artifacts. My mestizo friends suggested that he was an Indian and had spoken to me in his native language. There were still Otomí-speaking people living in the valley, they told me. They thought the old man's motivation was probably nothing more than his pride of the past, and that he had shared these elements with me as a courteous gesture. Nobody ever attached anything metaphysical to the moment but me.

That was the beginning. I have spent the past thirty-six years studying the ground, looking up only to encounter the Mesoamerican earth-colored people with strange histories, stories, and myths that even now continue to stir my emotions. Let the journey begin.

CHAPTER ONE

THE HOUSE OF GLOOM

San Miguel de Allende Project

SAN MIGUEL DE ALLENDE

Back in 1973, everyone in town knew the director of *Bellas Artes* (the National School of Fine Arts). In retrospect his name, Miguelito Malo y Bueno, fit his character appropriately. Miguelito, the diminutive for Miguel, was a small man, and, like all of us, he was both a little *malo* (bad) and a little *bueno* (good).

Don Roberto Lambarri, the town historian at the time of the tragedy, told me that Miguelito began his professional life as a pharmacist and suggested that was how Miguelito became interested in the pre-Hispanic history of the valley of San Miguel de Allende. Attending the ailments of *campesinos* (farmers) who had little money, Miguelito sometimes accepted pieces of pre-Hispanic art in exchange for medicine and services.

Whatever the circumstances, Miguelito put together a collection of artifacts and created a small museum in the corner room of his house. He never tired of dragging visitors off the street into his home, where he forced them to view his collection.

Once I met a couple from the United States on the corner of Hidalgo and Mesones, near Miguel's home. They stopped me to ask directions, and during the conversation they mentioned an interest in pre-Hispanic art. So we crossed the street and knocked on Miguelito's door.

It was impossible not to admire Miguelito's enthusiasm. We spent an hour in his house. After showing off his little museum, he took us into a bedroom and began to pull pieces out of drawers. He showed us, among other artifacts, a necklace of small, intricately carved jade seashells. I suspected they did not come from any of the sites in the local valley. Then he took us down the narrow patio to the far back wall where we climbed two small flights of stairs. On the roof was a small locked room. Inside, the floor was covered with piles of broken bones and pottery. Almost everything in the room still had patches of damp earth stuck to them, making the air musty. The space was so crammed that there was only a small dusty area in the center where we could stand single file among the artifacts. I noticed that three neatly bound boxes near the wall by the door were addressed to a museum in Houston, Texas. The top and front sides of the boxes were captioned in English with the notice, "Fragile–Talaveraware."

As we returned downstairs I asked, "Don Miguel, ¿Qué vas hacer con todas esas cosas?" (Don Miguel, what are you going to do with all those things?) He smiled and explained that when he died he was going to leave a museum to the community. "Pero no las piezas buenas!" (But not the good pieces!), he exclaimed, pointing downward to the landing we had reached. Below, I noticed a series of *tragaluces* (skylights) that indicated a room underneath the landing. "Las cosas buenas van enterradas conmigo" (The good things are going to be buried with me), he added, stamping his right foot emphatically upon the landing. I remember thinking that somewhere in his passion for the pre-Hispanic, Miguelito had crossed over the line into madness. I was also very curious about the contents of the room below us. Unfortunately, I never had the opportunity to find out what was there.

A few months later, in the patio of his house, Miguelito Malo y Bueno shot himself in the mouth in front of a federal agent and an archaeologist from the National Institute of Anthropology and History (INAH). His suicide was provoked by the new laws passed by the federal government concerning Mexico's national patrimony. As it turned out, Miguelito was just one of the twenty-two foreigners and Mexican nationals in San Miguel who were under investigation by the federal government in connection with the indiscriminate looting of pre-Hispanic sites and unregistered collections; some were accused of trafficking artifacts.

Miguelito's tragic suicide brought gloom and despondency to the community, and it was difficult for the residents of San Miguel de Allende to understand. He was a highly respected man in a community so small that everyone knew practically everyone else, and every third person was a cousin. Was not Don Miguel a pharmacist, a teacher, a historian, and the director of Bellas Artes? Was he not a humanist? Did he not treat the poor with charity by giving free inoculations and medicines when necessary? Did he not correspond with the great archaeologist Alfonso Caso, publish a guidebook, and write articles on the pre-Hispanic history of San Miguel?

Since then, I have often asked myself, "Why did Miguel, the illustrious son of the village, take his own life?" I figured that though it was a day like many others, he was caught in the middle of change. One day his activities were not illegal and the next day they were. Aside from this, I would love to excavate his cemetery plot to see if someone made good on his wishes.

In the community's mind the government was responsible for the suicide. The INAH was blamed, especially the archaeologist who was present at the time of Miguel's death.

The massive disappearance and/or destruction of the archaeological patrimony along the middle portion of the Río Laja took place during the twentieth century from the late fifties through the early seventies. Every site in the valley was affected.

Dozens of these pre-Hispanic settlements disappeared under water when the Allende dam was inaugurated in 1969. Ironically, this may have been a blessing. While they are unavailable for investigation at present, the large amount of silt deposited on these sites over the subsequent decades may actually protect them for future research. The majority of the sites in the valley suffered damage due to "pot hunters." Although some of the looting was casual, there was a semiorganized group of individuals who in one way or another assisted in the systematic destruction of these sites. And it involved some of San Miguel's most prominent foreign residents: Stirling Dickinson, Robert Somerlott and Bob Scott, and Janet and Mack Reynolds, to name just a few.

While most of the campesinos in the valley call the pre-Hispanic mounds *cuecillos*, the people of Tierra Blanca de Abajo call them *panteones* (cemeteries). In personal conversations with me, they compared their involvement to that of a *tianguis* (market) around the cemeteries. The buyers from San Miguel would line up along the sides of the diggers' pot holes and directly purchase artifacts held up to them from the burials. The activity clearly shows the financial motivation of the diggers: they had a ready market for the pots they had dug up.

The acquirers' motivations were a bit more varied, though no less destructive. Some, like Miguelito, were academically curious about the ancient peoples of the valley. Others in the community were simply collectors and displayed the artifacts to curious visitors on shelves or specially made cases in their homes. Some, like the campesinos, were motivated by commerce and sold artifacts locally in their stores and shops. Still others shipped the artifacts abroad.

I knew many of these people personally, and their attitude about their involvement was nonchalant. Response to any criticism was answered with the packaged phrase, "Everybody does it!" They treated these excursions into the countryside as "outings" or picnics. "We went to the peanut fields near Salvatierra for a dig last Sunday!" one collector exclaimed.

Far from the legislative palaces and academic debate at universities concerning pot hunters, most of those involved locally were stunned in the aftermath of the new laws governing the national patrimony. One of the intellectually curious, Robert Somerlott, confessed to me years later that although he had broken no laws prior to 1973, he felt guilty about the loss of information and the damage that had been done to the sites in the valley.

Ironically, Miguelito's death and descent into Xibalba had at least two positive results. First, the rampant looting of the sites in the valley stopped for nearly three decades. Second, since I accidentally inherited nine pre-Hispanic ceramic pipes from his collection, it indirectly inspired me to find out more about the pre-Hispanic history of the valley.

My mother-in-law, Doña Maruca de La Sota Zamorano, owned a bakery store across the street from Miguel's house. Although it was a small, one-room bakery, the property that extended behind it was large. One day she asked me to examine the property, as she was thinking of building some rooms back there. In order to get a better view of the property I climbed a ladder until my head reached the roof of the bakery. There on the roof in front of my eyes were pieces of broken pottery.

I knew immediately that at least some of the shards were pre-Hispanic. Deer antlers and primitive heads of birds and lizards were grouped together right under my nose. I was so excited that I completely forgot why I was standing on the ladder. I scrambled to collect the shards and discovered I held what appeared to be a number of broken ceramic pipes in my hands. There was no question in my mind that Miguel Malo y Bueno had thrown them across the street from the roof of his own house, perhaps on the very day he committed suicide.

I gathered up the shards and placed them in a plastic bag from the bakery. I spent the next few days patiently gluing the pieces together. When I finished, I had nine amazing zoomorphic ceramic pipes that I was afraid to show to anyone. In accordance with the new laws, I wasn't supposed to have them. At least that was what I thought at the time. Fearful that the *Federales* would descend upon me at any moment, I carefully wrapped them in paper, put them in a cardboard box, and stored them on a shelf in my library. They stayed there forgotten for some time until one day a young archaeologist friend, Ben Brown, asked if he could consult one of my books.

He returned from the library with the box in his hands and an accusatory expression on his face. After I explained how the pipes came into my possession, he suggested I get in contact with Emilio Bejarrano, an archaeologist who worked for INAH in the state of Guanajuato. I reluctantly agreed and asked Ben to introduce me. That was how I first met the young archaeologist who had been in the patio of Miguelito's house the day of his suicide.

Because of the rumors and gossip making the rounds of San Miguel after Miguelito's death, I was expecting a troll. The most disconcerting rumor was that Bejarrano had shot Miguelito in the face. I was very nervous that morning as I awaited his arrival.

Emilio, soft-spoken, patient, considerate, and extremely proper, was certainly not the monster I had expected. He listened to me attentively, joked, suggesting that I should be in jail, and then told me I had two options. I could either register the pipes and keep them or turn them over to the INAH. I chose the latter.

We took photos of the pipes and Emilio helped me write a letter in Spanish explaining how they came into my possession. Afterward, we took the pipes over to the small museum at Bellas Artes where I turned them over to an INAH staff member who gave me a receipt in return.

I thought that my association with the young archaeologist was over, but the road to Xibalba held many surprises.

THE PIT

Shortly after the appearance of the "messenger," I began to visit the countryside as often as possible. To get to sites in the valley I drove, walked, traveled by horseback, and twice flew over the intriguing ruins of the Cañada de la Virgen. On one trip we flew so low that my friends, seeing my photographs, thought I had visited the site on foot. Most frequently, I went with a friend.

Al Desmond, thin, white-haired, and goateed, looked like every drawing or sculpture I had ever seen of Don Quixote. Des, as everybody called him, lived in San Miguel long before I arrived. He was a veteran artillery officer during World War II and the calmest, most tranquil man I have ever met.

He lived meagerly in a small house that he owned on Calle Chorro. Where his money came from I never asked, and the little he had was spent on books and magazines. In fact, anyone visiting Des would have to remove batches of *Scientific American* and *National Geographic* from a chair to sit down. He was a self-trained Egyptologist and spent hours reading Egyptian hieroglyphic grammar books.

Our interest in the pre-Hispanic history of the valley of San Miguel called us to the countryside almost every weekend. Des had a funny-looking German vehicle called a Hauffllinger that looked like a cross between a Jeep and a foreshortened half-track. It wasn't very comfortable, but with its short wheelbase it would go just about any-where. We began to map the sites in the area and kept folders with drawings, notes, and photographs of the cuecillos that we visited.

Early one Saturday afternoon, returning from the countryside, we parked the vehicle behind the Instituto Allende and headed for the coffee shop. As we approached one of the back patios, we saw that workmen had removed a portion of the stone surface and had dug a large, square hole behind the eighteenth-century hacienda chapel.

"Wouldn't it be funny if they found something pre-Hispanic," Des joked, as we approached the area.

Curious, we walked over to the edge of the pit where, much to our surprise, broken pottery shards and bones were visible on the north and east walls of the hole. Stunned by the immediate confirmation of Des's prophecy, we stood looking down into the pit for several moments as if mesmerized.

I don't recall who spoke or jumped into the pit first but we found ourselves examining it in astonishment. By anyone's standards we were amateurs, but it was obvious from the pottery shards that we were look-ing at the remains of the same peoples we had come to know at other sites in the valley.

The workmen told us they were digging the pit to place a water stor-age container for the Art and Language School. I requested that they stop digging until I could talk with the owner, Doña Nell Harris Fernandez.

It turned out that Doña Nell was out on the golf course, so Des drove me to the country club. I walked around the fairways until I spotted Nell playing with her foursome. Tactfully, I waited until she made a good drive and then approached her.

"Don, what are you doing here?" she asked, surprised and even delighted to see me. Her smile made me relax. She was obviously in a good mood after her long drive down the fairway.

I quickly explained what the workmen had uncovered in the pit they were digging and asked if I could call the INAH in Guanajuato to see if the remains were important. I added that this might get the Instituto a little free publicity for the school. She cast a deep and piercing look into my eyes for several seconds, as if examining me for any hidden agenda, and to my great relief she smiled indulgently and agreed.

My departure for the parking lot was polite but abrupt. I wanted to give Des the good news.

When we returned to the Instituto, I went directly to the office of Stirling Dickinson, the director. He didn't have the phone number of INAH but suggested I call the famous muralist Chavez Morado.

Although I had never met the artist, I was familiar with his work in Guanajuato as well as his participation in the "Fountain of Rain" sculpture in the entrance to the National Museum of Anthropology and History in Mexico City.

Señor Morado listened patiently to my stumbling Spanish. Yes, he would report the find to an archaeologist and leave word with Stirling Dickinson about the date and time of the archaeologist's arrival.

In preparation, Des and I commandeered student volunteers. We made a long, narrow box frame and stapled a fine wire mesh to it as a screening bin. This was mounted on a single square leg and loosely bolted to the box frame above so that it could be shaken back and forth easily.

For the next two days we carefully screened the earth that the workmen had dug from the pit, and then the archaeologist from INAH arrived. It was Emilio Bejarrano. After examining the sides of the excavated pit, Emilio surprised me by asking, "What do you propose to do here?"

I was startled by his question. I didn't have any idea, so I winged it. "Well, I suppose the first thing would be to continue screening the piles of dirt surrounding the pit." Emilio nodded his approval and then told me that in the next few days while we were occupied with this task he would talk to the owner of the property and get permission from INAH to excavate the area.

I walked with Emilio to his car where he took a book out of the glove compartment and handed it to me. It was a hardcover first edition of Sir Richard Mortimer Wheeler's *Archaeology from the Earth*. He told me to begin reading it and that he would contact me in a couple of days.

The little group screening along the side of the open pit attracted a lot of attention. Between classes the students would stop by to see what we had found. We kept three cardboard boxes alongside the screening activity and allowed the curious students to reach in and handle the pottery shards, bone fragments, and worked pieces of stone. It was like putting gold dust in front of a prospector. Touching the artifacts gave the students the fever. As a result, more students volunteered than we could handle. When Emilio returned two days later, we had completed the task of screening the earth.

THE EXCAVATION

For the next few months, Sir Mortimer Wheeler was my god and the author of my Bible. I consulted *Archaeology from the Earth* every day, reading and rereading every chapter and paragraph. From the very beginning, I made photocopies of the chapters and handed them out to my student volunteers. Sometimes I was only a chapter ahead of them.

At the same time, I began to study everything I could get my hands on concerning Mexico and her pre-Hispanic past. The volunteer library in San Miguel helped get me started, and for a town of fifteen thousand inhabitants it had an exceptional number of relevant books for that purpose.

I started with Michael Coe's *Mexico* and *The Maya*, and from his bibliographies began to search for other books. It was Dr. Coe who made me aware for the first time of the Maya Otherworld, Xibalba. I couldn't wait to get my hands on the sacred book of the Quiché Maya, the *Popol Vuh*. But it was the magnificently illustrated adventure and travel books of Stevens and Catherwood that made me dream of the rain forest.

Meanwhile, under Emilio's direction, we laid out a string-grid of thirty-five square meters. Four students volunteered to work at the site before, after, and between their other classes. With Des and me there were six in total. Emilio instructed us to put two students in each square meter, and alternate each excavation unit like a chessboard. We started excavating at the maximum distance from where we supposed there might be something intact. Emilio stayed with us during the first week and after that he showed up once or twice a week to see our progress and look over our records and diaries.

The work progressed slowly and meticulously. Our lack of experience dictated that we be super careful. We measured, drew, photographed, and registered every rock, root, pebble, and stain. This was my opportunity to see the difference between the digging of the pot hunters and the disciplined work that surrounds an archaeological excavation.

The process was largely boring, but occasionally someone came up with a fragment of a human bone or a cluster of pottery shards and we attacked our chore with renewed enthusiasm. When we found our first complete artifact, the school's entire attention focused on us, and we were forced to isolate the area of the excavation with ropes to keep the rest of the students away. During this time Enrique Nalda, an archaeologist from the National School of Anthropology and History, visited the excavation.

After presenting himself to me he walked around the area, examining it thoroughly. Then he squatted down on the edge of the excavation and said, "This is great work. Too bad you can't work for INAH."

"Excuse me, why can't I work for INAH?" I asked.

"INAH doesn't hire gringos."

He said it quite matter-of-factly, and I didn't bother to question him further. I suppose I was still in awe of archaeologists and too timid to pursue the issue. But the statement "INAH doesn't hire gringos" took root in my brain, and I was bound and determined to find out why.

It took us so long to complete the work that the rainy season caught up with us and we were forced to construct a jerry-rigged canvas cover to protect the excavations.

Eventually we hit pay dirt, though it didn't appear to be very much. We found a thin section of very fine, white powdery substance. It was more than just a stain and extended in varying thickness for over a meter. At first we didn't know what to make of it. Only after another day of meticulous excavation did we resolve the mystery. The white substance was the remains of a stucco floor, and directly beneath it bones and pottery shards began to appear.

When we finished, we suspected that we had discovered a residential dwelling. It wasn't a very big area; an oval pit, no more than two by three meters and thirty centimeters deep, had been dug into the natural stratum of the local bedrock. The floor of the oval pit had been covered at one time with a layer of stucco. Beneath the stucco we found three separate burials cut into the bedrock.

The first one we excavated contained a complete and articulated skeleton that our reference books defined as a primary burial. At the feet of the deceased we found the partial human remains of another individual or a secondary burial. In total we found three burial pits under the floor, which contained two primary and three secondary burials.

In 1974 INAH had only a minor delegation in the state of Guanajuato. Emilio used his house as an office. Access to specialists, such as a physical anthropologist who could give us important information concerning the skeletons, was a problem. With no funds to pay for a specialist to examine the remains, our only alternative would have been to exhume, package, and transport them to INAH's labs in Mexico City. But with the growing idea that these burials should be on display to the public, we chose to wait until we could bring a specialist to the site.

Meanwhile, the restoration of the pottery from the burials took place in my home. This was the first of many times that my house would become the center and focus of INAH projects. Our colonial house on Calle Jesus had the typical large rooms and high ceilings of the viceregal architecture of San Miguel de Allende. In one of these large rooms we set up long worktables. Fifteen cardboard boxes filled with sand were the operation centers. We used each box of sand to reconstruct a specific pot by placing pottery shards upright into the sand. When we found the next corresponding shard it was balanced upon the other and then glued. This was both a balancing act and a gigantic, complex jigsaw puzzle. Small as our excavation was, there were thousands of pottery shards.

Emilio, after studying the ceramics, suggested that most of the pottery was made sometime near the end of the classic or beginning of the postclassic period. But there were a few unexplained Teotihuacán-type *floreros* (flower vases) in the burials from an earlier time.

Figure 2 Ceramic Laboratory (photo by author)

I am not an expert in ceramics. The discipline takes years and years of study and practice, and frankly, I don't possess the exacting patience required to be a specialist. Still, because of my outings with Des, by the time we started the excavation I was able to distinguish the pre-Hispanic shards from the ones of the colonial and modern periods. I also knew enough to distinguish intrusive shards that were not manufactured by the local culture. And by the time we finished restoring the pots from the excavation, I could tell the shapes of some of the vessels from the tiny shards I would see in the fields. The next step was to learn how these different shapes were employed by the pre-Hispanic peoples who lived along the Río Laja.

THE MUSEUM

I sat patiently waiting for Doña Nell to finish her scrutiny of the papers in her hand. When she finally looked over at me, she leaned back in her chair and appeared to relax.

"What can I do for you, Don?" she asked.

"I was wondering what you think about building a small local museum for the burials we have excavated," I said.

I could see she was beginning to reflect upon the request, and when the smile disappeared from her face I went on before she could say no.

"I was thinking that I could ask for donations from the students and community for the funds to build it. You know we have received quite a bit of attention with the excavations. I am sure people in town will want to contribute!"

She studied my face for a few seconds, and then responded. "Do you really think that anyone in this community is going to donate money for a building on private property? My property?" Before I could respond, she went on with the smug sarcasm of someone who knows what she is talking about. "I'll tell you what. When you bring me the first donated peso that comes from anyone in this community, I will pay for the rest!"

I couldn't believe my ears!

Nell Fernandez had a reputation with the students and a large part of the faculty as being a "tightwad." The students were always complaining that she needed to put more resources back into the facilities. The faculty complained about being underpaid. I suppose these criticisms are common in any institution in the world. But I knew one thing for sure: Doña Nell always kept her word. I couldn't suppress the widening grin that was swallowing my face.

I reached into the pocket of my shirt and handed her a $500 check from her neighbors, Les and Luella Hotsenpiller.

The look of astonishment on Nell's face will remain with me until the day I die. When she looked over the top of the check at me she began to smile, then she laughed.

"Don, you really sucked me into this one!" she said.

"Not intentionally, ma'am," I responded humbly. I resisted the temptation to point out that she had done it to herself.

"Okay. Bring me an architectural proposal and a budget."

"Thank you, I will," I said as I stood up to leave. When I reached the door of her office, she spoke.

"Don." She sighed, "Sometimes you try my patience. But I am glad that you work for the Instituto."

"Thank you, Doña Nell." That was the only time I ever received a word of praise from her.

Impatient to share the good news, I hurried out the door, across the patio, and up the back stairs to the site of the excavations where Des and some of the students were photographing the burials.

The walls of the new building went up while we were still excavating. In order to save money on construction materials, we used the stones from rubble that had once been part of the construction of the old hacienda. Once the roof was on, we began to work on the presentation of the findings for the public.

Emilio came up with the idea that we make it a small site museum, stressing the exacting procedures of an archaeological excavation. I suspect part of his motivation for such a theme was Miguel Malo's suicide and the subsequent gossip in the community. I didn't ask.

The museum covered about half the space of the excavation. The other half we eventually turned into a classroom, and, after communicating with a pair of isotope geologists from the U.S. Geological Survey in Denver, we installed a small lab for dating obsidian.

Doña Nell brought her friends to the dedication. Monseñor Mercadillo blessed the museum, and we opened the doors to the public. Most of the visitors were public school children and their teachers. Sometimes curious archaeologists from INAH would arrive to look the place over, but it was Joyce Kelly, author of *The Guide to Mesoamerican Ruins*, who gave the small museum some promotion. It was one of the first sites in Mexico mentioned in her book.

One day, shortly after finishing the museum, Emilio appeared, accompanied by a distinguished-looking gentleman who turned out to be Professor Gaston García Cantú, the director of INAH.

During the excavation and the building of the museum, I decided to study archaeology. Since I could not afford to go to the mountain, I brought the mountain to San Miguel. Once again I found myself in Doña Nell's office.

"The University of the Americas is going through a reorganization process and cutting many humanities courses from their curriculum.

This could be advantageous for the Instituto Allende."

"How could we possibly benefit from this?" she asked.

"Well, if they are cutting their Arts and Humanities departments then the Instituto might be able to pick up a number of these students. We already have art, history, and language and writing courses, so it is just a matter of getting the word to the students at the University of the Americas."

Then I brought up the underlying reason for my audience with her. "Also, we could add a few courses in anthropology and archaeology."

I could see from her expression that she was seriously considering my proposal.

"Don, you must realize that we don't have the classroom space necessary for creating new departments."

"Well, we don't need to construct any new classroom space if we start small. If we offer one or two classes, we can use the extra space behind the exhibition in the museum."

"Who is going to teach these classes?"

"With your permission, I can go to the National School of Anthropology and History (ENAH) in Mexico City and see if I can find professors for introductory courses in anthropology and archaeology."

"Well, as long as you make no commitments. First, find out if there are interested teachers and what they expect as salaries." Reflecting on the issue for a moment she added, "I suppose we will have to pay for their transportation to and from Mexico City."

Three days later, the first meeting took place in Mexico City at the Calle Reforma Sanborn's near the United States Embassy. One of the ENAH representatives who attended the meeting was Enrique Nalda. A month later, Manuel Gandara, an archaeologist, and Miguel Block, an anthropologist, were coming to San Miguel once a week to give classes at the Instituto Allende. Doña Nell agreed to pay their travel expenses.

To our surprise, the first students were mostly older foreign residents of San Miguel. Miguel Block was a social anthropologist trained with Marxist ideals, so the debates in his classes were often fascinating, and always exciting. For most of the foreign students who had been subjected to the Cold War, it was the first time they ever got a direct, full-strength dose of Marxist philosophy.

Although I didn't sign up for classes the first semester, I attended them every time I could. I intended to take the courses offered the next semester, but a telephone call to Yale changed my plans.

▦ ▦ ▦ LETTER CONTINUED ▦ ▦ ▦

I acknowledge that my first encounter with San Miguel de Allende was nocturnal and more than a little romantic in nature. I share it with you now because it remains the basis for my sentiment and passion for the Historic Center.

Thirty-six years ago I pulled into San Miguel at 11:30 p.m. on a Saturday night. It was in late May of 1970. I was a young man of twenty-seven. I drove into town on the narrow road that ran between what was then the single-lane traffic of Highway 57 and San Miguel de Allende. I entered the village on the northeast corner of the community.

Back then the cobblestones began out past Paco Garay's textile factory, where the asphalt pavement ended on the final curve. I had never driven on cobblestone streets in my life, and this jogging experience became a physical and audible background for the new images passing before my eyes. Indeed, every loose nut and bolt, suitcase and box in my brand new van began to vibrate and make noise.

Of course, I didn't know where I was going and drove past Calle Hidalgo and turned left up Calle Quebrada. I was more than just a little nervous because of the dimly lit streets. Adding to my anxiety was the fact that I did not see a car or a person on the street. My eyes searched every darkened doorway, niche, and side street for any sign of life. It appeared so devoid of humanity that I was beginning to think that I had either entered a ghost town or crossed over into the Twilight Zone. I began to question my decision for beginning this trip, "What have I done?"

When I arrived at the bridge overlooking Calle Canal I stopped and got out of the car to get my bearings as well as to look for someone to understand my gestures and answer my question, "Is this San Miguel de Allende?" There was not a soul around, but as I looked up Calle Canal, what I saw forever changed my life.

It was something comparable to walking into an art history book. The view was one of eighteenth-century images and textures. Stealing a line from Gabriel García Márquez, "Everything was so new I didn't even have names for them." Nevertheless, I began to take a visual inventory: the narrow cobblestone streets, the stonework, the ironwork, the wooden doors, the *bugambilias* cascading down textured walls of stucco, *cantera*, and/or adobe, the *cúpulas* of the churches, and the dimly lit *faroles* (streetlights). Most of the building facades were painted white back then, and the little light from the faroles created patches of friendly warmth for an otherwise dim, cool, and moonlit mystical scene. It took me a while to accept the visual shock. I actually thought a white rabbit might appear at any moment running up the street ahead of me like the one in Lewis Carroll's fantasy, *Alice in Wonderland*.

I got back in the van and at the next corner turned left off of Quebrada up the hill on Umarán. In less than two minutes I found myself in front of a gigantic, dark, and intimidating gothic cathedral. The blue moonlight accentuated the upper edges of the stones along the sides and front of the facade. I thought of El Greco's painting *View of Toledo*, but it would not have surprised me to have seen swarms of bats descending upon me from the belfries.

At first the plaza appeared to be as empty as the streets. However, when I was about to drive on, a shadowy figure began to emerge from the dark under a bronze sculpture of a friar and Indian. As the vague figure moved in my direction, I quickly ran through my head the only three phrases of Spanish I knew: "Buenos días" (Good day), "¿Donde están los baños?" (Where are the bathrooms?), and "Lo siento mucho" (I am very sorry). I decided that the situation called for the latter.

To my surprise, the person who walked in front of the lights of my van appeared to be a gringo hippie. This was verified when I rolled down my window and he spoke, "Hey man, you want a toke?"

I cautiously turned him down but decided immediately that this sleepy little hillside village was my kind of community. He kindly directed me to the hotel where he was staying, La Villa Hermosa. After helping me with the receptionist, we sat in my room and talked. I tried to get as much information as I could about the community before daylight.

The next day I discovered that San Miguel de Allende was not a ghost town but a small, lively community of fifteen thousand inhabitants. Later I learned that about 10 percent were originally from someplace other than San Miguel. Actually, there were almost as many transient students attending one of the art or language schools as there were foreign residents. I don't remember how many were enrolled in Bellas Artes or the Academia, but as I recall, there were close to eight hundred students taking classes at the Instituto Allende during those early years of the seventies.

As one might expect with so many young people in such a small place, the nightlife was awesome. However, how the participants moved from one place to another was always a mystery to me. I assumed that they walked, as there were very few cars in the village. Yet, I seldom ran into friends on the street at night. Occasionally one would encounter young native lovers in the doorways, framed romantically in eighteenth-century blocks of stone and completely wrapped up in each other.

On the weekends the principal hangouts for the foreign students and male nationals were two night clubs: the Fragua until midnight and then down the hill to El Escondido, where some remained dancing and drinking until daylight. Rarely, a young Mexican lady would be seen at these clubs.

Of course there were private parties almost every night during the week. A thirty-minute soda or coffee break in the Instituto Allende art store and coffee shop would generally provide an invitation and location of that evening's party. I sometimes didn't make it home for days at a time. For the students who attended the schools, San Miguel was heaven. Even teenage tourists managed to escape the scrutiny of their parents and were sucked into the hedonistic existence.

I recall one night in the Fragua listening to the conversation of two adolescent gringo girls at a table near mine. Neither of them appeared to be more than fifteen or sixteen years of age. I was wondering where their parents were when one of them, in a moment of pure youthful exuberance, declared to her companion, "God, I could never get away with this back home. My parents would kill me." I assumed she was referring to her age and the drink that rested on the table in front of her. For most of the foreign students, it was pretty much an atmosphere of *mota* (marijuana), sex, rock and roll, and artistic euphoria. Yet outside the student craziness, there was something in the dimly lit corridors of the cobblestone streets and my mind that slowly enveloped me. Eventually it dawned upon me: it was a sense of history and stubborn stability.

The moment I timidly began to make contact with the locals, I discovered a deep-rooted pride among them that crossed several generations of the town's residents: a pride for San Miguel's role in history and their families' participation in that history, as well as the subsequent respect and delight for the monuments and traditions built by their ancestors.

During the period of 1970 through 1985, the residents referred to San Miguel as their *pueblo* (village). The people of the village called themselves Sanmiguelenses. The people from villages nearby, like Comonfort or Dolores, called the people from San Miguel *Atoleros* because of the traditional beverage *atole* that was consumed in the community. The increase in the population during this period, if there was one, was not noticeable. In 1970, the community did not extend much in any direction beyond the sixty-eight square blocks of what is known today as the Historic Center.

The village was so small that my wife, Marisela, could tell me if I stopped to tie a shoelace or talk to someone during the four-block walk from the Instituto Allende to our house. In short, San Miguel was a place where you knew almost everyone you met on the streets and every third person was a cousin. It was easy to learn about San Miguel because Sanmiguelenses loved to talk about their history and brag about their ancestors. One of the first things I noticed was they were also quick to criticize the government even when members of their family were involved in it. I used to ponder how so many cynics could fit into such a small community. Apart from that, they were macho and adamantly defiant of almost all authority. I soon discovered that the people of San Miguel liked to party. And when it came to having fun, the gringos were amateurs in comparison to the Sanmiguelenses. There is nothing in the world like a Mexican fiesta. One year I made a calendar of fiestas and discovered that there were a total of 196 festive days that year. Ye Gods! Doesn't anybody ever work in the place?

A few of the young married Mexicans of my generation spent their weekend nights in a small club where Border Crossings is now located. It was called the Hosteria del Parque, and the rather plump Doña Josefina sang the most beautiful renditions of this generation's most popular songs. Sometimes, after midnight, the police would show up and ask us to lower the volume. Once they took the club's guitar, so I walked to our house and brought mine back, to a rousing applause from the fun-loving locals.

One of the great ironies of this period was that the police were the only authority we were not afraid of. They had no vehicles and carried no guns in the street. Some of them didn't even have complete uniforms. Their only armament was a whistle that they blew for their own comfort or during emergencies. Their most important task appeared to be arresting drunks during the Sunday market. The prisoners were kept in jail overnight and given the job of cleaning the streets the next morning. The one conversation I had with a policeman was pleasant. He was even sympathetic to my problem.

One night during my lustful youth, and before marrying Marisela, I tried to get Manuel Nava's grandmother to open the street door to her apartments (Farmacia Sta. Teresa). With a few tequilas between my ribs and spine, I knocked on the door rather loudly several times. About five or six minutes passed when a little window opened in the door and Grandmother, with an angry scowl on her face and a demanding voice, asked me, "¿Qué quieres?" It was more of an explosion than a question. I tried to explain that I wanted to visit the beautiful gringo girl that was staying in one of her second-floor apartments. She told me that nice girls didn't receive visitors at this hour and shut the window, leaving me standing in the street. Evidently, my loud knocks indicated that I was not her little grand-daughter with a basket, so she had called the police before answering me through her window.

The policeman arrived so quietly behind me that I did not hear his approach. My first realization of his presence was when he gently tapped me on the shoulder. When I turned and discovered I was being confronted by a policeman, I thought I was going to jail for disturb-ing the peace, so I began to repeat my intentions to him in almost a whisper. He smiled and raised his hands and shoulders and I realized that I was speaking in English and he had not understood a word. In my broken Spanish I tried to explain that I was sad because the old lady would not let me visit the young lady. He got the picture because as he led me gently away from the door he said, "Amor es muy dificil joven" (love is difficult, young man). I thought it better not to confess that love was not what I was looking for that night. The policeman walked with me up the street until we had crossed the *jardín* and he was certain that I would not return to bother Grandmother Nava and the residents of her neighborhood.

Every Sunday was market day and it extended down Insurgentes Street for blocks. All of the farmers, cowboys, and families came into San Miguel from their village on market day. The town would be full of horses and burros with an occasional goat or pig. It is true that the odor of the town changed on Sundays, but quite frankly I prefer the barnyard smell to that of the dog that has been defecating in the street in front of my house for the last two mornings. Of course there were dogs in the streets back then as well, and one in particular stood out from among all the rest.

Ralph was to San Miguel what the Tramp was to Walt Disney. Ralph owned the streets of San Miguel. This was an important accomplishment, as he was the alpha male for packs of wild dogs that roamed the streets. The dogs were probably the only thing that made me nervous walking the streets after dark. After most of the human population was inside their houses, the dogs would cluster into snarling packs around the fifty-five-gallon drums that were used for garbage. Ralph never joined these packs at night fighting over food. Instead, he made friends with people during the day and remarkably always found someone to invite him home for dinner. Sometimes he would spend a night or two but always moved on. At one point, one of the students donated a red handkerchief and tied it around Ralph's neck. He paraded around town in color for a short while. Ralph seemed to have a second sense about humans and joined them in places they liked to gather. One night at the movie theater he came in and sat in the aisle for a few minutes, intently studying the screen. Then, as if he was the *New York Times* movie critic, he began to howl. Everyone in the theater agreed with him and began to laugh. The movie was awful.

Another time I was sitting with a friend, Rick Rosemairn, in the restaurant and pharmacy of Barbara Dobarganes. A middle-aged and regal-looking gringo lady walked in with a toy poodle on a leash. She stood in front of the drugstore counter for a few minutes talking with the store attendant. Ralph came in and began to sniff about the poodle. When the lady discovered Ralph's presence, she scooped her precious little poodle up into the safety of her arms and looked back at Ralph with a superior sneer. Ralph calmly lifted his leg and peed on her shoes.

In spite of my great love and passion for San Miguel, my life was about to take another turn south—this time to Guatemala.

▣ ▣ ▣

CHAPTER TWO

THE HOUSE OF PORTALS

FLAAR Project

DR. MICHAEL COE

I suppose I was somewhat naive. I just kept thinking of Michael Coe's *The Maya*, and what I could do as an artist for his next publication. So I called Yale.

The secretary at Yale, who filtered all his calls, informed me that Dr. Coe was on sabbatical leave and would not be back until the following year. She kindly asked if I wanted to leave a message. What do you say to a request that will take a year to get a response? I thanked her for her time and politely asked for her to tell Dr. Coe when he returned that Professor Don Patterson had called from the Instituto Allende in Mexico. The word *Mexico* did the trick. She actually gasped, and within seconds I had Dr. Michael Coe's home telephone number.

I have often imagined the scene in the doctor's home that day. He was certainly not expecting a telephone call from me. He was probably sitting at his desk in a room full of books in front of his typewriter with his *Maya Scribe* manuscript scattered in piles before him. His reputation cast a huge shadow over the material on his desk, up the bookshelves, and on the outer edge of the ceiling. And at that moment it filtered even through the telephone wires. I was one nerve short of panic.

I was finding it difficult even to breathe as I introduced myself and offered my services. His momentary silence after I had finished was terrifying. Later I thought he was probably thinking of firing his secretary; instead, he politely informed me that he already had four artists working for him.

Not to be completely rejected, I bluffed: "I have ten artists at my disposal and could produce 4,000 man-hours of work per month."

"Wow!" he exclaimed. "I have an idea. Why don't you call Nicholas Helmuth at the Foundation for Latin American Anthropological Research (FLAAR) in Guatemala City? I talk with him often, and I'll tell him that you might call. I am sure he can use your services," he added.

I endured a few moments of excited silence as Dr. Coe looked for the telephone number for FLAAR. After he gave me the information he said, "If you decide to go to Guatemala and work with Nicholas, why don't you send me a resume with samples of your work from there?"

There it was. I was on the verge of changing my own life and those of a few others like my wife and six-month-old baby girl. Now all I had to do was convince ten artists to go to Guatemala, my wife that we should go, and the administration of the Instituto Allende to help. Easy.

Foundation for Latin American Anthropological Research

The Guatemalan ambassador to Mexico was most interested in our small group, especially in my Australian student, Morley Grainger, who handled his obvious flirtations with excellent diplomatic skills. Because of this, the formalities went smoothly, and in less than an hour all of our visas had been stamped in our passports. The courteous and flirtatious ambassador even suggested, since he would be in Guatemala during the Christmas holidays, that we contact him when we arrived in Guatemala City. He gave me his professional card and Morley his home phone number, in case of emergencies. A month later, just after Christmas of 1975, there we were—Marisela, our daughter Jessica, her nanny, Tere, and I—buried in luggage and seemingly a mile away from the Avianca ticket booth.

I couldn't believe the amount of luggage my wife had packed. We stood in line in the Mexico City international airport waist-deep in boxes, suitcases, and a motley assortment of other equipment that Marisela thought we would need. We would only be in Guatemala for three months, but it appeared to me that she thought we were never coming back. I kept thinking that all we lacked were fifteen porters to carry our supplies on their heads in order to make this a real safari.

We arrived at the airport in Guatemala City around 10 p.m., but we had so many bags that by the time the *aduana* (customs) had gone through them it was midnight. There were no taxis left to take us into town at that hour, so the head of customs gave us a lift in his Jeep.

We stayed in a small *pensión* (boarding house) until we found a house to rent. The Guatemalan ambassador, back in Mexico, had recommended that we contact the secretary of defense, General Santa Cruz, for a house. It turned out to be a two-story house in the tenth district—a nice residential area of the city. I didn't notice until later the bullet hole in one of the second-floor bedroom windows.

Marisela and I had arranged to meet the general at the bank to sign a contract and to make our first and last month's rent deposit. The general was a distinguished-looking gentleman, and although not in uniform his posture and bearing revealed years of military service.

After signing the deal, the general, with typical Latin politeness, offered us a ride to our new home. We accepted without realizing what was in store for us.

Neither Marisela nor I had ever been this close to so much power before. It began to surround and envelop us as we walked with the general toward the door of the bank. Plainclothes bodyguards suddenly appeared fore and aft, out of nowhere. Until we began to move I hadn't noticed them. The soldier at the door snapped to attention and saluted the general as we walked by. In the parking lot sat the new Mercedes-Benz with flags on the front fenders. A neatly dressed soldier opened the door for us. It turned out he was also the chauffeur. Two more cars filled up with the general's secret service personnel, one in front and the other behind us.

So there we were, on December 27th of 1975, crossing Guatemala City with soldiers on every corner coming to attention and saluting the passing Mercedes. It was like being in a parade. At first I was amused and then I found myself waving at the people in the street.

Wow, I thought, we could be taking over the country. Fortunately for Guatemala, this never happened. We never saw the general again. We just deposited our rent money in his bank account each month.

The foundation headquarters of FLAAR were located on the sixth and seventh floors of an office building downtown. The elevator only went to the sixth floor and then it was a walk up a flight of stairs to the seventh-floor penthouse.

The penthouse had a 180-degree view of the city and the mountains to the west. Barbara Hansen, the foundation artist, slept in the one bedroom at the far end of a hallway. Nicholas slept underneath a large table, where during the day graduate students worked on the foundation's publications and where they prepared for each evening's lectures. The inner walls were covered with bookshelves.

On the sixth floor were several small storerooms and one large room for lectures. When we arrived, Nicholas was supervising carpenters who made scaled bleachers to accommodate the sixty to seventy visitors who attended the lectures each night.

Nicholas was every bit the archaeologist. His first work on an archaeological site was as an architect at Tikal for the University of Pennsylvania. He earned his Master's in Archaeology at Harvard. His slight frame and aristocratic appearance belied his energy and stamina. I have never worked with any other archaeologist with so much going simultaneously. He ran a field study at the archaeological site of Yaxha in the Peten, published the FLAAR newsletter, guided rich enthusiasts of things Mayan into the rainforest, and at the same time ran the foundation with nightly lectures in Guatemala City. His failure to make sacred cows out of Ivy League institutions made waves in the academic world, and some called him "Peck's bad boy." But he didn't care and there were certainly no sacred cows to which he bowed reverently. He found it delightful to criticize the great scholars of the Mayan academic world. On the other hand, he set an example and demanded dedication and stamina from all of his graduate students and volunteers.

We were all eager to draw, but it was several days before we had the chance. We spent most of the next two weeks organizing the foundation archives. The library included hundreds of books, journals, and magazines. We maintained the organization established by previous volunteers and began arranging the material on the shelves according to subject matter and publication dates. The colored slides numbered into the thousands.

After work we attended Nicholas's nightly lectures. He or a graduate student presented one or two each evening for the first two weeks depending upon the subject matter. Tourists visiting the capital attended the lectures. Although the talks covered a range of subject matter, "The Rise and Fall of Mayan Civilization" and "Mayan Hieroglyphs" were the two that stand out in my mind, because beginning the third week it fell to me to give them.

One afternoon, Nicholas announced that he was taking a group of Mayan enthusiasts to visit the classic Maya site of Altar de Sacrificios, and then down the fabled Usumacinta River to Yaxchilan. He would be gone for a week. He asked if any of us had cooking experience. Charlie, one of my students, volunteered.

The chance to see the archaeological sites along the Pasión and Usumacinta rivers, which I had been reading about, would have been like a dream come true. At first I was annoyed and jealous. And when Nicholas informed me that I would be giving the lectures each night for a week, I laughed. When I finally realized he was serious, I panicked. For the next few minutes I gave Nicholas all the reasons why this was not a good idea.

"Aren't the graduate assistants more qualified to give the lectures than myself? Can't Barbara do it? What about training one of my students?" I was about to use my daughter's first birthday as an excuse when I enjoyed a stroke of genius. My questions turned to the undeniable and I pleaded with an expression blushed with humility: "I know almost nothing about the rise and fall of the Mayas and even less about their hieroglyphs!"

He looked at me somewhat amused and asked me what I had read.

"*The Maya* by Michael Coe and an English translation of the *Popol Vuh*," I replied humbly. He gave me two books by Sylvanus G. Morley and one by J. Eric Thompson and insisted that after reading them and attending his lectures I would know more about the Maya than any of the tourists who came to the lectures. That was on a Thursday night.

I remember little about what went on around me for the next several days. I took the books to the bedroom and bathroom with me. I made notes on numbered index cards. I paced the floor and stairs of the house and the sixth and seventh floors of the foundation. I lectured to myself in the mirror. And late Monday afternoon I arrived at the foundation to arrange two carousels, each containing one hundred colored slides that Nicholas had left for me on "The Rise and Fall of Mayan Civilization."

The carpenters had finished the risers and were cleaning up their mess of sawdust and tools scattered about the lecture room. They had built a stand with electric sockets in the center of the room for the slide projector. When I first arrived they had barely finished testing the leveling and height of the stand. As they busied themselves cleaning up, I selected slides that related to my note cards for the lecture, placing each one carefully in its corresponding place in the carousels.

I finished the job about thirty minutes before the time of the first lecture. Thinking to make one last check of the slides, I turned on the projector and discovered to my dismay that the bulb had burned out. I excused myself to the workmen who were beginning to sweep the floor and headed up the flight of stairs to the seventh floor of the foundation for a new bulb.

When I returned a few minutes later, I almost fell into a coma. There was nobody else there to testify to my shock. In the middle of the room, between the risers, were the overturned carousels. Two hundred slides were strewn around the floor. Before breathing I instinctively looked at my watch: seventeen minutes until showtime! Not only were the slides out of order, but also in the mixture were my note cards. This spelled disaster.

Fortunately, there was certain logic to the spill. In about ten minutes I had created two piles of slides. That was when the first couple arrived. I was on the floor with much of the evidence still around me. The man smiled, suppressed a smirk, and quickly ushered his wife to the highest riser at the back of the room. Soon after, more people began to arrive and I realized that it was going to take thirty or forty minutes to get the slide show organized and in sync with my note cards. Reluctantly, I put aside my note cards and began to replace the slides in the carousel as they came into my hand. By the time I had finished, the room was full. I was so nervous about what might happen, I couldn't look anyone in the eye. Maybe, since it was dark now, they wouldn't recognize me on the street in daylight. I purposely turned off the lights and started the projector fan before I introduced myself to them and announced rather squeakily the topic of the lecture: "The Rise and Fall of Mayan Civilization."

It would be nice to report that everything went well. It didn't. A large number of the slides were upside down and I had to change them. Of course they were also out of order for the lecture I had spent days preparing. I intentionally avoided the first-person pronoun, hoping desperately that the word "we" either covered up my ignorance or shared the blame for my mistakes. The audience, except for an annoying female graduate student, was either quietly attentive or asleep. In the dark it was hard to tell. Somehow I made it through the first hour and announced before the fifteen-minute intermission that I would answer any questions they might have. That turned out to be a big mistake.

From somewhere in the darkness a very young, critical, and precise female voice asked, "What is your opinion of the Rathjay-Sabloff model of trade and commerce among the coastal Maya?" God, how I hated graduate students!

Nevertheless, during the break, the audience treated me with amused respect. The second half of the lecture went fairly well and the graduate student was mercifully quiet. Just as I came to the end of the lecture with the question, "What happened to the Classic Maya?" the entire audience laughed. I was stunned. How could the disappearance of the Classic Maya be funny? As they continued to laugh I looked behind me at the screen. There on the screen was a small, polychrome, ceramic figure from the island of Jaina, his arms upraised to the height of his shoulders and with his palms turned upward as if to say, "Who knows?" I didn't.

QUIRIGUA, COPAN, AND THE VOICE OF GOD

Only a few days after Nicholas returned from Yaxchilan, he told me to select a couple of students for a three-day trip. Apparently, one of the tourists who had attended his lecture the night before wanted to visit the Mayan ruins of Quirigua and Copan. Since the client was paying for the trip, Nicholas wanted to take advantage of the journey and give us the opportunity to accompany them. He gave me instructions to rent a four-wheel-drive Toyota to accommodate five people. We would leave after his lecture that night.

John, the tourist, was dressed in a short-sleeved white shirt and khaki-colored slacks. He was a young man in his early twenties with closely shaven hair, as if he had just returned from Basic Training at Camp Pendleton. He didn't talk very much and responded with extremely polite "Yes Sir" and "No Sir" to our questions. He quietly listened to Nicholas, who drove and lectured for several hours during the trip that night. In contrast to the rest of us, John failed to ask a single question. He didn't look or act like he could buy us a drink, let alone pay for this five-day trip. He seemed intensely preoccupied with some urgent, private motive.

Shortly after midnight, Nicholas left the paved highway and we drove for about thirty minutes on a dirt road. The headlights of the Toyota revealed that we were in the middle of a huge banana *finca* (plantation). We spent the night near some railroad tracks in an abandoned United Fruit housing facility. The beds were wood frames with simple wire mesh where we placed our sleeping bags. Nicholas and John stayed in one room and the rest of us in another.

The next morning, before getting into the Toyota, Nicholas took me aside and said, "This guy John is *really* strange." He hesitated for a moment as if he wanted to explain, then changed his mind and without another word motioned for me to follow him to the vehicle.

The vegetation had changed since leaving the pine forests that surrounded Guatemala City. Daylight unveiled the tropical atmosphere we had entered sometime during the night. We ate a breakfast of bananas and oranges in our vehicle.

Quirigua was the first Mayan ruin I ever visited. I couldn't have had a better guide. Nicholas took us from stela to stela, altar to altar, monument to monument, explaining the history of every shape and line with patient details. For the first time, these ancient Mayan designs started to become legible to me. We toured the little site for almost three hours. Intently occupied with the information that was raining down on us, I filled several pages of notes. I had little time to monitor John's behavior or his reactions to the ruins. I do recall that his eyebrows were always furrowed as if something were disturbing him. Then Nicholas announced that it was time to get something to eat and continue on our journey to Copan, Honduras.

It was late afternoon when we reached the border, and our entry into Honduras was the strangest border crossing I ever made.

During the seventies a dress code appeared to be in place through-out Latin America for uniformed border personnel. They always wore brown, which coincidentally complemented the color of their skin. The border between Guatemala and Honduras was more of a clearing than anything else. There were forests around it, and the cleared area couldn't have been more than one hundred meters in diameter. There were four thatched roof *jacales* (huts) in the clearing, divided equally between personnel from the two countries. The first structure we encountered was the Guatemalan customs office. They searched our Toyota and everything in it. I was used to borders where everyone was searched upon entering a country. In Latin America they are usually looking for guns or drugs. Could it be that the Guatemalans wanted to keep these items in their country? After the search, we were motioned on to the next jacal, about thirty meters farther on.

Here was the immigration office. They checked our passports and visas, stamped them, and then requested that we fill out an exit form. Once again, this was a new experience for me. The exit form included the usual series of questions asked when entering a country. Carol, one of my students, filled in the space provided for "occupation" with a single word, "hedonist."

We were just about finished with the task when a Toyota carrying a government seal on the front door and a uniformed man with an abundance of gold braid on the brim of his brown hat pulled up to the front of the building sounding its horn. The immigration official hastily collected our partially filled-in exit forms and ran through the door. Anxious to be on our way, we hurried after him and climbed into our vehicle.

The official, still carrying our forms, ran to where a metal pole stretched across the dirt road in front of the government Toyota. With the help of a weighted tire on one end of the pole he began to raise it from the forked tree trunk upon which the other end rested. Just as the front of our vehicle closed the gap, the man dropped our papers, and in his effort to grab them lost control of the pole. The front end dropped on the ground and the driver with the gold braided hat ran over it.

Watching the ensuing scene from the sanctuary of our car, all of us except John roared with laughter. The man with the hat was giving the poor official hell. They removed the bent pole from the road, and as Nicholas drove forward the man with the gold braid raised his arm like a traffic cop, signaling for us to stop. He then commandeered us to help straighten the pole. The task took about thirty minutes, and when we finished the pole was replaced across the road. Then, with great formality and satisfaction, the pole was raised and we were allowed to drive out of Guatemala and across no man's land to the next border stop, only thirty or forty meters down the road.

The Honduran border was a mirrored reflection of the process we had just endured. The only difference was that the brown-uniformed Honduran border officials fumigated the inside and outside of our vehicle with DDT before allowing us to continue. Evidently, bugs and microscopic life between these two Central American countries preferred to hitch rides rather than fly or walk across the frontier clearing.

When we reached the village of Copan it was getting dark. We ate in a restaurant and Nicholas assigned us rooms at a hotel. For some reason he decided that I was to spend the night with John. After depositing our luggage in our rooms, my two students and I began exploring the village, while Nicholas and John went to see the director of the local museum. There was not much to investigate in the small community, so when we saw a relatively large crowd of men, women, and children lined up in front of an old, rickety wood building we went to check it out.

The dilapidated structure turned out to be both a barn and the local movie theater. A hand-painted sign announced that Sean Connery was starring, but we could not translate the feature title. Price of admission was equivalent to twenty-five cents, so we thought, "What the heck?" and entered the barn.

Instead of chairs for the moviegoers, there was a series of long, wooden benches. The projection unit, atop a wooden stable partition, made so much noise that none of the dialogue was audible, although it was in English with Spanish subtitles. The movie was projected onto wooden slats at the back wall of the barn. Though the slats were painted white, there were large spaces between them. During the night scenes of the movie, when the projected light was darkest, stars could be seen through the gaps in the screen.

Needless to say, no refreshments or popcorn were served during the intermission, while the projectionist changed film reels. Given the lack of luxury, the viewers that night gave the movie their fullest attention. There was even a splattering of applause when the movie ended. After the show the students headed for a cantina and I returned to the comfort of my hotel room.

When I entered the room, John was kneeling beside his bed like a statue of Buddha, with the palms of his hands pressed together, fingertips pointing upward. The deep furrows above his closed eyes, together with his piously arranged hands covering his nose, formed a large Y. His face suggested that his prayers were full of searching questions. Out of respect for his devotion, I tried to make as little noise as possible as I undressed and climbed into my bed.

It was several minutes before John opened his eyes and caught me watching him. He stood up and nervously fumbled with the light switch. He undressed in the dark and finally I could hear the squeak of the mattress springs as his body hit the bed. I broke the silence in the dark. "Where are you from, John?"

"Chicago."

"What brings you to Guatemala and Honduras?"

"God."

"Really?"

"Yes!"

"How do you know that God is behind your visit?"

"He spoke to me in a dream and told me to bring the gospel to these people."

"What people?"

"I am not really sure, but maybe the people of the village of Copan."

"Please excuse me for sounding skeptical, John, but how is it that God spoke to you and yet apparently hasn't told you which people you are to bring the gospel to?"

I will always remember the important highlights of his story.

His dream began with himself standing on top of a pyramid, high above a mass of brown-skinned people to whom he was to "bring the word of God." A voice told him that he was to go to seek out these people who built pyramids.

According to John, the next morning he packed a suitcase and went to O'Hare Airport. He lived by fasting at the terminal for several days. Having no money, he slept sitting upright in one of the waiting rooms and washed up in the public bathrooms. He repeated his dream and subsequent commission to anyone who started a conversation with him. Finally a man informed him that there were pyramids and brown-skinned people living in Central America, and suggested that John check the airlines that went to Guatemala City.

The first person who listened to his story in the waiting section of the Avianca airline departure gate bought him a one-way ticket to Guatemala City and gave him $1,000 to speed him on his way. You had to respect John's faith. The fact that he was actually in Central America by this strange metaphysical route was somehow unsettling, and it was hard for me to drift off to sleep that night.

I didn't mention his story to anyone the next morning, although I felt Nicholas searching my face for information. After breakfast we were off to the archaeological site of Copan, and John's strange tale was put temporarily aside.

While I had been impressed by the intricately carved low relief on the monuments of Quirigua the day before, I found the deeply carved monuments of the archaeological site at Copan awesome. The carved stelae were stupefyingly complex until Nicholas began his systematic explanation. He started at the top and came down the front of the first stela, describing every detail of the ruler's wardrobe and the accessories and their significance. As we moved across the parklike plaza, he gave us the opportunity to define the elements on the stelae for ourselves. By the time we reached the ball court, I was able to identify even the numbers and time-period glyphs.

When we passed the end of the ball court, the image before my eyes caused adrenaline to surge through my body. It was hard to believe that I was standing in nearly the same spot where Fredric Catherwood, more than one hundred years earlier, must have labored when he made his fabulous drawing of the stelae altar complex in front of the hieroglyphic stairway. Although mentally and physically exhausted by noon, I was loath to leave the archaeological site. It was the second Maya city that I had visited and the best day of my life so far.

After lunch John announced that he would not be returning to Guatemala City with us, so we parted company with this strange tourist. Only the gods know what became of him. Years later, after reading *Blood of the Kings* by Linda Schele and Mary Ann Miller, I wondered if John, like the ancient Maya lords, had let blood the night of his dream or vision.

Tikal

We flew into the airfield at Flores, the capital of the Peten province of Guatemala, and took a bus to Tikal. There was a landing strip at Tikal long enough for small passenger prop planes like DC-3s and other small private aircraft like Cessnas and Piper Cubs to land. Unfortunately, on the day we chose to leave the daily flight to Tikal was full.

The few tourist facilities at Tikal back then were clustered around one end of the dirt-and-grass airfield. The grass growing on the runway indicated that not many planes were flying into Tikal. There were two small rustic hotels, two palapa-style restaurants, a small museum, and a camping area. The camp area had no water, so campers drank soda pop purchased from one of the two restaurants. But what the facilities lacked in comfort and services was made up by the surrounding environment. It was all lavishly encircled by rain forest.

Nicholas stayed at the Jaguar Inn, and the rest of us stayed in tents at the campground. The hotel was so rustic that the only advantage over us was that Nicholas had a roof, a mattress, and running water. He let us use his shower at the end of each day. I suspect that he made an arrangement with the hotel proprietors before he left, because many of the tourists who stayed in the hotel invited us to use their showers before they checked out. As a result we managed to shower almost every day.

We ate breakfast, lunch, and dinner in one of the palapas near the airfield, and had a choice of chicken or eggs with tropical fruit. Sometimes there were beans and corn. There was never anything green on our plates.

The first day Nicholas gave us one of his well-informed tours of the site. But the sheer size and magnificence of Tikal and its surroundings overwhelmed even his exciting lecture. This was the first time any of us had been in a rain forest of such impressive dimensions. There was just too much to see and hear all around us. Flocks of parrots and other colorful birds flew overhead and we couldn't resist watching them. Loud growling noises interrupted Nicholas's lecture. The first of many times this happened I was sure that a jaguar would pounce on us at any minute. Seeing our lack of attention to his words, Nicholas explained that we were not to be alarmed. The noise came from mysterious creatures yet to be seen, howler monkeys. Still, each time it happened our attention would stray as we strained our eyes, trying to penetrate the thick, dark forest. We seemed to have short attention spans—as if we were small children. Surprisingly, through it all, Nicholas was as patient as a kindergarten teacher. He actually seemed to enjoy our childlike fascination for all that was around us.

We were so excited from the awesome experience that when we returned to camp for lunch we gathered around a table, eager to return to the site with our first assignments. Time passed quickly for us and we were so occupied with questions that we didn't notice the extremely slow service.

The thatched-roof palapa restaurants were small establishments, run in each case by a local man and/or his wife. There were no waiters. The process was something like a self-service McDonald's might be. When you ordered, you went to the person behind the counter. More often than not, that person was also the cook. The kitchen was along the back wall behind the counter, and you could see the cook preparing the meals. You collected your order at the same counter. Since there was just one menu, when you thought your order was about ready you kept your eyes peeled so that someone else didn't snatch it, or so that it was not left on the counter getting cold.

There was always a group of soldiers eating in the palapa at the same time as we did. The eight of them took turns, two at a time, guarding the entrance to the runway and community. The inside of their guardhouse was about nine square feet; outside it was surrounded on three sides by stacks of gunny sacks full of sand, which came up to butt level. The two men guarding the place made good use of the sacks. In one corner they had mounted a small, palm-leafed roof on a pole for shade. At the top of the pole, above the roof, they flew the Guatemalan flag. All of them carried automatic weapons. They were not sinister or threatening in any way, just young. On one occasion we found ourselves involved in a small misunderstanding with them.

It started out as a joke. The first morning, when we arrived for breakfast, we found a group of five young, blond gringo men in the palapa. They looked like they had just arrived from Muscle Beach and they towered over the Mayas, the soldiers, and most of us. One stood out among the rest, not only for his size but because of his loud and boisterous behavior. The boys, not accustomed to waiting on themselves, were making some very loud and crude statements in English about the service in the "dump." The giant, a couple of meters away from the other four boys, insisted directly and forcefully in the face of the cook that he wanted a hard-boiled egg. It was obvious from the blank look on the cook's face that he didn't understand English. The soldiers, as well as ourselves, quietly studied the boy's actions and manners.

After informing his friends across the room that he couldn't make the cook understand him, the boisterous giant ambled over to our table. Without any courteous greeting he came right to the point: "How do I say 'hard-boiled eggs' in Spanish?"

Nicholas grinned. He looked at each one of us as if giving us a chance to speak. Satisfied it was up to him, he turned in his chair and said to the kid, "That's easy, *huevos duros.*" Nicholas repeated the two words for the boy until he could do it on his own. As the boy walked back over to the counter, Nicholas was smothering a chuckle.

"Let's see what happens!"

The kid stood facing the cook.

"¿Tiene Usted huevos duros?" he asked in his loud voice.

The cook's expression was one of utter disbelief. When he did not immediately respond, the young giant became more agitated; thinking that the cook didn't understand his Spanish, he raised his voice another notch.

"¡Quiero huevos duros!" he demanded. This time he accented his request by slamming his fist on the countertop. In his frustration he repeated the phrase several times. Each time he slammed the countertop.

For a few seconds there was complete silence in the palapa as everyone's attention was upon the drama at the counter. Somewhere in the recesses of my mind I vaguely recall the scraping sound of moving chairs. But it was the clic-clic-clic sound of an automatic rifle being cocked that drew our attention to the soldiers.

The giant's four companions, sitting at the table next to the soldiers, were obviously shaken. They sat there stiff, erect, and frozen in a time warp, with their mouths open and eyes wide. They reminded me of icicles hanging from the limbs of a tree. The giant must have recognized

Figure 3 Nicholas Chelmuth (photo by author)

the sound of the weapon being cocked, for he had turned his back to the counter and stared at the soldiers.

Only two of the soldiers had stood up. Their faces were grim but their attitude not really aggressive. It was more a simple statement: "Don't give us any trouble or we will be forced to use our weapons."

Nicholas jumped to his feet and proceeded to influence the end result of a situation he had set up and perhaps even provoked. His joke was a play on words. "Huevos" in Spanish means eggs, but it also means "balls." In context with the word "hard," huevos always means balls. Nicholas cooled down the situation by explaining to the soldiers that it was all a misunderstanding and the young gringos didn't speak Spanish very well. The two soldiers sat down, leaned their weapons against their table, and returned to their plates.

Nicholas went over to the counter and informed the cook that the giant wanted *huevos bien cocidos*.

When Nicholas gave us our instruction that first afternoon, it turned out that all of us, except Marisela, would be drawing pieces located in the museum. Marisela was to be his photographic assistant.

Figure 4 North Acropolis (photo by Marisela G. de La Sota)

It was difficult to concentrate on the museum pieces with the flora and fauna of the rain forest and all of those wonderful buildings, temples, pyramids, reservoirs, and causeways to examine and explore just meters away. Every morning as Nicholas and Marisela disappeared into the rain forest in the direction of the ruins, our spirits darkened with envy. It took at least thirty minutes to shake off the envy and work up enthusiasm for our indoor tasks. Our day would end on the same note: Marisela returned for lunch with wonderful descriptions of the monuments and buildings that they had photographed that day. We listened and tried not to pout. Luckily for us, the museum was very small and we finished our first assignment in four days.

On the fifth day Nicholas told me that he had finished the photographic work that he needed to do and would be returning to the foundation headquarters in the morning. He would leave us documentation assignments calculated to take about two weeks. Back in the city he would arrange transportation for our return and send a message with one of the pilots beforehand to let us know the day and means of travel. If we had any problems, or if we finished the work sooner than he anticipated, I was to send him a message the same way.

Because I needed to supervise the students who would be working over a large area, Nicholas gave me only two jobs. The first was to measure and make a detailed drawing of Temple I. With the help of two of the students, I began.

I thought that measuring the pyramidal base of the temple would be boring. After all, measuring is fairly straightforward. But Temple I made it very challenging.

It was the tallest building I had ever measured. From the plaza floor to the top of the roof comb of the temple was 147 feet. Looking down at the plaza from the top, it seemed like even more. This presented some thrilling moments. Also, the main temple stairway extended well beyond the nine tiers of the pyramidal base, which became an obstacle on all but the bottom tier. In addition, there was always some strange new architectural element that we had heard about in one of Nicholas's lectures but until now hadn't been able to observe. Such was the case of the small stairs used by the workmen when they built the pyramid.

Nicholas had told us about these special flights of steps back at the foundation, but it was amazing to actually walk up them. The stairs were located on the side of and built into each of the nine levels of the pyramid's base. The original workmen used these small staircases to haul their building materials from one tier to the next one above it. The stairs were only a foot or so wide, so the workmen needed the agility of goats to keep from falling. We used these small staircases to get from one level to the next when we were measuring. By the time we reached the fifth level, we stopped walking up them. We cautiously crawled up. I thought that crawling up these stairs on the higher tiers was the bravest thing I had ever done in my life. I didn't feel that way very long. On the morning that Nicholas left Tikal, we began to measure the temple on top of the pyramid.

There, on the back side of the temple, I found myself with the measuring tape in my teeth, crawling on my hands and knees along a twenty-centimeter ledge 130 feet above the ground. I was too scared to brush away the sweat dripping into my eyes or the myriad of mosquitoes swarming around my face. My legs trembled and my hands became damp and slippery. I was constantly forced to look down to make sure that I placed hands and feet securely. When I did, the sight of the buildings and ground so far away below me made me so dizzy I had to close my eyes. About halfway across the ledge, my creeping motion was halted by resistance from the measuring tape in my mouth.

Almost immediately the voice of Charlie came from behind me, "Just a minute, professor. The tape is stuck in the reel." I heard Carol telling Charlie that he needed some slack in the tape line. "Slack," I thought. "Where in the hell is he going to get some slack? The end of the goddamn tape is in my mouth." I wanted to scream at them but couldn't for fear of losing the end of the tape and having to start all over.

After a few terrifying moments, Charlie yelled at me to continue. It wasn't until I reached the far end and called back the measurement to Charlie that the extent of my present predicament dawned on me. How was I going to get off the ledge?

Climbing up to the ledge had been scary enough. I was forced to hug the corners of the structure with both arms to get to the ledge. Now I was on its south corner with no room to turn around to climb down. I certainly didn't have the nerve to try to lower myself head first. Crawling backward across the ledge was out of the question. Or was it? It turned out to be my only option. After that experience I can honestly say that it was the bravest thing I have ever undertaken.

It took almost three days to measure Temple I.

After I measured the pyramid and temple, Nicholas had suggested that I make the final drawing back at the foundation, as he wanted to work on it with me. He gave me another task in his absence: to draw the main buildings of Group G. I loved it. There were howler and spider monkeys in the trees around me almost the entire time. I worked three days on the pencil drawing and made three attempts on one day at the final ink drawing. Twice the ink drawings were ruined by sweat rolling down my face and off my chin onto the drawing. Finally, I wised up and wrapped a bandana around my forehead. I put the date and my name on the drawing the day before I left Tikal.

Twice each morning I left my work for a while and circulated around the archaeological site, helping and overseeing the students' jobs. Sometimes I wandered off into the rain forest between visits. Most of the time I explored by myself. Other times I searched for Marisela to go with me. We never went very far; we had read that a young photographer had wandered off into the rain forest at Tikal. His body was found only a hundred meters from the main plaza of the site. Still, we managed to visit most of the ruins and climbed every unexcavated building and pyramid in the ceremonial center. The views from the roof combs of Temples IV and V were breathtaking. We often visited the site at night, and on one of those occasions as I stood in the main plaza looking at the rising moon behind Temple I, I thought of the words Teobert Maler wrote at the turn of the century about the Maya cities:

> The Mayas believe that at midnight (especially during the great festivals), their ancestors return to earth and, adorned as in the days of their glory, wander about in the forsaken temples and palaces, where their spirit-voices are heard in the air. Therefore all important ruins in this land are regarded as enchanted, *encantadas*, and timid people do not like to sleep alone in their desolate chambers.

I could swear I heard their voices.

Marisela convinced one of the guards at the site to accompany her on longer treks so that she saw a lot more of the rain forest than I did. She kept a record of the Maya names for all the trees and animals that she encountered.

Due to our untiring energy, the depth of concentration, and the fanatical need to document the monuments of the sites, Nicholas placed the germinating seed of an idea in my head: to create a team of documenters in Mesoamerican archaeology. Drawing the monuments was something I could do. On the other hand, I knew nothing about photography. Nicholas's aluminum suitcase, filled with Hasselblads and accessories, was something I needed to learn about.

EARTHQUAKE

On February 4, it was still dark at five in the morning as I slipped quietly out of my sleeping bag and left the tent. I recall making a hasty mental note to fix the tent pegs. Sometime during the night they had come out of the ground and the tent was sagging comically on both sides toward the center support pole.

Charlie, Ken, and Carol were already up and waiting with the driver who was standing by the door of the bus talking with a couple of soldiers. The guys were headed back to Guatemala City, on what we had calculated the evening before to be a fourteen-hour journey. A few minutes after my arrival, the driver entered the bus and started the motor. As they boarded, I gave the guys some last-minute instructions and messages for their companions back at the foundation.

By the time I returned to the camp, Marisela and the rest of the students were up and on the veranda of the jacal waiting for breakfast.

The cook had a radio playing soft music, and a refreshing early morning breeze moved the pointed ends of the palm thatching that lined the bottom edge of the roof. As I lowered my head and ducked under the thatching to join the group, I heard Marisela say, ". . . and the tent seemed to move!"

"Good morning. Did everyone sleep well?" I asked as I sat down beside Marisela at the long table.

The responses were all short and positive, except for Marisela who continued with her statement prior to my entrance. "I was just explaining that the howler monkeys and some birds woke me up just before dawn. They were very close to the camp. Then the tent began to shake. It made me very nervous. I thought the monkeys were trying to get into the tent!"

"That explains why the tent pegs were pulled out of the dirt. We must have rolled into the tent sides during the night. I'll replace the pegs after breakfast," I said.

Marisela gave me the special look that lets me know that my explanation of things doesn't jibe with her own assessment.

By the time breakfast arrived we were discussing the previous day's progress. Suddenly the cook hollered at us to be quiet. He turned up the volume on the radio. Either bad speakers or poor reception caused the voice to break up, and information came at us in spurts.

"... 8.2 ... Richter scale ... flattened the city. President ... has ... martial law ... cope with ... threat of massive looting ..."

We sat there in stunned silence as the reporter continued, "... the numbers of bodies under the rubble ... fear of outbreaks of typhoid ... other diseases ... medical units ... distributed ... city."

I looked at Marisela. The look in her eyes caused a great emptiness in the pit of my stomach. Without speaking, the one-word question, "Jessica?" flashed between us.

Between the bits and spurts of the radio we tried to assess our position. Apart from Jessica and Tere, there were three students back in the city. And there were also the three students I had watched leaving for the city that very morning. Did they have any idea of what was happening?

I don't recall the subsequent conversation, or when the decision was made, or even the long bus ride to Flores, the capital of Peten, but I suppose it was after the soldiers told us that there would be no flights in or out of Tikal that day. What I do recall is Marisela and myself standing in the small air terminal in Flores with dozens of others waiting to see if there were any flights back to Guatemala City.

Only two flights arrived and left Flores that day, and only Guatemalan nationals were allowed on the flights. Marisela and I were forced to return to Tikal.

When we arrived back at Tikal it was mid-afternoon. We didn't accomplish anything at the site that day. The owner of the restaurant was happy because we spent most of the time consuming food and refreshments as we sat glued to his radio. The news that filtered through the airways painted a very depressing picture of what was happening in Guatemala City and other areas of the country.

At first the radio reports, although constant, were contradictory and confusing. The voices of the newscasters were filled with such emotion that for a couple of hours we became infected with it. The estimates of those killed or wounded mounted higher and higher with each report. Outside the capital entire towns and villages had been destroyed. Landslides and ruined bridges made many of the major highways impassable. Concerns were voiced about the inability of people in the countryside to get access to food and water. I can't remember a single positive declaration.

Something happens to the sensibilities with so much bad news. After a few hours of panic, it makes you numb and jaded. On the other hand, numbness can be a good thing: anxieties are exchanged for the search for reasonable solutions.

By the time we sat around the campfire that evening, it was apparent that except for the grizzly, depressing radio messages, we were really isolated from the rest of the world. The news reported that there was no electricity in the capital and that the minimal phone service available was overwhelmed. The airfield personnel in both Tikal and Flores were clueless as to the possibility of any flights out of Peten the next day. A bus driver told us that rumor had it that due to avalanches and landslides, vehicles were only able to reach the eastern foothills of the Guatemalan highlands near El Progreso. If this was true, the three students who left that morning on the bus would have at least a three- or four-day hike across the mountains to reach Guatemala City. Although this gave us an option for getting out of Tikal, it was not high on our priority list. The dirt roads east into Belize were open but we lacked funds at Tikal to take everyone out that way. At best, we could send one or two students in that direction for help. Fortunately, during our discussion two young people joined us at the campfire. They were going out through Belize and offered to get a message to the Instituto Allende that we were stranded, and to inform the families of the students that we were all right. We finally decided I would go to Flores in the morning and if a flight came into the capital of Peten, I would try to get a seat. Marisela would stay close to the Tikal airfield and see if she could catch a flight. If either one of us got out, we would send help for the rest as soon as possible. So, early the next morning after leaving all of my money, except for the bus and airfare, I headed for Flores. Within an hour after arriving, I took a seat by a window on a DC-3, noisy and uncomfortable but dependable, and began winging my way back to Guatemala City.

Evidence of the disaster did not appear until we reached the mountains. The first thing that caught my attention was the highway. There were places where it had bunched up like an accordion. In other places the naked slope of mountains, now free of vegetation, had descended upon and covered the highway. As we approached the city I saw a large bridge twisted like a pretzel with its now independent large steel beams spiraling off in the air in various directions. I kept thinking that the view from the cockpit must have been awesome. Miraculously, the pilots flew over the barrio where our house and companions were living. It was a relief to see that most of the buildings in the area were still standing.

I was amazed that buses were operating and I took the first one heading north out of the airport into the city. When I calculated that the bus was nearing the latitude of our house, I got off. During the thirty-minute walk to reach the short western end of the block where our house was located, four tremors shook the ground. It was obvious that the ordeal was not over. Suddenly, in front of my face were the remains of a smashed car. The entire front of a building had collapsed and the weight of the debris had flattened the vehicle until the windows and even the outside rearview mirror, miraculously still connected to the chassis, were only a foot off the pavement. Panic once again rose in my stomach. Our house, still out of sight, was just around the corner.

Although there were various cracks and fissures, the house stood firmly and obstinately upright. The door was ajar and I noticed a lone tennis shoe on the floor, trapped between the door and its jamb. I pushed the door open and there was Tere holding our baby in the company of the two students, Francisco and Keith. I was ecstatic to see them and took Jessica in my arms. After warm and emotional greetings I learned that the boys had come to the house for supplies. They were living a block away, in a tent they had set up in the nearby park. Almost the entire barrio was living there. In fact, there were so many of these temporary camps set up around the city that we began to call the capital Tent City.

My next move was to the FLAAR offices. I was able to find a bus that took me within two blocks of the foundation. The bus ride was most notable because of the silence. The Latinos, usually very sociable and cheerfully pleasant, were quiet and sullen. No one spoke. We all just sat there looking out the windows, reflecting upon the fallen buildings and broken windows of the empty storefronts.

I stood there trying to get up the nerve to enter the FLAAR building. Finally, I walked through one of the paneless windows and went to the elevator. One look at the mechanism, along with a number of slight tremors and the close sound of breaking glass made me reconsider and I turned to begin my way cautiously up the stairs. I was out of breath by the time I reached the sixth floor but relieved to hear voices coming from the penthouse above.

Nicholas stood in the center of the largest room amid a pyramid of debris. The entire library of thousands of books, magazines, and slides was on the floor. Oddly, with the windowpanes gone the penthouse looked like a huge, open balcony.

Nicholas smiled when he saw me and when he reached out to shake my hand he looked down at the floor and said, "Welcome to the real world."

For the next several minutes we discussed the problem of my wife and the students trapped back in Tikal. We agreed that we needed to act as soon as possible. He would go to the bank for the necessary funds; then, I would fly to Tikal and bring them back to the capital. While Nicholas left for the bank I began to help clean up the mess.

I worked alongside Barbara Hansen, the artist who specialized in roll-out drawings of the Maya cylindrical vases. Her story of the earthquake was typical of a multitude of fascinating tales. She was awakened by the noise of the moving force of the earthquake and the exceptional cold breeze on her face. In the dark, she had no idea what was happening. She noticed that no lights were coming from the other buildings across the street from the penthouse. Then something heavy fell on her head. It turned out be a slide projector that had fallen out of the closet. Normally, her bed was three feet from the closet but because of the earthquake it had moved across the floor and come to a stop against the wall near the closet. Stunned by the blow to her head, she reached out to touch the wall, which was normally beside her bed. It was not there and she screamed. She told me that she didn't stop screaming until Nicholas arrived several minutes later.

By the time she finished her account of the earthquake, Nicholas returned with some bad news. The banks were not open and could not guarantee they would open tomorrow. He had checked with the secretary of transportation, who said Tikal might be accessed only by driving south into El Salvador and then turning east into Honduras. It would be a week before the government could repair the bridges, clear the avalanches, and repair the roads. Meanwhile, we were left only with the hope that the banks would open soon or at least that the telephone system would be up and working sufficiently to contact friends in Tikal. With nothing to be done, I returned to help Barbara.

While she continued her story, we began to pick up the magazines that had flown through the door of the penthouse and out onto the landing of the stairs. Suddenly, a noise much like a train in a tunnel blasted into our dialogue. It increased in volume, then the building began to move. I was squatting on the floor hanging on to the stair railing and looking over Barbara's head. I could see the distant mountains through an open balcony door. They appeared to move back and forth. First they disappeared to the right of the doorjamb, only to appear once again and disappear to the left. The building must have been swinging back and forth like a pendulum. The penthouse was clearly at the maximum arc of the swing. Somewhere below we could hear enormous amounts of glass breaking. We heard Nicholas yell, "Earthquake! get under a table!" He obviously wasn't talking to Barbara or me. There wasn't a table on the landing, and besides, I doubt I could have taken two erect steps, the building was moving so violently. Instead, we both hugged the iron banister railing of the stairs and stared at each other. The railing, made of forged one-inch steel, seemed inadequate and flimsy. I kept telling myself that given the opportunity, we should try to make it to a door where we could stand underneath a structural beam. Meanwhile, the constant sound of the earth's plates grinding against each other turned my legs to rubber.

The second earthquake, within forty-eight hours of the first, didn't last more than a minute, though it seemed much longer. It reached 7.6 on the Richter scale. The small dent the foundation staff had made on cleaning up the mess had to begin again.

My stomach told me that it was time to feed it, and my nerves told me to get out of the building. I told Nicholas I was going to the house to check on my companions and get something to eat.

He accompanied me down the stairs and when we arrived in the foyer, we could see Francisco and Keith standing outside trying to open the entrance door to the building, which had evidently jammed tightly shut in the latest earthquake. They exerted a lot of energy on the problem, but Nicholas and I simply walked through the vacant window space next to the door and greeted them with a smile. They looked at each other foolishly.

Keith was the first to speak. "Marisela arrived a couple of hours ago. She is back at the house with Tere and the baby."

"Thank God! Did she mention how the students at Tikal are holding up?"

"They were all fine when she left. She left them all of the money she had so that they would be able to eat for a few more days."

When they saw the concerned look on my face, Francisco spoke up. "Don't worry; they are fine. Marisela talked with the restaurant owner before she left and since he knows Nicholas he offered to feed them until help arrives."

Within five days the flock was back at the nest. Then a young man from Florida, Leon Rainer, arrived at the foundation. It turned out that he had a four-wheel-drive Bronco and wanted to see Tikal. He had come to the foundation to hire one of us as a guide. Instead, he offered to drive the circuitous route through El Salvador and Honduras to bring the students back from Tikal. In less than a week he had them back in the capital. The three lads who had left Tikal by bus on the morning of the first earthquake arrived in the capital three days later.

They had to hike over the mountains to reach the city. Food had not been a problem. Dozens of produce trucks carrying everything from bananas to watermelon and cantaloupes were stuck between avalanches and gave their cargo away to the hundreds of hikers trying to reach the city.

During the next two weeks the country experienced another earthquake as well as more than a thousand tremors. The ground trembled so often that we kept the doors propped open with boxes, shoes, furniture, and anything else we could find when we retired for the evening. The students kept a record of the tremors they felt during the hours we were awake. On the day we left Guatemala, their total was 1,212.

We decided to send Tere and baby Jessica back to San Miguel. Several of the students left as well. Those remaining went to work—not the work we had originally come to the country to do but, considering the situation, equally important.

In the mornings we scattered throughout the city and nearby countryside helping with the variety of chores necessary to help Guatemala get back on its feet. Some of us worked in medical units that the U.S. government had sent to Guatemala. Others packaged and boxed food under the supervision of the Guatemalan government or U.S. AID. Food was arriving from all over the world. Huey helicopters flew over the city every hour from noon until dusk. They delivered the food that had been packaged during the morning. We talked with the helicopter crews in the evenings. Many of them ate supper in the local McDonald's. It was a chore to get them to smile. They were always exhausted from delivering tons of food each day.

In the afternoons we helped restore the FLAAR foundation offices. At one point Nicholas approached Marisela with great enthusiasm. The situation that made Nicholas so excited was a by-product of the earthquake, which had smashed hundreds of pre-Hispanic pieces in a private collection.

The owner, a wealthy industrialist, owned one of the largest collections of Maya artifacts in the world. Nicholas had tried for years, without success, to get the man's permission to photograph some of the pieces. Now, because of the damage, the owner had called the foundation and asked for help. Nicholas was elated at the prospect. Unfortunately, Marisela and I were the only ones presently at the foundation with any experience working with pre-Columbian pottery shards, and this was limited to gluing together the two dozen pieces I had excavated back in San Miguel. Nevertheless, Nicholas introduced us to the industrialist as experts in restoration from Mexico.

I have never in my life seen the likes of such artifacts. As we walked through the house the man stopped in a room and showed us two large zoomorphic ceramic burial urns. They were large jaguars that stood as high as my waist. Some, if not all, of the burial contents were still in the urns. The most amazing features of the sculptured urns were the delicate claws of the jaguar, still intact.

When we stepped inside a long rectangular room on the roof, I felt like Howard Carter must have felt when he first peered into the tomb of Tutankhamen. There were hundreds of wonderful artifacts. Dozens of polychrome cylindrical vases, which before the earthquake must have stood like canned goods in a grocery store on shelves, lay broken on the floor. Hundreds of ceramic vessels with a variety of geometric, anthropomorphic, and zoomorphic motifs had also previously been arranged on shelves. Now the place was a complete disaster, and it would take an army of professional restorers months, maybe even years, to put everything back together again.

We explained the problem and apologized for not having more time but volunteered to help begin the process. It was agreed that in exchange for our assistance, Nicholas could photograph some of the artifacts. Marisela took charge, and with the help of a dozen hired men, we spent two weeks amid the shards, patiently gluing pieces back together.

Finally it was time to pick up and leave. Leon Rainer with his Bronco was once again the man of the hour. He offered to take us back to San Miguel in exchange for a tour of Maya archaeological sites in Mexico. He made me a deal we couldn't refuse. Marisela and I were as anxious for the opportunity as he was.

THE FLIGHT TO MEXICO

Traveling with Leon was a pleasure. He was thoughtful of others and a very good driver, but his smelly feet were a problem. The worst time was at night when we were all in the tent. Leon explained and even apologized for his affliction, and although we never got used to it, his good nature compensated for the odor.

Our first few hours heading back to Mexico were filled with reflection and conversation about what we had seen and were still seeing around us. As we passed the once magnificent village of Chimaltenago, we were again reminded of the disaster that had overtaken the country. The town was a sea of rubble. Here and there a doorjamb still stood proudly amid the mess. In the middle of the rubble, in what had once been the center of the village, stood a cast-iron bathtub with shower head and pipe still attached to it. It was a sculptural statement. It said, "Here is all that is left of modern urbanization in Chimaltenago."

Not far up the road we took a short detour to the southeast and the ancient capital of Guatemala, Antigua. We said good-bye to our friends Mary Lou and Jay at their jade market, then continued northward to Lake Atitlán and Chichicastenango. We stopped for a few moments at both and arrived at Quetzaltenago for the night.

Our first adventure came after leaving Quetzaltenago. We decided to take a dirt road north out of the city instead of the highway somewhat to the east. At the beginning the road was about eight meters wide, and the infrequent traffic coming down the mountain toward us was not a problem. Eventually, the road shrank to a width of six meters or less, and once or twice we were forced to drive into the vegetation alongside the road to let vehicles pass.

The road was flat as it left the plain of Quetzaltenago, but about an hour later it began to rise up a slope and into a pine forest. We spent another four hours climbing the winding road through the forest. At last the road broke onto a series of almost barren hills, and we could see for miles ahead. A small village spread across the upper slopes several miles away. A man, perhaps in his sixties, walked slowly up the road in front of us. I leaned across Leon, who was driving at the time, and asked in Spanish where the road was taking us. The pedestrian answered in a language unknown to any of us.

At first I thought he didn't understand my bad Spanish, so Marisela gave it a shot. He smiled and talked rather enthusiastically, in his own tongue.

At last it dawned upon him that we had a communication problem and he puckered his lips and looked off into space for a second and then grinned widely. "Buenos días." He managed the phrase rather hesitantly but when we responded with the same he became passionate. "Buenos días. Buenos días. Buenos días." He repeated to each of us.

With gestures we tried to explain that we were going to the village up ahead and he could have a ride. But his only response was a smile and more "Buenos días." I finally got the message across by getting out of the Bronco and making full-body gestures. When we reached the point where I had the car door open and gestured for him to enter, he still hesitated. Although I couldn't understand a word he said, I could tell by his voice it was a question. I got the drift. "Are you sure you are going to my village?" I assured him with a smile and quick little nods of the head, and he gingerly climbed into the car and sat down. I don't know if he had ever been in a car before, but he acted like he hadn't. He examined and touched everything around him.

By the time we reached the dozen or so *chozas* (huts) that made up the village, he appeared pleased with himself and us. He was especially excited when I reached across the back of Leon's seat to indicate how to open and close the door. He pointed to one of the huts nearest the continually narrowing road. As we pulled up alongside, a woman stuck her head out the window and, with a scowling face, began scolding our passenger.

Of course we didn't speak Mam Maya, so we didn't understand a single word of the conversation, but surely it went something like this:

"You are such a silly old man. What are you doing in that gringo contraption? You might have been killed. And stop that foolish smiling. What will the neighbors think of you making such a fool of yourself?"

I interrupted the monologue with another question that I expressed in sign language and gestures. How were we going to get back on a highway? I tried a series of motions, noises, and grunts trying to make the sounds that might give the old man an idea of a highway with lots of traffic. I found that making a prolonged "sh" sound as I moved my head rapidly from right to left sounded like a car speeding past. I repeated the sound and movement several times in succession to convey the idea of many cars. But I succeeded in getting only the woman's full attention. She looked at me from her secure position inside her house with an expression of utter disbelief. I am sure she thought I was a madman. Finally, by sheer luck and a last ditch attempt, I hit upon the sound. It was the sound of a large Mack truck changing gears. The moment I made the sound the woman spoke excitedly to the man. I made the sound again. He nodded his head and pointed to the east. We were out of there. The last scene I had was of the man standing in the middle of the narrow lane waving his arm frantically above his head and shaking his head rapidly. It was clear to us in the next few seconds what his gesturing was about. We ran out of road.

So we drove down the middle of a long, barren, and narrow hill that swept down eastward from the village. It couldn't have taken us much more that thirty-five minutes to make it to the very end of the ridge. When we arrived the ground dropped away quickly to the east and we could see that it was covered with a forest of pine trees and smaller growth. All three of us got out of the Bronco to take a look at the situation. It looked impossible.

The grade was steep. If the four-wheel-drive and brakes worked, we could make the descent. On the other hand, it was steep enough that the Bronco couldn't handle it if we were forced to traverse the slope but would simply tip over and roll down the hill with us in it. I had begun shaking my head when Marisela said, "Listen!"

It was the sound of a large truck changing gears as it climbed up a steep grade. "How very lucky we are," I thought. All the other creative sounds and swishes I had made were not in that village's vocabulary. Only the sound that reached their mountaintop from the highway below was understood. Taking the sound of big trucks as a good sign, we began our very rough descent.

It was just rough enough to be thrilling but not scary. We bounced over a few small, fallen tree trunks and did some serious damage to some of the secondary vegetation. Only once, when Leon accidentally released the clutch on an area of gravel, did it get iffy. The Bronco slid sideways down the slope for a few meters before Leon got it back in control. The last obstacle, a river at the bottom of the canyon, was shallow and presented no problems. Once across the river, the highway with its wonderful truck traffic was only sixty meters uphill.

Our next adventure was the border. It was an unpleasant experience. After spending the last two weeks in an atmosphere of friendliness, charity, and sincere courtesy among the struggling Guatemalans, the comparison was especially depressing for Marisela. I guess she took it so close to the chest because she was Mexican. The corruption of the Mexican border officials was especially vulgar that day in light of the fact that so many of the people crossing the border had been through the most devastating disaster of their lives.

We camped close to a lake in Monte Bello that night and visited the Mayan site of Chinkultic the next day. I was surprised that there were no guards or guides at the site. But I was inspired to buy a guidebook when we reached San Cristobal de las Casas. En route to San Cristobal we stopped in Comitan so that I could buy a hat. It had been made in Guanajuato!

In San Cristobal de las Casas I found a wonderful bookstore. Aside from a guidebook to some of the sites we planned to visit, I purchased several books. I couldn't resist J. Eric Thompson's *Catalog of Maya Hieroglyphs,* even though it looked baffling. What were all these prefixes and suffixes?

The next morning, on our way to Toniná and Palenque, we picked up a hitchhiker. He was a Chol Maya from a village about thirty kilometers up the dirt road. He was not like the Mam Maya we had seen the day before in Guatemala. He spoke Spanish fluently and rapidly. He loved to talk and told us he was returning to his village from a political meeting in San Cristobal. He was dressed in a cowboy shirt and Levi's. When I asked him if he ever wore his traditional clothing, he told me that it was no longer economically feasible to produce the traditional clothes. When we arrived at his village he invited us to stay for a while as there was a fiesta. I noticed that while the men were dressed similarly to our friend, the women wore their traditional *huipiles* (long embroidered blouses). I also noticed that all of the men spoke Spanish and the women did not. We had a long journey ahead of us, so after drinking some fermented fruit juice called *tepache* and smiling at everyone, we continued our trip.

At Toniná there was a guard. He had little knowledge of the history of the site, and not much had been excavated, so we spent only about thirty minutes there before moving on. We stopped briefly in Ocosingo for refreshments and then pushed on toward Palenque. We arrived at a campground just after dark. It reeked of marijuana.

That night, we discussed the possibility of going into the jungle and visiting the ruins of Bonampak and Yaxchilan, but decided that we couldn't afford the two or three extra days it would take.

We visited Palenque early the next morning and did everything every other tourist does there except eat the mushrooms. We descended into the belly of the Temple of Inscriptions to visit the tomb of an unknown Maya king, and clambered and crawled through the labyrinth of rooms around the observatory. We climbed the hill of the three temples. I didn't miss a chance to photograph the incised graffiti on the stucco walls. According to Nicholas, the graffiti was made by the common Maya peoples after the nobles had abandoned the buildings. I missed those wonderful lectures from Nicholas, as I had little idea of what I was seeing. After several unsuccessful attempts to find a glyph in Thompson's catalog, I gave up.

Nevertheless, we were filled with the awesome power of the ruins and our own reverence as we traversed the site.

We spent the next night with our tent pitched in the small plaza of Chicaná. There was a full moon, and the elaborate, mysterious carvings on the face of the building were magically highlighted in blue.

The next morning the caretaker at the site agreed for 100 pesos to give us a tour of Becan and Xpujil. When we got to Xpujil, I was at least knowledgeable enough to exclaim, "This is Río Bec style architecture!"

Our guide saw another opportunity and offered it. "I know the way to Río Bec. Would you like to see it?"

"I thought that it was lost and only recently found by archaeologists!" I exclaimed.

"What?! These foolish people showed up here a few years ago and made a big deal about finding it! We always knew where it was!"

His use of the plural made me wonder if he was with whatever group that had allegedly rediscovered it. But it was an interesting proposition, if only we had the time. He told us that it would take four hours to get there and back. It actually took six hours of traveling. We spent another hour at the site photographing the graffiti.

We headed due south of Xpujil at the nearest intersection. It was a well-groomed dirt road, over eight meters wide. We passed several lumber trucks going in the opposite direction. An hour and a half later and the great road ended when the guide motioned us to turn east. The new road was entirely different.

In a short time, it narrowed until it was just wide enough for the Bronco. Many times we were forced to stop while the guide and/or one of us cut a young sapling out of the road. Finally, traces of the road disappeared in a dense thicket, and we stopped. Taking water and machetes, we began to walk.

The guide indicated when we started the hike that the ruins were very close. An hour later, arms and legs worn out by the continuous effort of opening a path, we arrived in a small clearing. There was Río Bec. It was a small site . . . at least that is what we initially thought. The forest was so dense with underbrush we couldn't examine the area too far outside the clearing. However, Río Bec did have some wonderful ancient Maya graffiti and I spent a great deal of time with the camera. Especially interesting was the long, undulating body of a feathered serpent. Another graffiti showed a Maya lord on a litter carried by servants, with dwarves attending the procession.

It was early evening around dusk as we left our guide at the intersection with the highway. He was heading west back to Chicaná, another 100 pesos richer, and we were heading east toward Chetumal.

We spent what was left of the night in a hotel in Chetumal. But right after breakfast we headed back up the road to a sign that we had seen the night before, which bore a little picture of a pyramid and said "Kohunlich."

Ignacio Ik, the caretaker of the site, was the most talkative man we met on the trip. He never stopped talking. He proudly took us to the back of the pyramid where he and his pigs had found the first plate. His story was that he found the plate in a looter's hole, which he proceeded to show us. He told us he knew that it was something important the moment he found it. Not knowing what else to do with it, he took it to the municipal president. The mayor notified the INAH authorities and one day an archaeologist showed up looking for Nacho (short for Ignacio) Ik.

"I came back out here to this place with this bald archaeologist and showed him what I am showing you today. He asked me a lot of questions. He asked me how long my family had been working this land and he also wanted to know what the area was called. So I explained the generations of my fathers and then told him the place was called Nuevo Kajambrig. He got very mad at this name and told me it was not a good name for the city of our ancestors. When he returned the next time he told me the name of the place was Kohunlich."

"What was the original name you called it? I didn't understand."

He repeated, "Nuevo Kajambrig."

"What does that mean?"

He shrugged his shoulders and said, "I don't know. The people who lived close by called it that. They were English. Some of the people around here called them Mennonites."

It finally dawned upon me that what he was trying to say was in English. They had given the name of the area New Cambridge. We all had a laugh including Nacho. Then I asked, "Well, what does Kohunlich mean in Maya?"

"I don't know. This is the name the bald archaeologist brought back with him."

Once again his response brought laughter.

From Kohunlich or New Cambridge, we headed north along the Caribbean Coast. I tried to read the book I had purchased earlier that morning in Chetumal, the English translation of the *Book of Chilam Balam of Chumayel*, by Ralph Roys. Of particular interest to me were the suggested immigration routes he had mapped out in the back of the books. We stopped at a half dozen small Maya sites along the route. The sites not only were smaller than any we had seen, but had shrunk to the point that we had to get down on our hands and knees to enter some of the rooms. One guard told us that he thought the temples were for the Aluxes, and explained that Aluxes were little tiny people who had survived a great flood and wandered about the forest being mischievous. I had read somewhere of these tiny people before, but I couldn't remember where. In my mind, I compared the Aluxes to the Irish Leprechauns.

At Tulum we finally encountered more tourists. It was amazing, but we hadn't shared an archaeological site with anyone but ourselves since leaving Palenque. We spent two pleasantly social nights camped on the beach below Tulum.

We struck out west across the upper portion of the Yucatán Peninsula, and stopped at every site we thought was close to the road: Cobá, Chichén Itzá, and Uxmal. But, like pack horses heading back to the barn, our pace quickened and the stops became fewer and fewer. After spending the night in a hotel at Uxmal, we didn't stop again until we reached Coatzalcalcos in Veracruz. It turned out to be a bad choice for getting any rest.

We arrived the same night as the PRI presidential candidate. His entourage occupied every hotel in town. Finally, after dozens of inquiries, we found a small motel called the Pantera Rosa (Pink Panther) on the outskirts of town.

It turned out to be one of those "no tell motels." The traffic changed every thirty minutes or so, and every new group brought their own band.

After several hours of this, we decided that it must be approaching dawn so we packed up the Bronco and skedaddled. It wasn't until we were long on the road that we discovered it was only 3 a.m.

The rest of the trip was uneventful except for the usual getting lost in Mexico City. On top of that, somewhere downtown we attracted two motorcycle policemen. They insisted that we needed a special permit to carry all of the equipment we had in the Bronco. It was a real dilemma. Not a moral one but a truly economic challenge. It was Saturday, and the banks were all closed. We had just enough cash to buy the gas we needed to get back to San Miguel. I played dumb. I spoke in very bad Spanish and did a lot of gesturing, a talent that I had picked up on the journey home. I reasoned that if I played dumb they would get tired after a while and leave us alone. It didn't work. It seemed that their one assignment in the city that day was us.

Finally, it occurred to me that I had a few bills and some Honduran coins that I had not exchanged when we left Copan, Honduras, so many weeks ago. I spent the next thirty minutes convincing the policemen that the bills and coins were of great value, even more valuable than dollars.

They were skeptical but finally accepted them in payment of the alleged fine. Once they made up their minds, their sour character changed and they actually became friendly and offered to escort us out to the highway.

They moved along on both sides of the Bronco with pleased smiles on their faces and put magical spells on the traffic. It wasn't long before they indicated a ramp that took us to the highway that headed toward San Miguel de Allende.

After nine nights on the trip from Guatemala to San Miguel, home was like landing in heaven.

Leon spent several days in San Miguel with us. He purchased a number of woven woolen textiles and offered to have the various rolls of color slides I had taken developed back in the United States.

Unfortunately, I never saw Leon or my photographs again although we exchanged one or two letters after he left. I always get depressed when I think of all the unpublished graffiti that made up a large part of my more than two hundred photographs.

If Leon ever reads this I hope he contacts me. Not because of the photos, but because we shared an exciting time together.

THE PORTAL

We stood at the top of a ridge somewhere on the border between Quiche and Alta Verapaz, Guatemala. According to Morley, we were on the edge of two worlds. It was a place where pungent pine trees merged with decaying mahoganies. When I looked to the west, it was a place where the bright sunlight etched strong shadows on the forest floor. If I looked east, it was a place draped in perpetual twilight that smelled of rot and mold—a place that beckoned Xibalba. Directly below the west side of the outcropping of rock where we stood, two young Maya boys kicked a ball across a small clearing. The ball hit a tree and took an enormous bound upward in our direction before it disappeared into the rocks directly below us. The boys' gaze following the ball stopped as they took in our presence. They stood there and stared at us for a few seconds, until one of the boys shrugged his shoulders and they disappeared from sight as they went after the ball. Then they surprised us by suddenly appearing again, this time on the east side of the ridge below me. One of the boys carried the ball under his arm.

"How did they manage that so quickly?" I asked Emilio.

"Manage what?" he answered.

"How did they get to the other side of the mountain so fas—?" Startled at the sudden awareness of different surroundings, I didn't complete my question. Everyone around the campfire was staring at me. Disappointed and relieved, I realized I was back in Tikal.

"I think you have had enough of this very fine Tequila." Everybody laughed and I was not sure if it was at Emilio's statement or his highly accented English. He stood up and began to refill everyone's glasses. I had never seen him so gregarious before. When he reached me I refused a refill. He nodded approvingly.

"You'd better put a new Band-aid on your cut. It is beginning to bleed again."

I hadn't noticed. I looked down and saw that I had spilled small drops of blood on the legs of my Levi's and the ground in front of me. It was nothing serious but I knew from experience that I had better take care of it right away. The rain forest produces bacterial life quickly, even in cuts and scratches. Before I excused myself to fix my cut and retire for the night, I noticed one of the Italian girls making a move on Emilio. Emilio had noticed also, and looked very uncomfortable. He considered himself to be very proper and I expected that his fantasies were making him feel guilty. I smiled on the way to our tent.

I was asleep by the time Emilio came back to the tent so I don't know how long the party lasted. But Emilio had a big hangover the next morning. As he struggled desperately to get a sock over his toes, he looked at me and pleaded, "Don, please don't ever tell my wife about last night!"

"Oh, did you do something that she wouldn't appreciate?"

"I didn't do what you are thinking I did!" He almost yelled. "I just got drunk and acted foolish," he explained in a less exuberant tone.

"It's all right to act foolish sometimes. Actually, this was a pretty good time to do it. You were with a friend and a group of Europeans that you will never see again."

"Nevertheless, my wife has never seen me drunk," he confessed. "I have my reputation to think about."

As we were leaving Tikal on our journey south, I reflected upon what had brought me back to the site after having had to abandon it so suddenly three months before.

I found Emilio one day in San Miguel and he told me that he was setting up some INAH offices, and if there was money he would like to install a photographic lab. I remembered that Nicholas had a bunch of darkroom equipment that he had replaced with newer technology. I put the two men together over the phone. Nicholas ended up donating the equipment to INAH. Emilio got permission to go to Guatemala to pick it up and invited me to go along. We made the journey in a brand new blue Volkswagen Safari that INAH had supplied for Emilio.

Volkswagens are wonderful technology. They seldom cause problems and when they do they are easy to fix. Besides, hadn't I just read *How to Keep Your Volkswagen Alive*, by John Muir? The Safari didn't cause us any problems until we crossed the frontier into Guatemala. For some strange reason the Guatemalan border officials didn't want the governmental vehicle to enter their country. They told us that we couldn't bring it into their country unless Emilio produced a letter from his boss. Emilio argued that he was the boss and took them out to explain the seals on the doors.

"See that? That is the Mexican flag. Can you read what is written above it? It says 'Executive Power'! I am the executive in charge of the state of Guanajuato."

They finally gave us the necessary vehicle permit to enter their country.

The dirt road between Flores and Lake Isabel was the worst road I have ever taken. Of course it was the rainy season and large portions of the road were now swamps. When we weren't floating we were bouncing.

At one point the motor just quit. Then we discovered that the battery under the back seat had bounced up and welded itself to the metal springs causing a short circuit in the electrical system. I had never seen this happen before or since, but once we pried the battery away from the springs the engine turned over on the first attempt.

We picked up the equipment from Nicholas at the foundation, stopped by for a short visit with Mary Lou and Jay at the jade shop in Antigua, and then headed home.

As we passed a sign for Coban, I asked Emilio if we had time to visit the community. He said he was sorry but he needed to get back to Guanajuato to work the next day. I was disappointed, but my reason for wanting to go there sparked a lively discussion. For the next thirty miles we talked about the creation myths and the Hero Twins in the *Popol Vuh*. I asked him if he had read it.

Emilio was well read and we began our discussion of the creation myths with his question to me: "What is the common factor in each of the creation attempts that the gods made before the present one?" My mind began to reel back over the ancient text. "Let's see now . . . in the first creation man was made from mud . . . in the second man was made of wood . . ." While I was still absorbed with the first question, Emilio spoke again.

"Let me put it to you another way. What was the motive for the gods to make man?"

"That's easy, they wanted adoration. Each time they failed to achieve this goal in their creation they destroyed it."

"Correct. But they mentioned some very specific demonstrations of adoration, right?"

I couldn't agree because I couldn't recall. But Emilio did and he proceeded to tell me: ". . . and sacrifice. I doubt if we will ever know for sure if there is a connection but this desire for blood offerings may have been generally accepted by different cultures over a large portion of Mesoamerica."

There were some long, comfortable moments of silence after this exchange, but after a few miles I interrupted our reverie.

I began the discussion of the Hero Twins by explaining the daydream I had at the campfire back in Tikal. I confessed that the story had been on my mind lately and probably provoked my daydreaming. "Recinos, Goetz, and Morley suggest that the Quiche had a real geographical place in mind for the location Xibalba. In one of the footnotes of their English translation of the *Popol Vuh*, they claim the portal to Xibalba is located somewhere near Coban."

"Oh? If I recall, yes, the priest from Chichicastenango . . . What was his name? Father . . . Father Ximénez I believe it was. Ximénez compared Xibalba to our Christian myth of Hell."

He went on. "Not exactly the same of course. For example, you can't avoid Xibalba as Christians avoid Hell by being good in this life. I don't know if it was a real place or not, but I do think the message in the *Popol Vuh* is that everyone has to journey through Xibalba and they can only leave by being smarter than the Lords of the Underworld."

"Smart? Or maybe the message is just being more deceitful?" I suggested.

Emilio laughed. "Maybe you are right. It would appear that is the way it works in our world."

▦ ▦ ▦ LETTER CONTINUED ▦ ▦ ▦

By now, Jessica, you should begin reading the *Popol Vuh*. You are lucky because the manuscript has been retranslated and edited recently by Dennis Tedlock. It is so much easier to read than the edition I first encountered. Pay special attention to part three and the story of the Hero Twins.

▦ ▦ ▦

CHAPTER THREE

THE HOUSE OF JAGUARS

Yaxchilan Project

Just before dark, a small group of Chol Maya men visited our final campsite before Tenosique. The camp was located seven days downriver from Yaxchilan near the confluence of the Chocol-Ha and Usumacinta rivers and along the northern banks of the smaller tributary. The Maya brought the alarming news that a body had been spotted floating in the Chocol-Ha by one of the village members and that they had come to investigate in order to determine if it was one of their people. They walked downriver without seeing anything and eventually arrived at our campsite. It was then that we realized that Enrico was missing.

TENOSIQUE, TABASCO

After my adventure into the world of the Maya in Guatemala and Honduras, San Miguel seemed boring. The lure of getting to Yaxchilan and the Usumacinta River became an obsession with me. So I began to research the possibilities of getting there.

Preparations for the Yaxchilan project took the better part of a year. First we needed to get permission from Roberto García Moll, the archaeologist in charge. This involved visits to Mexico City and the National Museum of Anthropology and History. Roberto's office was in the basement. His consent depended upon a proposal and a positive response from the general director of INAH, Professor Gaston García Cantú.

Upon my return to San Miguel de Allende, Barbara Dobarganes, the acting director of the Instituto Allende, and I wrote a proposal for a documentation team to work at the site. Two weeks later we returned to Mexico City and presented it formally to the director of INAH in his office at Cordoba 47. Professor Cantú represented the very best of Mexican executive authority. He received us graciously, and after listening to Barbara and me and discussing the possibilities, he agreed to our proposal and directed us to make a contract between INAH and the Instituto Allende. He made a phone call and sent us down the hall to the office of his administrative secretary, Lic. Eduardo Villa Kamel. They were preparing the contract when we arrived.

The next step was to canvas the Instituto Allende campus for students interested in a holistic learning experience and adventure. More students were interested than we were prepared for and with the permission of INAH we extended the program a few months to accommodate most of the interested students in a second group.

I arrived on the train from Mexico City with the first group of ten students in Tenosique, Tabasco, in the middle of a wet January night.

"Féosique" (meaning Ugly Town), as we decided to call the community, is set on the eastern shore of the Usumacinta River and the northern edge of what were once the great rain forests of Chiapas and the Peten of Guatemala. Much like Peter Mathiessen's jungle settlement in his novel *At Play in the Fields of the Lord*, the community in 1978 was the jumping-off place for bush pilots, missionaries, jobless drunks, and smugglers of everything from drugs to animals and their skins.

It rained for three weeks. We tried all three of the modest hotels in Tenosique during the first week. In the first hotel several students found crab lice in the beds so we changed to another. We spent one night in the second hotel.

At two o'clock in the morning Tenosique is asleep. The municipal government shuts down at 5 p.m., leaving a casually uniformed policeman on duty by the front door. By seven the owners locked up the shops, stores, and markets. Two drugstores, a few restaurants, and a number of bars remained open until midnight. After that the town was still. The only lights left on were for the countless drunks trying to find their way home. Many of them didn't, and their snoring bodies could be found on almost every street in town. The missionaries were asleep, too, exhausted by their efforts at saving the community. Even the municipal policeman in charge of guarding the courthouse was asleep. It is possible that the smugglers were still up and about, but they were no less startled by what happened than the rest of us.

On the second morning, one of the students started to get out of her bed at 2 a.m. to go to the bathroom. As her bare foot touched the concrete, the floor moved. Startled, she flipped on the light switch in time to see hundreds—or possibly thousands—of cockroaches scurrying into cracks and little areas of darkness in the floors and walls of the room. Her yell and a subsequent stream of vengeful threats when she discovered the insect body parts and entrails clinging to the bottom of her foot woke up a sizable portion of the community. At first everyone but the young lady thought it was funny until the sound of loud voices from the hotel lobby downstairs penetrated through our laughter. When I went downstairs to investigate I found the small room full of local citizens, and the mayor was interrogating the night receptionist regarding the noise. Our group got back to sleep after negotiating a deal with the sobbing student and reassuring the community that no one had been murdered. Her roommates agreed that she could sleep with a light on in the room, and I offered to look for another hotel in the morning.

The third and last hotel in Tenosique did not have crabs or cockroaches but neither did it have any beds. We slept in hammocks.

By the end of the second week the students were running out of funds so the pilot of the project, El Capitán Pedro Joaquín, allowed us to stay in his small but clean warehouse at the airfield. Here, eleven of us slept on gunnysacks of corn or upon the leaves of the *chate* ferns. We showered under the drainpipes of the roof and the constant scrutiny of a platoon of soldiers assigned to the airfield.

Apart from the hotels, two things stand out in my memory of Tenosique: the coffee klatches in El Café and the customs/immigration officers.

The local gang, full of ancient wisdom and current knowledge, hung out in El Café every morning. The group was a motley assortment of prominent men in the community such as retired politicians, older ranchers, pilots, and smugglers. Men who could afford to spend two or three hours every morning gossiping about agriculture and smuggling, but mostly local politics. A few of them returned for an additional couple of hours before dark.

Occasionally outsiders would stop by El Café to request information. Often the municipal government had sent them, with the assurance that someone in the group would be able to solve their problems or answer their questions. The visitors were usually concerned about the route to and location of some small community in the municipality.

The visitor who most impressed me was the Lacandon Indian who appeared early one morning. He stood silhouetted in the entrance to El Café before walking over to our table. This was my first encounter with an indigenous person of the rain forest, and I examined him thoroughly.

The Lacandon could have been the prototype for the carved monuments of the classic Mayan world. He had the typical high forehead and cheekbones of the Lords of Palenque. His long black hair hung down the back of his off-white huipil halfway to his waist. The huipil was cut just below his knees, leaving his legs and bare feet exposed. Most remarkable was the contrast of the rest of his apparel and equipment. On his left wrist he wore a gold Rolex watch, and he carried a Standard toilet lid cover in his hand. In the other hand he carried a crude bow and several arrows. He spoke directly to Capitán Pedro Joaquín, whom he obviously knew, and requested in Spanish a flight into his village. Satisfied with the answer from El Capitán that he was in no danger of missing his flight, he crossed the street in the rain and entered the marketplace.

Every weekday the chief of customs ritually searched us out and counted us. What distinguished him from the other males in town was his much-used government-issue brown hat and shirt. I don't know why it was important that we were all accounted for; perhaps we changed hotels so often he became suspicious. At any rate, we saw him every day. The day I left for Yaxchilan I waved good-bye to him from the window of the plane.

His counterpart in charge of immigration was much younger and wore the rest of the government-issued uniform—the brown pants. Usually intoxicated, he did not venture out into the street, instead staggering to and from his jacal behind the two-meter-square room that was the immigration office in Tenosique. On one occasion I accompanied one of the female students whose visa had expired to that office. Everything seemed to be going fine. It took the official an hour, but he finally managed to find a new visa form and even get it into the ancient typewriter. Then he discovered that although she was a student, she had entered the country on a tourist visa. We had not counted on this obstacle. For the official it was an opportunity. At first I tried to play dumb as if I didn't understand where this was going.

I tried understanding, sincerity, dismay, and even anger. I offered logical and illogical solutions to the problem, to no avail. Then, unexpectedly, Roberto, the director of the project, entered the office. Informed of the situation, he expressed to the official the importance of the INAH project and even suggested that the official was standing in the way of progress. When this did not work, Roberto walked out the door in disgust and anger.

The official kept clicking his tongue on the roof of his mouth, shaking his head and repeating over and over, "No, Señor. This is a serious problem." The silence between his mutterings was broken by the sound of a single cricket under the nearby wastebasket. For some reason this chirping made me nervous and added to my inner tension.

I knew that sooner or later that I would have to face up to the fact that I was going to offer him a bribe and I hated myself for it. When gringos stressed the endemic "corruption" in Mexico, I always countered with, "Who is more corrupt? The person who offers the bribe, or the one who takes it?" The cricket reminded me that I had no excuse. The student had the wrong visa and we were in reality asking the man to bend the law in our favor.

Somehow the man must have guessed my unvoiced decision. He suddenly stood up and, smiling, motioned for me to follow him.

Going through the small back door I found myself in a dirt yard with a turkey and several chickens pecking about. A woman, whom I assumed was his wife, was washing clothes on a large rock in front of a thatched roof jacal.

The official stopped in the center of the yard and turned to face me. Simultaneously I reached for the wallet in my back pocket. To my surprise he detained my arm and shook his head.

"I don't want your money, mister. We can work this out another way."

The quizzical expression on my face prompted him to continue.

He tilted his head toward the office, then leaned forward and whispered, "¿Y esta güera?" (And that blonde?)

I was shocked. I stood there for several seconds trying to close my mouth. His intentions overwhelmed me. Embarrassed and dumbfounded, I glanced over to the woman to see if she was aware of her husband's request. My mind was in torment. Then, without being aware of where my thoughts were taking me, I heard myself ask, "If you had to buy la güera, how much would you be willing to pay?"

The man didn't hesitate. "300 pesos!" he exclaimed with a broad grin on his face. I reached into my wallet and took out the 300 pesos and put it into his hand. I glanced once again at the woman washing clothes. Without waiting for an answer, I turned my back on the official and walked back through the door and into the office.

As I entered the office, "la güera" looked at me nervously and asked what had happened. I shook my head and indicated that we should wait. In less than a minute, the official returned to the office, sat down in front of the typewriter, and filled out a new visa.

As we walked into the street we saw Roberto waiting for us. "What happened?" he asked.

When I told him that the new visa cost 300 pesos he became quite upset. "We will never get out of this bureaucratic corruption as long as you gringos continue to bribe the officials," he stammered.

"Look, Roberto, it was either 300 pesos or a tryst with la güera," I responded. I felt guilty as hell and wanted to point out that Mexicans had a history of *mordida* (bribes) long before me.

Figure 5 Capitan Pedro Joaquín (photo by author)

La güera looked shocked. "What?" she exclaimed. Trying to be philosophical, I told her, "Well, at least now you have a fairly good idea where the bidding starts in this community." None of us ever mentioned the incident again. I never again saw la güera anywhere near the office of immigration.

The sky began to clear and we made two attempts the third week to get off the muddy ground. Each attempt ended with all of us standing amid the supplies and around the plane, while the pilot and the mechanic stared woefully at the overcast sky.

THE AIRFIELD

Finally, late Saturday morning, Capitán Pedro Joaquín announced that there was enough ceiling for him to make a couple of runs over the mountains. With our dampened spirits slightly dried out we began, after removing three of the seats, to load supplies into the Cessna 180. Then Roberto instructed me and two students, Iñigo de Martino and "Hollywood" Harry McKnight, to climb into the plane on top of the supplies.

The flight from Tenosique to Yaxchilan takes about forty minutes. As Pedro Joaquín flew over the Usumacinta River I kept thinking of the Credence Clearwater Revival song "Proud Mary."

Pedro Joaquín, I was to learn during the next few months, was the respected "Dean" of the bush pilots flying into the rain forests of Chiapas and Central America. He noted our extreme interest in the tropical forest below us and pointed out several places that he thought we would find interesting. Except for the long seam of the Usumacinta and its lateral sides of white sand, the rain forest was a vast unbroken sea of green vegetation as far as the eye could see in any direction. At one point Pedro Joaquín lowered the plane and flew between the ridges surrounding the river to give us a dramatic, eye-level view of Busil-ha (smoking waters) waterfalls. We crossed over the river several times during the flight en route to Yaxchilan. Sometimes the captain took us over the Peten of Guatemala and other times over the forests of Mexico. At one point, on the Chiapas side of the river, he pointed out a large lagoon, Santa Clara, which apparently was the property of a ranch family that lived near Tenosique. I noted ominous little streams of smoke rising from fires in several locations around the lake but made no comment.

The dirt airstrip at Yaxchilan is barely more than 400 meters long, so Pedro Joaquín, after climbing over a ridge above the river, immediately cut his engine and lowered his flaps in order to avoid running out of runway. The treetops passed no more than a meter or two below the landing gear of the plane. Even though there was not much view in the approach, it was apparent that the runway was clear for landing. But by the time we taxied to a stop near two overgrown palapas, a hundred hungry and cheering workmen surrounded us. In less than ten minutes the enthusiastic workmen had unloaded and carried off the badly needed supplies from the plane. The captain took off into the wild blue yonder, pledging to return in about three hours.

As we stood watching on the edge of the runway, our contact with civilization disappeared into the horizon. A workman, pointing to his chest, succeeded in identifying himself as Zotz (Yucatec Maya for "bat").

He tugged on my arm and in broken Spanish asked if I would like to see the "Cristiano" in the river.

Whatever the dead man's religion, he had gone to meet his maker. The little body, riddled with bullet holes, was obscenely bloated from being in the river for several days. He was lodged in the rocks near the shore just out of our reach. Iñigo found a tree branch nearby and Harry and I used it to dislodge the body in an attempt to bring it onto the shore. Unfortunately, the branch broke the moment the body was freed from the rocks, allowing it to drift into the current. We stood there quietly, watching the corpse float downriver until it disappeared from view.

We jabbered excitedly for several minutes, speculating on the man's identity. Was he a smuggler? Was he a revolutionary? Who had shot him? Had he been shot in the river? Was he dead before he reached the river or did he die in the river trying to escape his adversaries? Suddenly the magnificent tropical forest seemed sinister, and goose bumps tingled my arms and the back of my neck.

Zotz, patiently listening to our excited conversation, again tugged at my arm. Although he spoke no English, he obviously understood the drift of our conversation. With a very serious frown on his face, he gestured toward the Guatemalan side of the river and made motions and sounds imitating an automatic weapon.

There were questions that I would have liked to ask Zotz, but neither he nor we spoke enough Spanish to communicate beyond a few words and gestures. With fearful glances over our shoulders, we solemnly climbed back up the riverbank to the edge of the runway.

By the time we reached the river edge of the airstrip, we were breathing heavily, sweating profusely, and had not even begun to leave behind us the experience of the "Cristiano" in the river.

Harry took us by surprise when he broke the silence with one word, "Listen!" It was the faint hum of an aircraft.

It took us several minutes to locate the position of the plane. Harry had worked in both Chicago and Denver as an air traffic controller and after a few minutes identified the aircraft as a Twin Otter.

The plane circled overhead, and with each circle, much like a duck descending upon a pond, approached closer and closer. Suddenly Harry exclaimed, "Run! The fool is going to try to land!"

Without hesitation we dashed across the airstrip and into the protection of the trees on the uphill edge of the runway. When we turned around my first reaction was to motion for Zotz, who had obviously not understood Harry's exclamation. But Harry grabbed my arm and pointed down the runway. I looked just in time to see the left wing of the Twin Otter hit the top of a tree on the river side of the airstrip. The plane angled down onto the mucky runway gouging out deep ruts of mud with its landing gear before finally coming to a halt. The pilot managed to taxi the plane around at the end of the airstrip and within a few minutes the door of the aircraft opened and the copilot let down the metal stairs. Immediately, twelve German tourists descended onto the runway. As we watched, our mouths hanging open, the passengers, obviously well disciplined, formed a single line and their tour guide began to spray them with insect repellent.

Without another word they marched off into the rain forest in the direction of the ancient Mayan ruins. The pilot, white-faced and trembling, descended the stairs and walked straight to us. His first words were, "Does anyone have a smoke?"

Whatever the pilot thought about his previous lack of judgment he never expressed. Nor did we. He immediately focused upon his next problem: how to get the plane out of there. Evidently a Twin Otter is designed for taking off and landing on short airfields, but his problem was that the wingspan of his aircraft was too wide for the narrow runway. He requested my help.

I was stunned by his request. There I was, with less than an hour in the middle of the rain forest. I knew only a few phrases of Spanish. I had already dealt with a dead body in the river. I had a hundred workmen ravenously devouring all of the foodstuffs. I had twelve German tourists with whom I could not communicate; when they returned from the ruins they were obviously going to be anxious about their future. And finally, I had two students and Guatemalan pilots awaiting my reply.

Oh, shit! I rubbed my eyes vigorously with the heels of my palms as if I had just awakened from a very bad dream. This was not the laid-back "Mañana Land" that I had come to appreciate and love in San Miguel. This was more like Mexico City! What to do?

Fortunately, as I looked up again, the first thing that came into focus was the smiling bat. Throughout the whole ordeal Zotz had remained on the other side of the runway. His smile said, "Welcome to the rain forest." It was enough to set me into action. Without replying to the pilot, I hurried across the airstrip and tugged at Zotz's arm, motioning for him to follow me down the runway.

We stopped about three-quarters of the way down the field and in front of the tree where the Twin Otter had taken the hit. Motioning with my hands I tried to convey the concept of topping off the tall trees on that side of the airfield.

I believed Zotz understood, because he took off with amazing alacrity in the direction of a few Mayan workmen sitting on a fallen tree trunk near a thatched roof jacal. As I waited, my gaze turned up the airstrip to where the copilot squatted upon the left wing of the Twin Otter. He was patching the hole made by the tree with some of Harry's duct tape.

Meanwhile, Zotz had returned with a group of five smiling Mayans with machetes. I stayed there with the men and watched their progress, trying not to get in their way. After cutting off about two meters of the tops of a dozen of the tallest trees, the pilot walked over and requested that we also cut some of the taller underbrush from the edge of the runway, about three meters wide and one hundred meters long. Two hours later we were still occupied with this chore when once again we heard the hum of an approaching aircraft. It was Pedro Joaquín with more supplies, two more of my students, and, much to my relief, Roberto, the director of the project.

I was expecting either criticism for destroying the rain forest or some kind of praise for taking charge of the situation, but Roberto offered neither. Instead, after listening to the excited report, he calmly informed me that, depending upon the weather conditions, the rest of my students and more supplies would be coming into Yaxchilan during the next couple of days. He pointed out the two organically tangled palapas near the river bank where my students and I would be living. Then, much to my surprise, he informed me that I was to accompany Juan, the project's paid hunter, early the next morning eighteen kilometers upriver to a Chol Mayan village to buy corn. He then turned away and headed for his jacal on the other side of the airstrip.

With our small crew of five, we spent the rest of the day cutting and prying the rain forest loose from our new homes. We were constantly on the lookout for snakes, scorpions, and the large, gray, flat and crablike spiders whose resilient webs were everywhere. Zotz, seeing how long we were taking, arrived with a short, forked branch and a machete. In less than five minutes he showed us how to cut away the undergrowth without exposing our arms and legs to the tangled and varmint-invested mess. Our confidence soon overcame our reluctance and we began to make real progress. Our strategy for acclimating to the heat and humidity was to take a dip in the river every couple of hours. We would be sweating profusely again by the time we climbed back up the riverbank to the palapas. Just before nightfall we had eliminated the flora and fauna from under one of the palapas.

Exhausted, I reclined in my hammock just after dark. The students had built a small fire and were excitedly discussing the day's activities and the fact that the wild still surrounded us very closely on all sides. Since I was to travel upstream in the morning, I asked them to take charge the next day to recruit any more students who arrived to clear out the other palapas and the area surrounding them both for about two to three meters, and to build a latrine as well. After that, I was too tired to participate and was asleep within minutes. I didn't get a chance to see the ruins of Yaxchilan until the third day.

THE RIVER OF THE SACRED MONKEY

The pirogue was long and narrow in the dark, and extremely delicate in balance. With the aid of flashlights, and after a little stumbling around, I was able to find a seat on the wooden thwart in the prow.

Figure 6 Usumacinta (photo by author)

To say that my companion was a man of few words was an understatement. Juan was a very silent man. Even if he had spoken, I could not have heard him during the journey because of the noise of the small craft's motor. The trip upriver took four hours. So, without the intrusion of conversation, I was able to study the rain forest and river with great intensity.

The Usumacinta is a large river and the volume of water is tremendous. The upper portion forms the frontier between Chiapas, Mexico, and the Peten forests of Guatemala. Within this section the river cuts through a series of small hills, mountains, and serpentine cliffs, creating a wide diversity of boating conditions. Below Yaxchilan the river is seldom navigated by the locals. In fact, a number of years ago the authorities at Tenosique denied access to this portion of the river because of various tragedies at one of the rapids called Chicozapote falls. But in the section above Yaxchilan the river is gentle and even tempered. Only during the dry season, when the water level is so low that it exposes numerous rocks and boulders, does this section contain many hazards. Even though it was technically the middle of the dry season, the last two weeks of winter rains had raised the water level to the point that there were few visible rocks or sandbars to obstruct the pirogue's advance.

Nevertheless, enormous amounts of vegetation came down the river with the current. Juan skillfully avoided the larger tree trunks and branches. The current had dislodged a large number of snakes from their resting places along the banks of the river. I counted forty before I became bored with the effort.

The forest was like a dense and dark jungle curtain on both sides of the river. I was not a complete novice to the rainforest, having worked in Mayan archaeological sites in Peten, Guatemala, and I could identify a number of the trees. I soon recognized ceibas, cedars, mahoganies, and ramons (breadfruit). Frequently, flocks of parrots flew noisily across the river. In one tree I counted more than fifty long, bulbous, hanging nests of the yellow-tailed *oropendolas*. Occasionally, howler monkeys sent out their roaring challenge and more often than not the response came from the opposite side of the river.

The monkeys reminded me of the story about the twins in the sacred book of the Quiche Maya, the *Popol Vuh*. I had imagined the twins traveling down the eastern slopes of Alta Verapaz, Guatemala, and then down the Usumacinta on their journey to Xibalba, the Mayan underworld. I asked myself if their final destination had been Yaxchilan or Piedras Negras. Perhaps their fateful ballgame had even been played on the ball court of Yaxchilan. These two ancient Mayan cities, located upon the banks of the Usumacinta, were where Dr. Tatiana Proskouriakoff found evidence that enabled us to identify the historic nature of the texts carved on their stone monuments. Especially important was her identification of the name glyphs, allowing us to establish the historic nature of the texts. From these texts modern man uttered the name Bird Jaguar, and as one author put it, "he became the first Mayan Lord to have his name spoken in over a thousand years." Hopefully, as the epigraphers revealed more from these carved texts, my wild speculations might be resolved.

As we came in sight of the Chol village on the Mexican bank, the river widened and great exposed sandbars extended down its middle. Juan expertly directed the pirogue toward the right shore, where several Chol men stood quietly, as if awaiting our arrival. As we neared them, Juan gave the small motor more throttle and then tilted the engine up in an effort to beach the craft on the sand of the shoreline. Unfortunately, he miscalculated the force that was needed and the current was so strong even in this shallower water that without the motor the bow began to turn back downstream.

Juan jumped in the water and tried desperately to stop the craft from drifting back down the river. I saw that he could not handle this by himself so I quickly took off my boots and socks and jumped overboard to help. By the time I did, the bow was heading downstream, and Juan grabbed the bowline of the pirogue while I filled the position on the stern. He pulled and I pushed. There was no great distance between us, but the water was up to my waist and I tried desperately to grab the bottom of the river with my toes as I shoved and he pulled.

Finally, I could see that we were making progress. Just as he had the bow of the craft within a few feet of the shore, one of the Chols ran to the pirogue, grabbed my boots, and ran with them over the beach in the direction of the village.

Juan let go of the bowline and took off after the man. The last glimpse I had of the drama was Juan making a tackle that would have made a linebacker for the Green Bay Packers proud. Meantime, I had encountered a more serious situation.

When Juan let go of the bowline the current had swept the prow of the pirogue around and I found myself digging in my heels trying to keep the craft from heading back downriver to Yaxchilan. I remember loud voices behind just as my feet were lifted from the river bottom, and I was left hanging on to the boat's stern. Suddenly, several brown bodies surrounded me.

I vaguely recall my fear. For a moment I thought that Juan was dead and these Chols were going to kill me and steal the boat. Fortunately, this train of thought quickly abated as the men, completely ignoring me, began to struggle in an attempt to turn the craft toward the shore.

Juan stoically waited on the shore, holding my boots out in front of him like some kind of trophy. The thief was nowhere in sight. I thanked Juan twice with a "Muchísmas gracias" as I accepted my boots and then turned and thanked the solemn-looking faces of the diminutive men who had helped me save the craft.

Juan grabbed my arm and pulled me around to face him. He pointed to my watch and then my pocket. I got the idea and removed my watch and hid it in the front pocket of my dripping jeans. Then without a word he handed the bowline, with an air of complete confidence, to one of the village men who had helped me save the pirogue and started walking up the bank in the direction of the village.

During the Mexican presidential administration of Luis Echeverria, hundreds of Chol Maya from the highlands of Chiapas had been relocated into the tropics of the eastern portion of the state. The Chol village that we were visiting was one of these relocated communities. In 1978 the village was called Frontera Echeverria. Today it is known as Frontera Corasal.

It wasn't much of a community. We passed fewer than a dozen widely separated thatched-roof jacales as we crossed the village. Like so many of the Mayan villages I had visited, the houses were scattered around the family plots with a few small *milpas* (cornfields) close by. The nearest neighbor was fifty to a hundred meters away. In many places the rainforest still penetrated the community among the different parcels. There was no electricity, though there had been an attempt by the government at urban planning. The urbanization consisted of two square blocks of dirt streets cut out of the rainforest. The dirt roads were wide enough for traffic, but it didn't surprise me that there was no sign that vehicles had ever been here. Even if someone in the village had owned a truck, it would have been useless that day. After the two weeks of rain, it would have taken an army half-track to maneuver them. Juan cleverly kept off the streets and led me down a well-worn and easier path along the edge of the rain forest.

As we passed the first couple of jacales, the women grabbed their children and ran into the houses. Some of the children peered out from the darkened doorways with fearful yet curious faces as we walked by.

Finally, we arrived at a small clearing where one cow and a few pigs were busy eating corn stubble stocks. This was the western edge of the community. On the front of the clearing a man appeared and motioned for us to join him near the entrance to his jacal. We sat down on small tree trunks, the only furniture to be seen in what was the front yard. Chickens and a few wild birds, known as *chachalacas,* were feeding on grains of corn that had been scattered about the front of the house.

I had expected a change in Juan's character when he found himself with another who could speak the same language. Yet few words were spoken, and we must have sat there in silence for over an hour. Juan obviously knew this man, as we had gone directly to his parcel without speaking to anyone. There didn't appear to be any kind of negotiating going on. After the man's wife brought us a cup of *café de olla,* she disappeared into the jacal and did not appear again. I spent the hour smiling at the stern-looking gentleman each time our eyes met, and drawing doodles in the dirt with a stick on the ground in front of me. I doubt a dozen words were exchanged.

Finally, an adolescent appeared with a small paper sack and gave it to Juan. Juan peered into the sack. After examining a handful of corn that he had poured in his hand, Juan nodded his head. We stood up and the younger man directed us to a small shed behind the jacal, less than twenty meters from where we had been sitting. The shed contained twenty or thirty gunnysacks full of corn. Apparently, the price the project paid for the corn did not include transportation to the river. Juan and I made several trips to carry a dozen fifty-kilo gunnysacks through the muddy community and down to the river near the pirogue. When we finished, Juan began to open the gunnysacks and empty their contents into the bottom of the pirogue. He returned the sacks to the young man who appeared on the upper bank of the river.

Returning to the boat, Juan motioned me to the front of the pirogue and we drifted into the current of the Usumacinta.

The trip back downriver to Yaxchilan was a time of quiet reflection for me. I could not remember a day in my life that I had said so little and listened so much. I had been told by various teachers and professors during my school days that if I talked less and listened more, I would perhaps learn more. Yet the simple truth was that I understood very little of what had gone on that day.

One thing I had unconsciously observed was that nobody had smiled. Except for the children, all of their expressions were the same. They reminded me of Grant Wood's early twentieth-century painting "American Gothic." Their fight for survival was obviously a daily struggle, so I reasoned that they had little to smile about. From an early age the Indians learned to be suspicious and even fearful of strangers. I did not realize it at the time, but dark forces were taking shape under the perpetual twilight of the rain forest canopies in the villages on both sides of the river, forces that would bring tragedy and chaos to their villages and keep most of these peoples from smiling for the rest of their lives. Many of them would die; however, that was the future and this day was not over yet.

Near dusk, about thirty minutes shy of Yaxchilan, we rounded a bend in the river and came upon a large rubber raft. The occupants, all young gringos, waved us over. When they saw me they all began to speak at once in a torrent of English.

Apparently, they had been camped four nights previously on the Guatemalan side of the river only a few kilometers upstream from the Chol village we had just visited. They had been sitting round the campfire smoking pot when they heard the nearby sound of automatic weapons downriver.

Within minutes, soldiers dashed into their camp carrying weapons, and the group, being stoned, became paranoid and panicked. One of their companions jumped into the river and was fired upon by the soldiers. The rest had been tied up and led through the night to a small village where they were locked up in a jacal. They were guarded for two days and fed by the soldiers. Finally, a Guatemalan immigration officer appeared and, after questioning them, released them and ordered them not to come back.

Although lacking most of their supplies, they had been able to rescue their raft and had chosen to continue downriver in hopes of finding their missing companion.

I asked for a description of their friend, thinking that perhaps he was the body that we had dealt with the day before, but their description did not fit the "Cristiano."

Since they were short on supplies, I suggested that they could camp that night at Yaxchilan where the students and I could provide them with a limited amount of food. I also warned them about the rapids downriver. They seemed hesitant, so after waiting for a few minutes I turned and pointed downriver to Juan, and we took off.

It was dark by the time we passed the ancient stone pilings in the river in front of the ruins of Yaxchilan. After we landed the pirogue on the beach by the camp, Juan pointed to my pocket and then my wrist. I had completely forgotten my watch. I took the watch out of my pocket and handed it to him. It was the only time in the four months I shared with him that I saw him smile. It wasn't a big smile, but to me it was a great privilege. Unfortunately, I never learned his last name. Most of the workmen in the camp simply referred to him as the Guatemalan or *El Cazador* (the hunter).

I never saw the young American rafters from Arizona again; however, I did meet their lost companion the following day.

THE RETURN OF THE GRINGO RAFTER

Something was moving about. I opened my eyes and there was Andy Rakcozy grinning down at me. "Don? Don, get up! Roberto told us that breakfast is at five thirty." I lay there looking up at his teeth and replied, "Andy, get out of my face." He straightened up but stood there grinning.

"Professor, you don't want to be late your first day of work!" He accented *Professor*.

"Andy, when did *you* arrive?"

"Yesterday I came on a flight with Linda and Marion. Have you seen the ruins?" It was both a question and an enthusiastic declaration.

Andy, a photojournalist who specialized in wildlife photography, had been my friend for several years. He had returned from Vietnam in 1970 and a year later ended up in San Miguel de Allende. He had learned photography in the army at Pleiku, where he was in charge of a battalion darkroom. He claimed to have stolen enough film from the army to last for years to come.

I sat up and swung my legs over the side of the hammock. I reached down in front of me and picked up a boot, turned it upside down, and shook it vigorously.

"What are you doing?"

"Shaking out little rain forest creatures," I responded as I reached for the other boot. As his expression remained puzzled, I added, "Scorpions, Andy, huge black scorpions!"

He looked around the palapa in disbelief. I immediately recognized the changes, as well as more hammocks strung up under the palapa than there had been the day before.

"Iñigo built us a shower out of that bucket over there in the corner and Linda Anderson had Iñigo, Harry, and me dig a latrine back there in the jungle."

As I dressed, Andy showed me the work that the students had accomplished yesterday. Even the dirt floor of the palapa had been swept immaculately clean. The rain forest that had previously encroached around and within the palapas had been removed for about three to four meters all around the structures.

After dressing I took off in the direction that Andy indicated for the latrine. I came upon a long trench about a meter deep and there relieved myself. The latrine had obviously been used several times. It was about two meters long and the excavated dirt was used as refill.

When I returned to Andy, he said, "Linda says we can recycle the shit to grow flowers around the palapas." Walking across the runway in the direction of the dining room, I made a mental note to leave Linda in charge of our portion of the camp.

The camp was laid out along the uphill length of the airstrip.

Only our palapas were located on the riverside and near the end of the runway. The two palapas had been built a few years before our arrival by Captain Pepe Martínez, a pilot out of San Cristobal de las Casas. During the next five months the Mexican military, against our protests, appeared twice and fumigated these palapas with DDT. Our protests were very polite, with huge, friendly smiles. True, no one in our group came down with malaria and several of the Mayan workmen did. Nevertheless, there was a full day of grumbling by the students after each fumigation.

Three thatched-roof jacales made up the nucleus of project activity. They were built on concrete foundations with walls that extended halfway up to the roofs. The remaining distance was screened in with a fine wire mesh.

One of these buildings had two rooms and served as the bedroom for the Mexican students as well as the dining room. Attached to the dining room end of the jacal was an open-air kitchen.

To the right of this building was another jacal, a single-room storehouse with a covered veranda extending out on the riverside. Here, all of the carved stones and material found in the excavation were cleaned and studied. In front of the veranda was a hitching post. Below the warehouse was the third jacal, the bedroom of the project director, Roberto García Moll, and his assistant. There was also a small, covered veranda where two hammocks were hung. Inside was the short-wave ham radio with which the director contacted the pilot, Pedro Joaquín, every night at 7 p.m. Outside of a few small villages upstream, it was our only contact with civilization.

In the rest of the buildings in Yaxchilan, most of the crew either ate or slept. Behind the director's abode was the largest structure of the camp, a rectangular palapa that served as both a kitchen and dining room for the eighty workmen from Tenosique. One end was partitioned off with cloth drapes; behind this was the makeshift bedroom of the cook and her assistants. On weekends this space experienced a lot of solicited traffic.

Behind the workmen's dining palapa was another smaller one, where the workmen hung their hammocks and kept their personal belongings. Perhaps a hundred meters down the runway were three jacales where Zotz and another twelve Mayan workers from Oxkutzcab slept. These men were the expert restorers of the project.

Farther down the runway was the jacal of Luis Cuevas and his family. Luis was one of the guardians of INAH at the ruins as well as the second hunter of the project. Luis and I spent a lot of time together and remained in contact for years. Just a few days before his tragic death on the Usumacinta, he spent the night in my apartment in Mexico City. Years later, when I returned to Yaxchilan, it took me more than thirty minutes to remove the rain forest to reveal his grave. Memories of our shared time together filled my thoughts while my eyes filled with tears.

My students were seated at the long table and had already eaten. Roberto introduced me to the cook, Señora María de la Cruz. She smiled shyly when we shook hands. Later I found out that she was Luis Cuevas's sister-in-law.

I sat down to eat. There were scrambled eggs, beans, and tortillas on the plate in front of me. María brought a small cup of café de olla. In addition, a large bowl filled with animal crackers was waiting as dessert. While I ate, Roberto began to speak.

"Some archaeological students will be arriving today, and as you can see there are not enough chairs in here for everyone to eat at the same time. Beginning tomorrow, breakfast will be served between five and five forty-five a.m. Therefore, if you want to sit down to eat, get here early. I expect everyone to be at the site by six o'clock and we will quit working at 2 p.m. We will have lunch at two thirty. Today you can finish organizing your camp and use the rest of the day to familiarize yourselves with the ruins. Oh, you had better take flashlights," he added.

With that he got up and left for the site.

By the time he left, I was starting on dessert. Thorrun, my student from Iceland, looked on in disgust. "I refuse to eat those things!" she exclaimed. "They have absolutely no nutritional value!"

I didn't bother to answer and instead reached for an elephant.

Harry examined a refrigerator that stood at the end of the long table on the back wall of the dining room. "Too bad," he said. "We could have used this thing for storing cold beers."

"Yeah, why can't we?" I asked.

"There is a large diesel generator back in the rain forest a few meters but Roberto allows it to be used for only an hour each night in order to save fuel."

We talked for about thirty minutes, discussing our various adventures of the last few weeks, laughing and making fun of each other. Afterward we walked back down the hill and across the runway to our palapas.

Our camp area was so clean and efficiently organized that after examining what the students had done the day before, I congratulated them and then proposed that Linda Anderson be in charge of all maintenance and changes that the rest of the group desired. They unanimously agreed on this, so I went over to one of my metal ammo boxes and took out a map.

"Let's go visit Yaxchilan," I said.

The map I had brought along was a copy of a topographic map of the site originally made by Ian Graham of the Peabody Museum in Massachusetts the year before. The small photocopy I had made was difficult to read and before the visit was finished we realized that we had underestimated the elevations.

Still, we managed to find most of the numbered building complexes indicated on the map. Yaxchilan sits on the edge of a horseshoe formed by the wandering Usumacinta doubling back on itself. The river had come within a few hundred meters of making the site an island. The main civic-ceremonial center was located on the eastern edge of the horseshoe, or the western bank of the river. Investigators suspected that the general population of the center probably lived across the river in Guatemala. Large visible stone pilings marked the spot in the river where a bridge or dock had connected the halved community.

The two main plazas of Yaxchilan ran along and above the western bank of the Usumacinta River. We entered the first plaza from behind the left side of the structure numbered 19 on Ian's map, and descended a small flight of stone stairs to gather around one of the two doors in the facade of the building. I recognized it immediately as Teobert Maler's "Labyrinth."

Teobert Maler was one of a handful of nineteenth-century Mayanists whom I truly admired. He is the one who gave the ruin the name Yaxchilan, or "small green stones." He arrived at the ruins in 1896 during the rainy season, having begun his adventure downriver from Tenosique, Tabasco, where he received reluctant permission from the local authorities for his expedition. His publication, *Explorations of the Upper Usumacinta,* contains the best photographs ever taken of dozens of the carved monuments at the site.

There was no whistle to announce the end of the day's work, but the mass exodus from the site was punctual. As the hundred laborers started back to camp, each picked up a stone from the tons of rubble that poured out of the rain forest along the lower edges of the buildings.

These stones were to be used for the construction of buildings for a new camp. During the five months I was there, we carried enough stones, one at a time, to complete two of the proposed new buildings.

When our crew returned to the camp, the first thing we did was head for the river, not only to cool off but to soothe the insect bites we had acquired during the day. By the time we climbed up the back to the edge of the airstrip, we were sweating again.

When we arrived at the dining room for lunch, there were two unexpected faces. Pedro Joaquín, still delivering supplies for the project, was sitting with Roberto and two guests, one of whom was a bush pilot out of Palenque and the other his client, a young and very blonde American in search of his rafting companions.

The kid repeated his story without reluctance. He admitted that he panicked that night and, as he put it, "preferred to die in the river than rot in a Guatemalan jail." So, with bullets flying overhead, he dove into the Usumacinta hoping to make it to sanctuary in Mexico.

Luckily for him, the river formed a large gravel and sand bar downstream from where he entered and he was able to reach it with the help of a back eddy in the otherwise strong current. Exhausted and cold from his endeavor, he hid and tried to sleep among the larger rocks and boulders of the gravel bar until daylight.

In the early morning light, he was able to see another large gravel bar downriver from his hiding place. It appeared to extend closer to the Mexican bank, so he committed himself once again to the river. By late morning he had managed to make it to the Mexican side of the river by gravel-bed hopping, arriving on shore about a kilometer short of the Chol village of Frontera Echeverria.

Three days of walking and hitchhiking took him to Palenque. After spending a night of remorse about abandoning his friends, he hired the pilot to help him find them.

I have thought of this young rafter many times since then. I never found out whether or not he got together with his companions, but I suspect he did.

The Mesoamerican Watering Hole

There are times when our differences stand in the way of the common good [of the project].

—Diary: Feb. 14, 1978

There were both upsides and downsides to the rain forest.

In the positive column, it was beautiful. Everything was lush and green, and there was much variety and density of vegetation. At times it was overwhelming. This was especially true for my Icelandic student, Thorrun. For the first two weeks one would have thought that she had never seen a tree before. Because she was always looking up, she constantly tripped over the myriad roots that crossed the trails. Moss, ferns, and Bejuco vines were more plentiful than I had ever seen. Orchids bloomed everywhere. The forest produced so much oxygen that every breath was a pleasure and each thought clear and sharp. On the surface it was like a tropical Camelot. As one might expect, I caught all three of the male students at one time or another beating their chests in poor Tarzan imitations.

But there was also a dark and sinister side to the rain forest that made me uneasy, maybe because I had read Ferdinand Anton's description when he visited the archaeological site eight years before:

> Nobody had warned me about the poisonous spiders the size of eggs, which spin their webs everywhere; nobody mentioned the masses of bats in the vaults, or the hundreds of loathsome toads the size of chickens, which swarm at night over the moist earth. None of these, however, constitute a serious danger, any more than the few prowling jaguars, or the numerous snakes, which abruptly slither away from underfoot. The only danger is getting lost.

The forest also produced a variety of night-flying biting insects that could penetrate your Levi's, leaving large, burning welts. Everybody in the camp scratched. But worse still, the rain forest was a force, a living force whose dense, entangled roots, moss, and vines created an impenetrable wall between civilization and us. It encroached slowly but steadily into the very social structure of the small encampment, compressing life and art into a condensed relief, just as it had in Yaxchilan on the lintels and stela over a thousand years ago. There is something awesome about ancient cities in the rain forest; the rain forest slowly and relentlessly, millimeter by millimeter, takes control. For over a thousand years, it alone decided what would be destroyed and what it would embrace with protective arms.

Iñigo, depressed by Lavinia's rejection of affection, had wandered off into the rain forest early one morning and gotten lost. He managed to keep his cool and by sheer luck stumbled back upon the ruins in the late afternoon. With his body badly bruised, battered, and scratched from the rain forest trek, he had just returned to the camp dining room.

Though still depressed, it was apparent he was relieved to have survived his ordeal. He had missed lunch and hungrily attacked the unfinished bowl of animal crackers on the table.

I looked across the table at Iñigo. "We've been here over two weeks and it has turned out to be something even more exciting and magnificent than I had ever imagined." I was consciously trying to be positive.

"Yeah, right!" Iñigo commented caustically. "Especially the food: beans, eggs, tortillas, and animal crackers. We eat three meals a day and they are exactly the same. All they do is change the serving order. Yesterday I saw the workmen unloading three large sacks of these damn animal crackers from Pedro Joaquín's plane. I thought Thorrun was going to have an epileptic fit." He immediately followed with, "Do you know what Xoco calls Coca-Cola? The black waters of imperialism!" he answered himself indignantly.

So there it was, the cold war beginning to creep into the cracks and crevices of Yaxchilan. I was not surprised. I thought of the Russian linguist Yuri Knorosov sitting at his desk somewhere in Moscow daring to suggest to the Harvard Mayanist, J. Eric Thompson, that Mayan glyphs were phonetic.

"Jesus, Iñigo," I said. "What did you expect? Of course you could swim across the river into Guatemala and if you did stumble upon a village over there they would be sure to have Coca-Cola. Which kind of proves Xoco's point, doesn't it? More than likely you would just get lost again. You were very lucky today. On the other hand, we have Roberto's example. He is a socialist and, like the Coke commercial, the '*Chispa de la Vida*' (the spark of life). In fact, he should be making commercials for Coke. Have you ever seen a bigger addict?"

Looking past Iñigo through the screen mesh of the dining room, I said, "Look at what Harry is doing down there at the palapa!" ("And it isn't going to help the situation," I added under my breath.)

I had been watching Harry working by himself all morning, and I tried to figure out what the hell he was doing. When Iñigo mentioned the black waters of imperialism, it suddenly became clear what Harry was building.

"What is he doing?" Iñigo began to grin as he asked. The nice thing about Harry: he was very bright. He was also strange, but everyone enjoyed his not-too-subtle caustic wit and quirky mannerisms.

"While you were looking at the sacks of animal crackers," I said, "I am surprised you didn't see the three cases of beer that Harry had flown in yesterday. He was probably inspired by Roberto's decision to run the generator night and day in order to refrigerate the children's medicine. I imagine that Harry is bringing capitalism to Yaxchilan. Isn't that beginning to look like a cantina? How do you think our socialists are going to react? Let's go see if we can talk him into at least being reasonable with the prices."

"Did you miss me?" Iñigo asked, obviously in better humor as we opened the screen door of the dining room and started down the hill.

"I didn't even know you were missing until lunchtime," I replied over my shoulder.

The only thing that the 130 souls that inhabited our camp had in common was Christianity. The men outnumbered the women almost ten to one. Apart from this, we were divided into at least five groups, through division of labor, our living quarters, and even the rain forest. This all exacerbated our differences both at the camp and the site.

The largest segment of the personnel was the eighty mestizo laborers from Tenosique who slept, ate, drank, fished, worked, whored, and fought together. They were the ones who cleared the tons of rubble that had once been the roof combs, walls, and decorations from around the structures, the most labor-intensive activity in the ruins, a difficult as well as dangerous process. First, the underbrush had to be cleared from the mountainous slopes. Then, cubic meter after cubic meter of rubble was carefully extracted and separated by hand. This work exposed their bodies to snakes, scorpions, tarantulas, and other rain forest life too numerous to mention. Constantly fearing the possible fatal bite of the Fer de Lance, or *Nauyacas*, as the Mayans call them, they overreacted and killed every snake they encountered. Once they bragged secretly to Andy that they had killed 108 snakes that week.

The mestizos worked hard during the week. But from Saturday

afternoon until they finally retired Sunday evening, they drank. There was an abundance of booze, which came across the river every Saturday like clockwork. The Guatemalan smugglers filled their long, narrow dugouts with liquor, cigarettes, and women. The workmen from Tenosique lined up on the beach like it was the Tuesday market in San Miguel. For those workmen who spent their salary on women, alcohol would come from a homebrew made of fermented fruit called *tepache* they produced in their palapa. Differences over the women sometimes resulted in fights.

The twelve Yucatec Mayans stuck together as if they were all related, and many of them were. Although none of them was over five feet four inches tall, their contributions to the project were monumental. After the workmen from Tenosique exposed the intact areas of a structure, the little Mayans would begin the painstaking chore of consolidating it. Under Roberto's guidance, they became so proficient as a team that they are now hired for investigations throughout the Maya area. They were the most tranquil of all the segments in our camp. Although Paul Sullivan had not yet published his wonderful book, *Unfinished Conversations: Mayas and Foreigners Between Two Wars*, I had read accounts of the savage conflicts during the Caste Wars of the Yucatán. Out of curiosity and the desire to converse with these people whose cultural ancestors had built these strange ruins at Yaxchilan, I spent more time with this group than most of the others did. It was from Luis, Zotz, and their companions that I began to learn my first words of Yucatec Maya. It was clear that they preferred the company of the foreign students and kept a restrained distance from the mestizos from Tenosique.

The Mayans didn't drink or whore but liked to gamble and spent hours pitching pesos in front of one of the jacales where they slept. But what they loved most was baseball, and almost every Sunday they chose sides and organized a game at the end of the runway. They invited people from the other groups to participate, and students from both the Instituto Allende and the National School of Anthropology occasionally joined the game.

The ten students from the Instituto Allende were in charge of the graphic documentation of the project. Two of them were photographers and the other eight were artists and draftsmen. They came from all over the world and their backgrounds were varied. They were the capitalists, although all of them, with the exception of Harry McKnight, were left of center.

The six archaeological students from the National School of Anthropology and History oversaw the work done by the groups from Tenosique.

President Echeverria had filled the National School of Anthropology and History with Marxist anthropologist professors. As a consequence, the students, along with Roberto, were the academic socialists of the camp and they wore Levi-Strauss on their shirtsleeves. Naturally, the archaeology students were from the very beginning suspicious of the motives of the imperialistic foreigners.

Personally, I admired Xoco. She was the idealist among the Mexican students, and she put her education and philosophy into practice. One day she announced to the workmen that every evening they were invited to attend classes where she would teach them how to read and write. It was truly inspirational to see eighteen or twenty workmen go into the dining room every evening for an hour. I suspected, however, that one of her motives for doing this was to show the "imperialists" her devotion to her *raza* (race). As it turned out, she also utilized her classes to express her socialistic ideas.

One evening, as the class was ending, I lay in one of the hammocks in Roberto's jacal, talking with him about the site. One of the workmen approached us with his head slightly bowed and a depressed look upon his face.

"Professor, excuse me for bothering you tonight, but I have a favor that I must ask of you." Obviously embarrassed, he kept his head down with his hat in his hands. His fingers played along the upper edge of the brim as he spoke.

"Of course, Pepe. What is it that I can do for you?" Roberto asked.

"Well, Professor, I need to go home and was wondering if I could catch a ride back to Tenosique with El Capitán next time he flies into Yaxchilan."

"I think that we can arrange that for you. Are you sure you must leave us? Is a member of your family sick?" Roberto questioned him with concern in his voice.

"No, Professor, but thank you for inquiring. It is because Xoco told us that the communists are coming and I would like to be with my family when they arrive."

I do not recall Roberto's precise response because I turned my head away and concentrated on swallowing a laugh. I do remember he softened Pepe's concern by telling him that the communists were not going to come for some time yet. After Pepe left, so did Roberto, in the direction of Xoco's classroom. Although sympathetic to her position, he explained to her in a voice that could be heard throughout the camp that Karl Marx was frightening away the workmen.

In spite of Roberto's and my social-economic differences, our common love of Mesoamerica cemented us together. I owe a great deal to Roberto. He showed me the mechanics and nature of being in charge of an archaeological project under the most remote and stressful conditions. By placing me in situations requiring instant decisions, he gave me the opportunity to learn something about myself. Years later, Roberto became the general director of the National Institute of Anthropology and History. But at Yaxchilan he was caught up in the spirit-deadening onus of his task. Sometimes it came upon him from unexpected and apparently innocent sources. One story that helps explain Roberto's character came from someone outside the camp.

Late one Sunday morning a young medical doctor arrived at Yaxchilan by pirogue, accompanied by a man and two small children, a boy of eight and a girl of ten. The young doctor, after graduating from the university, was fulfilling his social service obligations in the rain forests of Chiapas. This work was either very easy or nearly impossible to accomplish, depending upon the professional ethics of each graduate. This young doctor was idealistic enough to think he could make a difference.

He had come downriver to Yaxchilan because he had heard of our refrigerator through the pilot who brought him the necessary medicine for his project. Apparently, a rabid dog had bitten both the children. This required that they be injected with serum once a day for seventeen days. It presented a problem for the children because the medication they desperately needed was sensitive to the heat and required refrigeration. It also presented a problem for the doctor, whose service was required over thousands of square kilometers of the Lacandon rain forest.

Roberto agreed to keep the generator going night and day for the children's medicine, and Andy offered to make the daily injections over a seventeen-day period so that the doctor could continue his rounds of the villages. The doctor expressed his gratitude and then suggested enthusiastically that he had time to stay for lunch. Nobody objected to his request. In fact, everyone grinned, knowing what was in store for him. To our surprise he attacked the meal with gusto, and afterward, as we all headed for the door, I saw him stick a handful of animal crackers in his pocket. I began to realize that perhaps we were better off than most of the people out there.

After lunch several of us sat on the concrete edge of Roberto's veranda or lay in one of his hammocks, listening to the doctor talk about his experiences in the Lacandon rain forest. Obviously bored, Roberto yawned, stood up, and announced that he was going inside to take a nap. After he left, the doctor told us how lucky we were to be working with Roberto. It was obvious that the doctor admired Roberto, and he began to tell us a story.

THE DOCTOR'S TALE

"Last year about this time I was visiting the site. And just like today we were sitting on this veranda when a faint sound was heard over our conversation. Ta tat ta ta tat ta ta tat ta—the noise became louder and louder until finally Roberto spoke up, 'It's a helicopter.'

"Sure enough, within minutes a government helicopter appeared overhead and began its directed descent near the palapas at the end of the airstrip. A man in a white Veracruz *Guayabera* shirt stepped out of the chopper.

"'It is the governor,' remarked Roberto. 'What the hell is he doing here?'

"The governor and two other officious-looking men joined us at the veranda. One of the men held a three-quarter-inch video camera. After introducing himself and the two television reporters, he laid out the purpose of his visit. The president of Mexico, Luis Echeverria, was to visit Yaxchilan the next day, and the governor was acting as an advance guard for the occasion. He had come to see what the site offered. He requested that Roberto show him a portion of the site that the president could view in a couple of hours.

"Roberto agreed, so the governor, along with the two reporters, followed him down the trail in the direction of the ruins.

"By the time they returned, everybody in camp knew that the president was coming to visit the site. I was excited about the proposed visit. It would give me the chance to tell the president of the medical needs in the villages, so I decided to spend the night.

"When the governor and reporters returned to the camp with Roberto, they stood around chatting with all of us for a few minutes. Looking at his watch, the governor turned to Roberto.

"'Is there anything you need or that I can do for you and the project before I leave?' he inquired.

"Much to our surprise as well as the governor's, Roberto responded, 'Well, yes sir, there is something you might be able to take care of for the project.'

"We all looked at Roberto curiously as he continued, 'See that jacal across the river? Miguel de la Cruz, a Mexican national, lives over there in Guatemala because there is an order of apprehension waiting on him on this side of the river. Unfortunately, the man has been smuggling scarlet macaws out of the rain forest on both sides of the river and nobody has been able to catch him.'"

At this point in the doctor's story, I held my breath. I knew why there was a warrant for the arrest of Miguel de la Cruz. He had killed a man. The story told to me by Luis Cuevas (Miguel's brother-in-law) was that Miguel had sold one of the carved monuments at Yaxchilan to a gringo a few years before. The gringo flew the sculpture out of the rain forest and Cruz wasn't paid. The stupid man returned a year later and Miguel shot him. I waited anxiously for the doctor to continue his story.

"'What can be done to stop him?' Roberto asked the governor.

"'Well, just get me a boat and I will go across the river and get this settled right now!' replied the governor, with a determined scowl on his face.

"After Roberto arranged for the governor's transportation for crossing the river, I watched the scene partially unfold from the veranda. When the governor left for Miguel's jacal, the reporters began a filmed interview with Roberto. I listened from time to time, but my real attention was on the other drama. I could not see the pirogue cross the river because it was out of sight below the bank on the Mexican side. But when the governor and the two boatmen beached the craft, I watched as they walked across the gravel bar and into the Guatemalan rain forest. From time to time I could catch glimpses of color through the trees as they moved uphill toward Miguel's jacal. Eventually, the governor appeared in the small clearing in front of the house and then disappeared into the darkness of the door.

"About twenty minutes later I looked down at the river and saw the heads of the two boatmen as they appeared above the embankment across the airstrip. The interview had ended by that time and the reporters were idly chatting with the small group. I interrupted the conversation with, 'Here comes the governor!'

"Everybody looked down the hill as the governor appeared carrying a large bamboo cage. Inside was a scarlet macaw. The governor went straight to the helicopter and got in. The embarrassed reporters excused themselves and flew down to the airstrip and the waiting chopper. I looked at Roberto, who was coiled up in rage. The anger was so apparent that I don't think anyone ever dared to mention anything about the incident. I certainly didn't.

"Later that afternoon a platoon of soldiers arrived from upriver and set up camp near our palapas.

"The next day, the president arrived with his entourage. They came in two small aircraft and the same helicopter the governor had used the day before. Surprisingly, the governor was with the president. Apparently Roberto's outrage the day before had subsided, and he met them graciously, and then the group headed down the trail to the archaeological site. I was treating a workman with a bad cut on his leg and did not see them visit the site, but when they returned I was lying in one of the hammocks and got up to greet them. There must have been twenty or thirty workmen and staff members who had the same thought as myself. This was a chance to see a president up close. I arrived in earshot just in time to hear the president speak.

"'You have done a great job here, Professor. Keep up the good work. Is there anything . . .'

"I must have gulped loudly for I did not hear the rest of the president's question. I could not believe my ears. I just caught the end of Roberto's reply, '. . . Cruz and the governor are smuggling macaws.'

"I stopped breathing. Echeverria turned slowly toward the governor, who, caught by surprise, was standing there with his mouth open. Echeverria is not a big man by your gringo standards. But to the governor he must have grown three feet.

"The president didn't say anything to the governor but when he turned to face Roberto, he said, 'Let me assure you that it will never happen again. Will it?' He shook hands with Roberto and then they all walked down the hill to the runway.

"Two reporters were standing fairly close to me and I heard one of them exclaim with a big grin on his face and admiration in his expression, 'What balls!'"

Shortly after finishing his story, the doctor informed us that it was time for him to leave, as a small community downstream had several cases of malaria requiring attention. As he stood up he asked sincerely, "Would anyone mind if I took a small bag of those animal crackers with me?"

The Stalactite and the Throne of Bird Jaguar

I can't even remember the day of the week let alone the date. I'm tired, so tired . . . I've almost completed the stalactite. Just seven small pieces to ink and it will be done.

—*Diary: April 1978*

The students from the Instituto Allende organized themselves in work just as they had in cleaning and maintaining our camp. They also fell into a monotonous routine: work and scratch, scratch and work.

Everyone was in the ruins by 6 a.m. each morning, leaving the camp almost empty except for the cooks and the ladies who did our washing. Once in a while, two of the Mexican archaeology students spent the day in the storage jacal cleaning and marking the pottery shards that had accumulated during the excavation and restoration.

The project photographers, Andy Rakcozy and Marion Piorezyaski, shuffled between the ruins and the camp "darkroom," a black changing bag where they developed their film. Printing was done on Andy's small enlarger, which he kept in his tent. They rigged up a line from the generator and for an hour every night printed the photographs taken that day. One of their chores during the day was to produce enough clean and filtered water to make their prints. This they did by filtering the river water through a series of cotton cloths several times. It was tedious and time consuming, but the results were well worth the effort.

Rakcozy seldom frowned. Nor did he smile; he grinned. He was especially happy when one of the workmen brought him a snake. One day he was grinning so much that I asked Marion why. She took me over

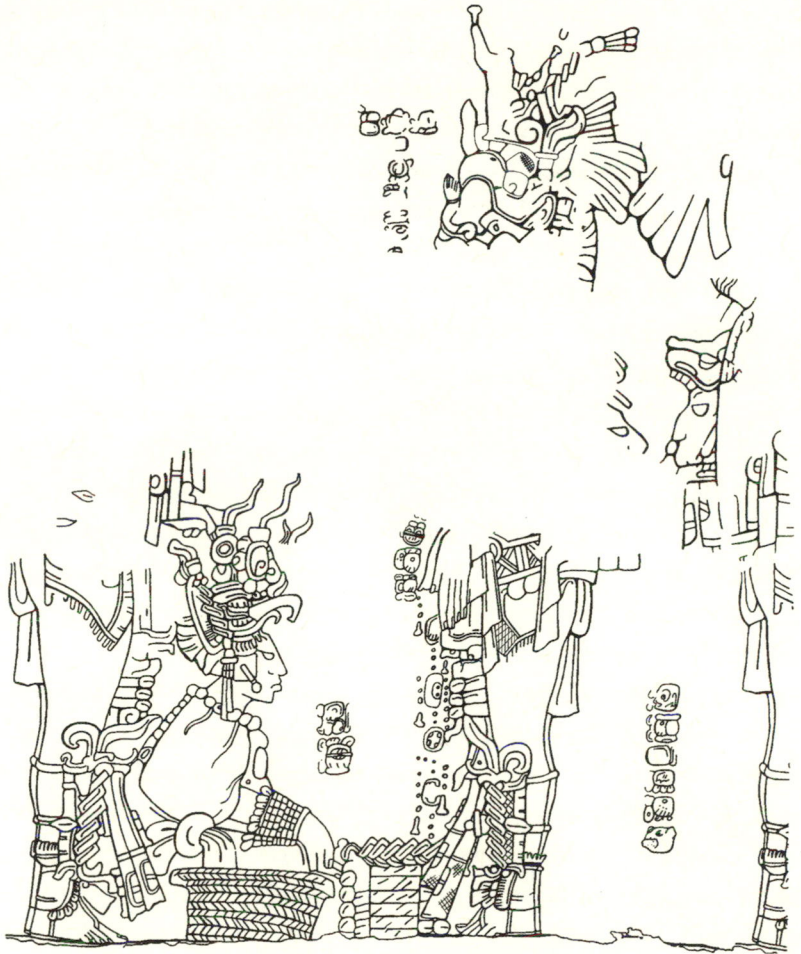

Figure 7 Stalactite Temple 33 (drawing by author)

to his tent, opened the door flap, and asked me to go in. "Be careful," she remarked rather casually. Andy had seven snakes stored in gunnysacks in the tent. She explained that he was paying the workmen a peso for every snake they brought him. He stored them in the gunnysacks until he found the right place in the ruins with the right light so that he could photograph them. Then he turned them loose.

Thorrun, Harry, and Iñigo sketched the structures while Mary, Linda, Peggy, Sandy, and Lavinia made rubbings of the carved monuments that Roberto wanted documented. In the afternoon they transferred the rubbings to pencil drawings on transparent paper. The drawings were returned to the monument and corrected the next day. When the students were finished, they traced their corrected drawings in ink on a clean sheet of paper.

One day I went to check up on the work being done at various locations within the ruins and spied Thorrun sitting up on the roof comb of a temple, intently drawing the building below. Her back was to me as I climbed up behind her to see her progress. I noticed that she was eating something from a small plastic bag lying on the stone where she sat. When I got closer, I stifled a laugh. They were animal crackers.

I usually took one of the tougher jobs and every so often visited the others to see if they needed anything. I can't recall any monument I have documented in Mesoamerica that presented more problems than the stalactite in front of Temple 33.

The stalactite was incised with figures and glyphs that completely encircled the stone. It stood about seven feet tall and the upper half, constantly exposed to the rain and sun, had exfoliated badly. The stalactite bore a series of undulations and the incised carving frequently disappeared into one of the small hollows in the stone. Due to the character of the stone, it was impossible to discern the details of the sculpture.

I ordered some white cotton sheets from Tenosique, and one day Pedro Joaquín stopped by Yaxchilan to deliver them to me on his way to Miramar to pick up a load of chate ferns.

I soaked one of the sheets in water and with the help of a student forced the wet material into the hollows of the stalactite until it was completely encircled.

I used the green leaves of the begonia flowers that fortunately surrounded Temple 33 to make the rubbing. I did this so that the coloring agent, being vegetable, would not have adverse effects on the badly eroding stalactite.

The sheet had to be constantly wetted to stay in place. This meant that the rubbing had to be finished in one day.

I waited impatiently until about noon the next day for the cotton sheet to dry enough to begin tracing it on paper. I worked on a large table in the storeroom all day, not even stopping for lunch. That evening Roberto came in to see how the work was going. He stood beside me looking at the drawing for a few moments, then announced, "We are going to shut down the generator in about ten minutes." He made no comment about my drawing. Instead he said, "Ian Graham drew this stalactite last year. I was not satisfied with his drawing."

I stopped work and straightened up. "Well, I am sure he will have to correct the glyphs that I have drawn. They are so small and badly eroded it is hard to tell what was intentional and what has been caused by erosion."

"What do you suppose those shapes being dropped into the basket are? Blood or corn?" he inquired.

I had been thinking about these objects on the monument for several days. "I really don't know. Perhaps they are both," I replied. "I do know what Nicholas Helmut would say: 'blood.'"

I worked on the pencil drawing for three days and two nights. Each morning I took the drawing to the site to compare it with the original. At night I worked with the help of a small gasoline generator and one lightbulb, moving the light with my left hand as I peered into the cracks and crevices of the stalactite in order to discern the details. It took still another day to transfer the then ragged and smudged pencil drawing to ink. I was extremely proud of my effort, but at the same time very anxious. It was important to be faithful in every detail so that the archaeologist and/or epigrapher would benefit and not be misled by my labor.

Years later, my wife, Marisela, and I had a visitor to our house at Jésus 21 in San Miguel. It was Dr. Carolyn Tate from the University of Texas. Tate was an epigrapher who had studied under Linda Schele, coauthor of the book *The Blood of the Kings*. Dr. Tate was on her way to Yaxchilan to study some of the glyphs on the carved monuments and had heard that I was a friend of Roberto's. During the course of our conversation, she showed me drawings and photographs of various monuments that she would be studying. At one point she pulled out a photocopy of my drawing of the stalactite. Recognizing it immediately, I asked, "Where did you get that drawing?"

"Ian Graham at the Peabody gave it to me just a few days ago. Why?"

I can recall with great clarity the days excavating and the subsequent nights drawing and photographing the throne of Bird Jaguar III. In the world of the classic Maya, Bird Jaguar was the Lord of Yaxchilan during the eighth century after Christ.

Roberto gave me the opportunity to excavate the northwest exterior corner of Structure No. 7. This structure, known as *Templo Rojo de la Rivera*, was famous because Teobert Maler spent nights in this building in his renowned explorations of the late 1890s. As anyone who has read Maler's *Explorations of the Upper Usumacinta Drainage* will confirm, his photographs and descriptions of most of the carved lintels and stelae of this site are unequaled even today. This information alone excited me, but this was nothing compared to what was about to take place.

I found the throne by mid-morning of the first day of the excavation. The work was quite enjoyable even though nine pairs of scarlet macaws in a nearby ceiba tree continuously criticized my efforts. The throne began to show up less than ten centimeters below the actual ground level. As my brush began to reveal the undulating surface along the sides of the first of two large stones beneath the soil, my excitement rose. At moments like these, controlling your impulse to attack the dirt like a dog looking for a bone is very difficult. The next hour seemed like an eternity before enough dirt was removed from around the edges and the full-figure glyphs were exposed. I was ecstatic. At that time there were few places apart from Copan, Honduras, and Quirigua, Guatemala, where full-figure glyphs had been found on carved stone.

When the complete throne was freed and I saw the glyph for Bird Jaguar, I thought there would never be another moment in my life such as this. But of course I was wrong. Still, it was a major thrill, and I can picture myself at night, alone, underneath the protection of the

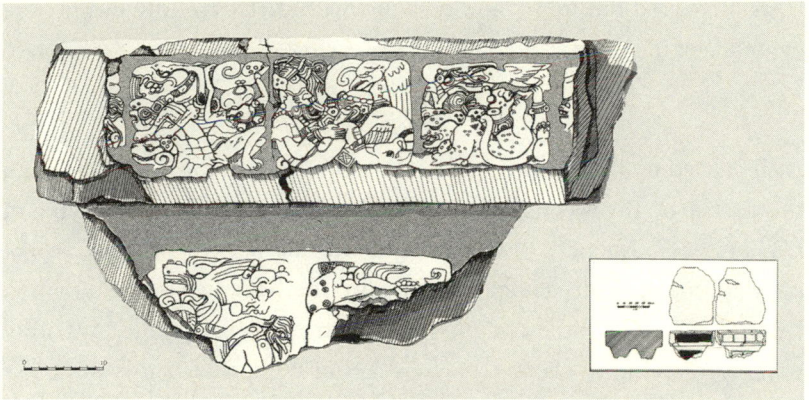

Figure 8 Throne of Bird Jaguar (drawing by author)

mosquito netting and with the small, noisy gasoline generator providing light for me to draw. The air was so heavy with moisture that even
at night I had to be careful not to put the drawing anywhere beneath
my dripping nose and chin. The insects clustered upon the outside wall
of the mosquito netting until I had to stop and shake them free of the
netting to let enough light into my little world to see what I was doing.
Sometimes I even had to shut the generator down so that the insects
would momentarily abandon the area. When I did, the background was
orchestrated by dozens of unidentifiable rain forest night sounds. Finally,
I brought the light under the mosquito netting with me and found that
I was able to control the insect problem as well as improve the light for
my drawing.

I knew that when the Peabody Museum got wind of the throne
and its full-figure glyphs, it would not be long before Dr. Ian Graham
would show up at Yaxchilan. His *Corpus of Mayan Hieroglyphs* was like
a bible to me, and my respect and admiration for his tireless search for
these ancient writings had been one of the motivations that brought
me to the world of archaeology. After drawing and photographing the
throne, I wrote a short message to Dr. Graham and stuffed it in a plastic
35-millimeter film canister, placing it near the top edge of the stone.
Then, because the throne was so close to the river and susceptible to

theft, I covered the stones and message with dirt, carefully hiding any evidence of the excavation.

La Guardia

It all started on the runway early one Saturday evening. I was crossing the airstrip on my way to Roberto's jacal, where I could see him lying in his hammock. About halfway across the field, one of the mestizo workmen approached me. He had been drinking heavily. Normally when I found myself in these circumstances, I tried to disengage myself by politely agreeing to every tepache-reeking request. On this occasion the drunk was adamantly pulling on my shirtsleeve and insisting that I understand. It took a lot of fidgeting patience, but finally, after about thirty minutes, I got the gist of his message.

He was offering to sell me some artifacts from the site. When I refused, he insisted that it would be all right, as he had already sold some things at a good price. Unfortunately, he had spent his money on tepache and a woman. "You are a gringo and have a lot of money to buy such things," he declared.

When I declined, like a used car salesman he changed his approach. "There is very little time left because soon everything will be gone," he prophesied.

I was convinced that I had not understood him. "What do you mean that everything will be gone?"

"The Guatemalans are crossing the river tonight to steal the objects from the tomb," was his reply.

"Oh, shit!" was all that came out.

Gently but determinedly, I removed his grasp on my shirtsleeve and continued quickly up the hill.

As I approached Roberto he smiled, and asked in jest, "Selling booze to the workmen, are you?"

When I revealed the conversation that had just taken place in the middle of the runway, Roberto became very serious and said, "I hope that you misunderstood what he told you, or that he is so drunk he is imagining all of this. If not, we have a big problem. Go get Luis

Cuevas and bring him here to my jacal. In the meantime I will try and find the Guatemalan."

As I started down the runway, Iñigo joined me. As we walked down the field I explained what the workman had told me. To my surprise, Iñigo was aware of the situation and confided in me that the same workman had approached several of the students with a similar offer. I was appalled.

"Good God!" I exclaimed and then hesitantly inquired, "Did any of you buy anything?"

"Not that I know of," he replied. "I think everyone reacted pretty much the same as me. It was embarrassing to me because he kept insisting."

"Well, I hope and pray that you are right. I don't know what Roberto has in mind, but you and I are going to get Luis Cuevas, and Roberto went to fetch the Guatemalan."

As we entered the area in front of Luis's jacal, it came to me that these were the only two people in the camp with guns. I was becoming more nervous by the moment.

We found Luis out back placing the last palm leaves over a roasting pit. Thin wisps of gray smoke rose among the leaves. Luis greeted us with his usual smile and proudly announced that we were going to have barbecued pig for dinner tomorrow.

"Listen Luis, Roberto wants to see you as soon as possible," I told him. "There is a problem. He sent me to get you and he has gone to look for Juan."

I noted that Luis had suddenly become serious. "Here. Help me by putting these last few palm leaves over the pit and I will be right back," he said, and disappeared into the back door of his jacal.

It couldn't have taken more than a minute for Iñigo and me to cover the pit with the few remaining leaves. As we were finishing, Luis returned with his single-shot 20-gauge. Looking at our work, he smiled a little condescendingly, and after adjusting a couple of the palm leaves motioned for us to join him on the runway.

When we reached the veranda of Roberto's jacal, he was nowhere in sight. By then it was dark, and just as we arrived we heard the big generator start up. Within seconds, the lights came on inside. Luis rested his shotgun against the wall of the jacal and then sat down in one of the hammocks on the veranda.

"Do you have any idea what this is about?" he asked. As I was about to answer him, I saw Roberto and his assistant Ernesto walking toward us from the direction of the river. I motioned with my head, and Luis turned to look down the hill. Arriving at the edge of the veranda, Roberto checked his watch, and after a terse greeting asked us to join him inside the jacal.

He walked directly to the small table where the ham radio sat and flipped the switch on the front of the box. As he sat down he pulled the microphone closer to his face and began to give Pedro Joaquín's call sign.

Suddenly, Roberto's expression changed. Deep furrows showed upon his brow as he began to tap the microphone with his index finger. He blew into it a couple of times and then turned to Ernesto. "Bring me a screwdriver from the tool box." Something was obviously wrong.

In less than five minutes Roberto removed the case and by then all five of us had clustered around the short-wave radio. We peered into the damn thing and it didn't take an expert to see what was wrong. There was a tube missing from the set.

At first we all were silent as the implication of the missing tube began to settle into our minds. Somebody did not want us communicating with the world outside.

"I don't want a word of this to leave this room," was the first thing Roberto said. Then he turned to Luis and the Guatemalan to give them instructions.

"We have to stand guard over the excavations tonight. Take your weapons with you, leave the jacal separately, and take separate routes to the site. Luis, you leave first. You better tell your wife that you will not be home tonight. Juan, you leave in about ten minutes."

"Who could have done this?" asked Ernesto.

"It doesn't matter right now," replied Roberto. "The first thing we have to do is protect the excavations."

I spoke up. "What can I do?"

Roberto smiled slightly and said, "Act as a lookout. Wait for a while and then take Iñigo and another student you can trust with you. Set up positions down by the river and if any of you hear or see any pirogues crossing the river to our side, beat it back to Juan and Luis to let them know."

I was both excited and relieved. Excited by the participation and honestly relieved because of the fear and guilt that one or more of my students might have involved themselves in the worst of possible crimes given the circumstances: the trafficking of pre-Hispanic art. My mind swirled with questions and decisions that I would have to make.

Who could I trust? I went over and over the names and personalities for each student. None of them, I decided, would intentionally do something illegal. I then began to question myself. Had I made clear the federal laws in Mexico concerning pre-Hispanic pieces? My heart sank as I realized that I had never discussed the question with them.

After Luis and Juan had left, Roberto turned to me and added another burden to my already trampled soul. "You had better hope that you misunderstood the accusation that somebody in the camp has purchased one of the artifacts. If Pedro arrives in the morning I am going to leave with him and check this workman out. If I find anything, I may have to return with the federal police or soldiers to search the camp."

The Guatemalan was probably the only person in camp, aside from Roberto, with a watch. The need to know the exact time really had no meaning in Yaxchilan. I do know that it was the longest night of my life.

There were only two or three places that a boat could land on our side of the river. One was directly in front of our palapas, which was out of the question for anyone planning a surprise visit to the site. Another location was farther upstream, just south of Structure No. 7, near a fallen stela and almost at the end of the lower plaza. The third was some distance farther south and about two hundred meters from the end of the main plaza. Sandy and I took up our position near the bank of the river at the first location and Iñigo volunteered for the potential landing spot farther south.

Sandy and I made no pretense at remaining quiet. We talked almost all night, and from time to time turned on our flashlights. It helped us to keep awake, and at the same time our voices carried out across the water, acting (we hoped) as a deterrent to anyone approaching the shore.

The rain forest is not quiet at night. Looking back on that night, I remember it as an orchestra. It is amazing how many sounds and little noises the forest produces. There was the noise of the river. It gurgled, bubbled, lapped, and hissed constantly. Occasionally, an object floating downstream would hit a rock or root of an overhanging tree and startle us. Each time this happened we strained our ears and eyes, hoping that no boat was approaching. Sometime early on our watch, the sound of a motor starting upstream in the distance set every nerve ending to tingle with excitement, and our hearts pounded with an intense adrenaline surge. But the noise slowly faded, and it soon became apparent that the craft was heading away from the ruins.

There was not even a slight breeze that night, so the soft sound of insect wings buzzed relentlessly in our faces and around our ears. They flew into our eyes, ears, and mouths, and everything that moved seemed to bite. The earth itself was another source of sound. Little creatures constantly scurried, scuttled, and rasped the leaves of the forest floor. One unidentified flying thing made a sound like a Japanese wind chime, pinging from place to place around us. We constantly brushed moving things from our arms and legs, too terrified even to want to know what they were.

But the real terror was of humans. I began to speculate on what to do if indeed someone approached. We had been given the instruction to inform Luis and the Guatemalan if this happened. Still, we did not know their exact location near the tomb in Temple 33, and even if we had they had already left Roberto's jacal before he gave us this instruction. What if in their excitement they fired upon us? Or, worse still, what if looters had overcome Iñigo and approached the plaza between us and the hunters? I fantasized every imaginable horrifying scenario.

Fortunately, nothing happened, and at first light when I saw Sandy's face, I was shocked. Her eyes and cheeks were so puffy that it looked as if she were squinting. I didn't mention my concern, and she returned to camp to get some sleep. I headed upstream to find Iñigo.

I came across him on the trail heading back to the plaza. He had survived the night, but just barely. His face and ankles were swollen from insect bites. He had obviously suffered even more than Sandy.

His natural good humor was completely gone.

"Jesus Christ!" he exclaimed through his teeth. He tried to move his face into a frown. "I never ever want to go through this shit again!" he hissed. "This is insane!"

He blamed everyone and threatened to kill at least a dozen persons, including me, for his condition. "You don't look so good yourself," he finally conceded, after exhausting his complete vocabulary of swear words.

I tried to console and placate him but to no avail. When we finally reached the palapas, Iñigo refused to answer the questions being thrown at him by his companions, and after a quick trip to the river he went straight to his hammock where he remained most of the day.

Breakfast was served at 7 a.m. on Sundays, but since I wanted to talk to Roberto before then, I waited until Ernesto appeared on the veranda of their jacal and then I went to see Roberto.

It was obvious that neither he nor Ernesto had slept much the night before. Roberto's stern countenance inspired me not to mention much of my experience. He just looked at me as if I were a stranger, and then suggested that plastic surgery might help. Evidently, nothing had occurred that night in the camp, so we headed for the dining room and breakfast. I do recall that the animal crackers were unbelievably delicious.

As it turned out, we had some luck. Pedro Joaquín, concerned that he had not heard from us on the shortwave the night before, flew in to Yaxchilan to find out if there was a problem. Roberto left with Pedro about 11 a.m. for Tenosique. I stood on the end of the runway and jealously watched their departure. As they flew over, Roberto leaned his head against the window of the cockpit and waved good-bye. I spent the rest of the day in the river trying to soothe the insect bites, and in my hammock trying without much success to get some sleep.

At dusk I saw Luis heading toward the ruins with his shotgun. I intercepted him and asked how it went the night before. Looking at my swollen face, he smiled and said, "There are not as many bugs up the hill as there are close to the river."

Ernesto recruited two of the Mexican students to stand guard that night. I noticed that he did not volunteer to go himself. I didn't volunteer, either.

The next day the work around the tomb was accomplished with some urgency. But they did not finish, and Roberto did not return until Tuesday.

He arrived mid-morning with two policemen from Tenosique, and they headed for the ruins and returned quickly with the drunk workman. The policemen boarded the plane with the workman and left.

Later in the day, Roberto explained that the same workman had been fired from the project in Palenque when it was discovered that several artifacts had mysteriously disappeared from the storeroom.

Encounter with *Nohoch Balam*

Late one Friday afternoon I filled the old army knapsack with a few items that I thought I would need, grabbed my bow along with six arrows, and, ignoring the quizzical looks from the students, stepped out of the palapa and disappeared into the fog. I made my way down the runway to the jacal of Luis Cuevas. I didn't return until Sunday afternoon.

The Guatemalan had already arrived and was sitting on a log in the mist in front of Luis's home. He acknowledged my arrival with a single nod of this head and pointed his finger at his watch. As I got closer I could see seven dogs were lying around his rustic chair. Two of them rose to greet me and began to growl. Luis, hearing the dogs, showed up in the darkened doorway as I entered his dirt front yard.

"¿Tush ka' bim?" (Where are you going?), he asked in Yucatec Maya.

His question took me by surprise, as he was the one who had invited me on this trip, and he knew better than I where I was going. Satisfied with the serious furrows above my eyebrows, he grinned.

Juan and Luis spent most of their time hunting to satisfy the workmen's carnivorous demands. They were usually successful, and returned to camp with birds, deer, javelin, and sometimes fish and/or a large crayfish called either *langostina* or *pigua* from the river. Occasionally, when the game was large or plentiful enough, after the workmen finished, the students and other staff members were given a chance to eat. Otherwise, for us it was eggs, beans, tortillas, and animal crackers.

Roberto allowed only the two men to hunt on the omega of Yaxchilan. But recently game had been scarce, and they had to travel up to five kilometers away to be successful. Luis explained that it was due to the weather.

It had not rained for about a week, but for the last several days a heavy mist the Mexicans call *neblina* had settled over the rain forest. The sun never appeared. The sky never changed. For days the sky, the river, and the rain forest were no more than slightly different tones of Payne's gray. Night and day the mist descended and retreated in slow motion, rolling up and down the arroyos toward the river. Then it seemed to pile up on the river and condense and engulf the omega. It gave the camp and ruins an eerie feeling. It reminded me of an old black-and-white Boris Karloff movie. Visiting the lower plazas and stelae of Yaxchilan in this fog was an experience.

It was so mystical that I expected that the carved stone lintels and stelae of Yaxchilan to release the bodies and spirits of Bird Jaguar, Shield Jaguar, and Lady Xoc. They seemed to resurrect, magically appearing out of the gloom. The constant mist left a humid spray in the air that the Mexicans called *chipi chipi*. I called it *la chinga quedito*. On the positive side, there were no flying and biting insects. Visibility was in front of one's face. The fog was so thick in the arroyos that Luis and Juan were having difficulty seeing the game.

Figure 9 Yaxchilan in the Fog (drawing by author)

Because of the heavy fog, Luis told me that they were going into Guatemala on a hunt that night. He and Juan knew of a small lagoon downriver where their chances of locating game were better. Also, it was closer and they could use a dugout canoe to bring back the game. He asked if I would like to go along. I didn't hesitate to accept.

It was crowded in the dugout canoe. We hadn't brought many supplies, but with three guys and seven dogs? Luis put me in the bow of the dugout with a headlamp and belt battery. I placed my bow and arrows close to me as I got in the canoe, but just before we shoved off, Luis brought me his single-shot, 12-gauge shotgun. Juan took the pole in the center of the canoe and Luis got in back in order to use the homemade paddle as a rudder. The dogs got comfortable in the bottom of the dugout among us. From stem to stern, the homemade craft approached four meters.

The big thrill heading downriver in the dusk was my constant and extreme preoccupation for the stability of the craft. It didn't take much to make it rock. And it rocked constantly as one or more of the dogs would scratch for fleas or bite at the tick sucking between its ribs. Once a dog stood up and the canoe rocked so badly that I turned my head back to see if the others were as preoccupied as I was. I caught Juan nodding and scowling at the dog. The dog understood and immediately lay back down. This did not surprise me. Juan seldom spoke. He had hundreds of expressions and gestures with which he communicated. He had, in his world, almost done away with the need for speech.

Part of my job was to notify my hunting partners if there was anything ahead of us that they needed to avoid. I did this by extending my arm and pointing either to the right or left. At the same time, I searched the river and both banks, whenever I could see them, for deer or other game that might be crossing the river undercover of the fog. Nothing did.

At last, we beached the dugout around a bend in the river near a large outcropping of rocks. Behind this lay a strong back eddy, caused by a low-pressure area in the river that had created a medium-sized sandbar. We camped there on the sandy beach for the night.

While Juan gathered driftwood for a fire, Luis took me back down to the dugout. He pointed out the extent of the back eddy through the mist and told me that when the current took me past a series of exposed boulders in the river, I was to harpoon langostina.

"We only need three," he said, and started back toward the small fire that Juan had going. Luis stopped and turned back to me. "Oh yes, be careful: *Nauyacas* also have red eyes."

"Thanks a lot, Luis," I thought. Until he mentioned them, poisonous snakes had not been my immediate preoccupation. My first concern was how to keep from turning the dugout over; the second, how to utilize the back eddy without entering the main current and ending up back in Tenosique; and the third, how to manage the current and canoe and still harpoon langostina. The first time around the eddy I didn't even bother to pick up the harpoon, yet I still came close to capsizing several times. Each movement aboard the craft had to be slow and deliberate. I had to strain to focus my eyes intensely on the surface of the water, and in doing so learned that the fog not only dissipated but actually stopped a few centimeters above the water.

How to harpoon a langostina? As I began to float past the boulders in the shallows, I turned on my headlamp. It took a few minutes to adjust my eyes to the circle of light in the fog and find the river bottom. Almost immediately thereafter, two bright red orbs caught my attention. Before I could raise the harpoon, I had drifted past. It took several attempts before I found it was necessary to be poised with the harpoon in order to be able to get off a thrust. Unfortunately, by that time the eddy had taken me past the boulders and rocks and I was once again heading downriver.

On the next attempt I succeeded, but by the time I removed the langostina from the end of the harpoon I was once again beginning to circle downstream. "I've got to thrust, pull, and remove the prey faster," I thought.

On the fourth pass I managed to harpoon the two that I lacked, but as I poled the dugout toward the shore where Luis waited, I tipped it over.

It could have been a real disaster, but I managed to grab the craft before it drifted away. All of its contents fell into the water: pole, paddle, harpoon, and langostina. Fortunately for us, the equipment floated, and we patiently waited for it to come by us again in the eddy.

My pride and clothes were all wet. When I returned to the comforting embers of the campfire, Juan said nothing. But as I removed my wet clothes I kept wondering what he thought of this apparent greenhorn. I had spent over an hour trying to provide a meager dinner and failed. Luis joined us about twenty minutes later with three large langostina. They helped fill our stomachs but did nothing for my self-esteem.

The next morning, they were up and moving about in the eerie diaphanous light that announced the beginning of another day in the fog. By the time I got enough courage to put on my still wet and cold clothes, breakfast was ready. Luis had harpooned three more langostina and roasted them like the night before in the coals of the fire. Ten minutes later we were on a trail. At least I hoped it was a trail. Visibility was less than four feet.

Walking through the rain forest at any time is an amazing experience. What made this trip special was the fog. First, I was forced to look at the ground in front of each step, not where I was going. When I looked up, I invariably tripped over one of the hundreds of roots that covered the path. There was only a space of a few feet in which to adapt to any change in the direction of the trail.

Juan took the lead with the dogs. They put me in the middle. Luis brought up the rear.

We moved along the trail very slowly. Juan advanced a few paces then paused. Remarkably, the dogs did the same. Each time he stopped, all of the dogs, whatever they were doing at the time, put their noses to the ground and sniffed around the trail.

We ascended the ridge on the Guatemalan side of the river and began our descent in less than an hour. Finally, the trail began to get very soggy. When I looked up, Juan and the dogs, less than three feet away, stood on the edge of a lake.

There was no real shoreline, as the rain forest grew to the edge of the water. Branches and bejuco vines draped out over the water. Strangely, the visibility across the small lagoon was better than it had been on the trail, and I could make out the ghostly shapes of the forest on the other side, about twenty meters away.

When I turned around to make a comment to Luis, he had disappeared. Surprised, I turned back and looked at Juan. He spoke softly, and as was his custom, minced no words: "He will be back shortly."

We did not have to wait long. Luis appeared in less than ten minutes and said one word, "*Javelin.*" There was a brief and whispered conversation between Luis and Juan. Then Juan and the dogs took off back up the trail and Luis motioned for me to go, too, in front of him.

As I followed along behind Juan and the dogs, the latter kept my attention. They never moved very far from Juan. Occasionally, the obvious leader of the pack would trot ahead for a few paces, but never out of Juan's sight. Most amazingly, they acted like Juan. They were very quiet dogs. Not once did they whine, bark, or growl. They reminded me more of a pack of hunting wolves than dogs, and I thought they might do well in a rerun of the *Hound of the Baskervilles*. From time to time one or another fell back around me as he sat down to scratch or bite a tick. Recovery was always quick, and soon he caught up to the pack around Juan's legs. Scratching and nipping were the only sounds they made.

We traveled along less than five minutes from the lagoon when Luis made a *ppsst* sound, very much like a Mexican trying to catch the attention of a waiter in a cantina. Juan stopped and moved to the right of the trail, where Luis was pointing. Juan stooped down in some tall grass at the bottom of a huge outcropping of rocks only a couple of feet off the trail. He picked up some dirt and held it for a moment next to his nose. He turned and looked at Luis, and his head bobbed down very slightly. Then, to my surprise, he bent down and whispered in the ear of the lead dog. The dog shot up the trail. The other dogs that had been sniffing at the ground around Juan's feet and legs took off after him. In seconds they had silently disappeared into the gloomy, tree-curtained mist.

We followed behind at a quickened pace. This time there were no pauses to stop and listen. We hadn't traveled very far when we were brought up short by the sound of a dog. It wasn't a howl like a Hound of the Baskervilles, but instead a short yelp. The immediate silence that followed made the hair on my arms and the back of my neck stand up. It was the abrupt stop of the sound that made my skin tingle. Juan looked back at Luis and uttered one word, "*tigre!*" and began to run up the trail. We followed.

We came across the lead dog about sixty or seventy meters later. He lay on his side with his tongue hanging out, panting loudly. He had been taken by surprise at the foot of a large boulder. His stomach had been ripped open from his crotch to his front legs, and his intestines poured out on the leaves of the forest floor. By the time we arrived he had bled all that he could, and I think that his lungs were pumping nothing but oxygen into his emptied veins.

Juan hunched over the animal and caressed his head for a moment and then took out his knife and slit the dog's throat.

The signs around the scene were obvious, even to me. The big jaguar, instead of running or climbing up a tree, had laid an ambush for the dogs. When the first dog came by the boulder, the cat had pounced on him and then quickly took off running once more up the trail with the other dogs right behind him.

The second dog had died in the bottom of a small ravine. Here the cat had run up the ravine and then scrabbled up the side of the bank. It then turned around and lay down at the edge to wait. When we found the third dog, he was lying at the base of a huge white ceiba. The roots of this magnificent tree began on the trunk, well above our heads. They slowly extended out forming a kind of vault, like a Gothic cathedral, around the dead dog. This one, like the other two, had been gutted. The cat must have been frustrated and angered by this time, for he had ripped open the dog's neck as well as racked his belly with his hind claws.

Juan opened his shotgun, removed the single shell, and blew down the end of the barrel.

The noise coming from the gun sounded amazingly—and I might add appropriately—like a ship's foghorn. He then sat down near the base of the ceiba, where we joined him.

I asked Luis why Juan had blown on the shotgun. "He called back the other dogs. If he didn't, the jaguar would kill them all. This tiger is big, smart, and has been hunted before." He looked at me seriously and added, "After he kills the dogs, he will come back for us."

In spite of the fog, it was one of those days in the rain forest that when you walked, you sweated. When you sat down, you got chilly. I figured that that was the reason for the slight shiver that swept over my body.

In about twenty minutes, three of the dogs returned. They wagged their tails and clustered around Juan's legs as if nothing had happened. He patted them affectionately and we waited another ten minutes for the other dog. When he did not show up we started back down the trail toward the lagoon.

"Pinche Luis!" All the way down the trail I kept looking back over my shoulder and each time I did, Luis just grinned.

It was mid- to late morning, and the mist had begun to roll back up the ridges. When the forest permitted, visibility extended to about twenty meters. The ground had flattened around us and the smaller vegetation increased, indicating that we were approaching the lagoon. Suddenly, the ground and lowest vegetation to the right of the trail exploded. Squeals, grunts, and snorts accompanied the movements in several directions. The three remaining dogs shot past Luis and me and left the trail above us, into the forest on our right. I did not realize it at the time, as things happened so fast, but the dogs, acting like sheep dogs, were sandwiching the animals between the lagoon and an outcropping of rocks and ourselves. They effectively blocked the javelins' only escape route.

Although I had knocked an arrow and had patiently drawn the compound bow back fully, I never got a glimpse of an animal to shoot. Both Juan and Luis did, and their shotguns went off within seconds of each other as I strained to get a view.

We gutted and cleaned the two small pigs where they had fallen. While we were occupied with this, Luis and I talked about the events of the last hour and a half.

"The pigs probably spent the night beneath the outcropping where I originally picked up the scent and tracks," he began. "By the time I arrived, they had heard or smelled our presence, and the herd began to move up the trail. They did not get very far before they sensed the presence of the jaguar and cut through the forest, heading down the gentle slope toward the lagoon. After the dogs picked up the pigs' scent, they had started up the trail and came across the scent of the jaguar, which had probably been stalking the javelin, and unfortunately they took off after him."

Afterward, Luis and I packed the pigs on our shoulders, Juan carried our weapons, and the three hunters and three remaining dogs headed back to the river. When we arrived, a surprise awaited us. The dugout was gone.

Luis had hidden the dugout back in the edge of the rain forest about fifteen meters from the beach. The human tracks and the deep ruts in the beach sand caused by the dugout told the story. Four persons had stolen our craft.

While Juan and Luis discussed our plight and planned our strategy for returning to Yaxchilan, I sat down on the beach, exhausted, and tried to light a damp cigarette. Before I finished it, Luis came over to where I was sitting and began to explain our problems and plans.

It would be dark long before we could reach the shore on the Guatemalan side of the river in front of Yaxchilan. Even then, we would still have to cross the river with the remaining dogs, equipment, and dead pigs. Therefore, they decided to spend the night where we were and begin the journey at first light. Luis, always optimistic, thought we would be home by noon the next day. While he explained this, I watched Juan begin to cut the hind leg off of one of the javelins. They were right, of course, and from my point of view a good meal of roasted pig, followed with a good sleep, would help. The unpleasant thought of tramping through the rain forest in the dark with two dead pigs began to retreat into the darkening recesses of obscurity.

We had gathered around the small fire and were about ready to eat when Luis looked over his shoulder and motioned us quiet. The soft murmur of voices floated over the river and out of the mist, and the dogs began to growl softly. Startled, we turned and looked upstream. Eventually, dark gray shadows slowly emerged from the fog. Four men were coming downriver in a dugout. It turned out to be ours.

When at last they were close enough to shore, I began to see details and I became very apprehensive. Three of the men were seated in the bottom of the boat nonchalantly carrying *Cuernos de Chivo* (AK 47s) slung over their shoulders or across their laps. The fourth man poled the dugout onto the beach. Juan reached over and touched my leg as he stood up. "*Cierra tu boca*," he whispered. "*Todo está bien*," he added thoughtfully.

Although neither Luis nor I could understand the few words of Chol the men exchanged with Juan, they appeared formally at ease with one another and that was comforting. They had extended hands, and after a few minutes Juan helped them beach the dugout and then brought them over and presented them to Luis and me. Introductions were made in Spanish and very timid and limp handshakes were exchanged. I was still nervous, and not only because of their weapons.

It was obvious that they were poor. Their clothes, tattered and torn, were old and colorless from years of use. Three of them were barefoot. The fourth wore an old pair of wet boots. The boots had no laces but were fastened at the top with thin strands of what appeared to be bejuco vine. All three exuded a strong odor that smelled like a mixture of moldy bread and smoke. But it wasn't their poverty that made me uneasy. It was their animal nature. Their small, thin bodies were coiled like snakes and had a catlike tenseness, as if they might spring upon me at any moment. Their eyes could penetrate concrete. So intense were their stares around the flickering light of the campfire that I found it difficult to maintain eye contact with any of them. Perhaps it was paranoia, but they seemed to ignore Luis and focus their attention on me.

To my relief, Juan sat down next to the fire. This interrupted the mutual examinations, and the rest of us did the same. Without another word we began to share the leg of roasted pig.

It was a long time before the atmosphere loosened up. Very few questions and monosyllable responses were made while we ate. However, after we had lit up and offered cigarettes to the guests, a noticeable change took place. There is something unique about a campfire, a full stomach, and a cigarette. It didn't happen as quickly as I had experienced in other wilderness areas of the hemisphere; still, with each word and puff we began to lay aside our fears and suspicions.

It was Luis who broke the ice. More talkative than Juan, he recounted our adventures of the day. And when he made a big deal out of my apprehension about the jaguar following us down the trail, they reacted with great amusement. Laughing, one of the men clutched the front of his throat with one hand and pointed the forefinger of his other hand at me.

With everyone laughing, I thought it was time that I could finally ask the question that had bothered me since their arrival. "What do you hunt with your Cuernos de Chivo?"

The laughter stopped and their concerned expressions took the smile off my face. They stared at me intensely, producing more anxiety. Juan tilted his head ever so slightly and one of the men took this as his cue and answered with a single word, "*wachos.*"

I had never heard this word before and when my eyebrows furrowed, the man explained with another single word, "soldiers."

I wasn't surprised. But the confirmation of my suspicions didn't exactly make me feel better. These men were revolutionaries, and whatever grievances they had with their government, I had found myself a part of them that night around the campfire.

Fear kept me from asking questions about their life and their cause. Nevertheless, during the limited conversations that night, I found out how they came to be at our campsite.

They belonged to a larger group of revolutionaries that encompassed several different linguistic indigenous peoples in Guatemala, extending from the Peten into the highlands of Alta Vera Paz. They and their companions, a contingency of eight, had been distributing propaganda at a village upriver a few weeks ago. After getting supplies from people in the village sympathetic to their cause, they made camp a league or so downstream near the river. During the night they were surprised by soldiers and five of them had jumped into the river. The next day the four of them had gotten back together and traveled down the Mexican side of the river for two days. They crossed back over to Guatemala at a place where there were old ruins. There, hunting and fishing for survival, they hid among the ruins until two days ago. They decided that enough time had passed and they could make it back to their own village. Earlier that afternoon, they found the dugout and thought they could harpoon some langostina with our equipment.

Although I thought once again of the "Cristiano" in the river the day of my arrival in Yaxchilan, I didn't mention him. Instead, I inquired if they all had families they wanted to get back with. They did. Then, for some strange reason, the words of the late Jim Morrison came to me, ". . . death makes angels of us all."

During the conversations that night, I asked if they had any fear of the Mexican authorities when they had traveled downriver on that side of the border. One of the men responded, "It is not the rivers that divide our nations."

When I awoke the next morning, one of the pigs and all four men were gone.

Looking back on it now, I can see that the rain forest and villages were in crisis. A few years later it would explode upon the international scene. In 1978 it was, for the most part, still in defense mode. It was and is a simple question of survival. Perhaps the jaguar could even be the metaphor.

When a jaguar screams, it sends out a message that keeps other males and predators from his territory. His tactic works most of the time. The louder, deeper, and closer the threat, the more you tremble. Nevertheless, this is his defensive gesture. When all else fails, he uses his claws.

The peoples of Mesoamerica have been observing and using the jaguar as a role model for centuries. Warriors, priests, and even gods took on his name and attributes. His name appears in the titles of their literature and sacred books, *Chilam Balam*. At some point, a group of people took the name *Balam* for themselves and their descendents ruled over the city of Yaxchilan. The record left behind by the Jaguar Clan of Yaxchilan attests to their amazing accomplishments.

This was the last trip I ever made with Juan, and I never saw his friends again. Juan was from the little co-op Mayan village across the river and just upstream from Yaxchilan. In 1984 the wachos shot up the villages along the border. More than four thousand Guatemalan refugees crossed the river into Mexico at Juan's village and settled in the camp and ruins of Yaxchilan. Was Juan one of these? Or was he one of the hundreds of unclaimed bodies that floated down the Usumacinta? Or maybe he joined other Mayans in Mexico and now wears a ski mask.

▣ ▣ ▣ LETTER CONTINUED ▣ ▣ ▣

Hopefully there will never be closure to my relationship with Yaxchilan, the river, and its occupants. I have revisited the ancient civic-ceremonial center many times since the 1978 field season.

During the 1980s my business partner Steve Korhner and I made several rafting trips down the river from Yaxchilan to Tenosique. These seven- to nine-day rafting trips gave me a chance to observe and speak with the village people along that stretch of the Guatemala-Mexico border. The last trip of this period was in 1989. By the next year the violence that had begun on the Guatemalan side of the river had finally spilled over into Chiapas, making it difficult to find clients for river trips. On our last trip during this period, Steve, in the supply raft behind the rest of the group, was fired upon from the Guatemalan side of the river and we were unable to visit Piedras Negras because of the land mines that the Guatemalan soldiers had allegedly planted.

Also, the rain forest was disappearing at a speed that could almost be measured in megahertz. When I first flew down the River of the Sacred Monkey with Pedro Joaquín, the forest extended like a great sea in all directions. Today, on many parts of the Mexican side of the border, the rain forest is a one- to two-kilometer veneer along the river.

I also returned to work at Yaxchilan, once in November of 1997 and again in February of 1998. The directors of the project, Mario Perez Campa and Daniel Juarez, invited me to make some drawings of newly discovered lintels and stelae. On the first trip I mostly took photographs of the carved stones. On this trip, with the company of my archaeologist friend from San Miguel de Allende, Luis Felipe Nieto Gamiño, we watched the migration of tens of thousands of raptors flying south along the river for more than thirty minutes. Five years later, you joined me for a bitter-sweet journey down the Usumacinta River. From villagers along the banks we learned that we were the first rafting team to descend the Usumacinta since 1996.

I don't know if you noticed, but several times during the hour-long walk we took to the village that dreadful morning, I looked back to see how you were taking it. I was not worried about the hot and humid climb up the mountain and through the rain forest, but rather what was surely on your mind as well as everyone else's on the expedition—that Enrico was missing, and based upon the information that the Chols brought to our camp, he was probably dead. The main thing on my mind was the general predicament: our extreme isolation and the slow wheels of Mexican bureaucracy combined to trouble me with terrifying scenarios. I could imagine the horrifying consequences of being held up with the group at the campsite for days while a thorough search for Enrico was made and all of us questioned by the authorities. Although running out of food was a possibility, the thought of Enrico lying in the 105-degree temperature hastened my pace. I actually prayed for divine assistance. When we finally returned to San Miguel, I wrote the following description of the events that took place that day:

> Upon arriving at the jacal where the telephone was located, we were surrounded by a couple dozen curious villagers, mostly women and children. The sun was already burning hot and Steve sat down on the single bench with his head bowed in a gesture of complete and utter exhaustion from lack of sleep, the long walk, and grief. Jessica and Kenzie made small talk with the villagers as I entered the jacal and tried to make a telephone call for help in Palenque. My first several attempts were unsuccessful. Finally, one of the local schoolteachers arrived and assisted me in getting through to one of the few telephone numbers we had. By either the grace of God or some amazingly good luck, Julie Morales answered the phone.
>
> The phone in the jacal was located on the left and near the one door of the long single-room building. In the small space, at my left elbow, between the telephone and front wall, a bag had been hung. The bag contained an angry turkey. Between the frustrated gobbles and the distracting synchronized echoes

Figure10 Lintel Yaxchilan (drawing by author)

of both our voices, I told Julie that Enrico was missing and that the authorities should be notified. She told me that her husband, Alfonso, was at the archaeological site but she would contact him on his cell phone and call me back in twenty minutes. I went outside to inform Steve and the girls of the conversation. I really didn't want to make the next call and procrastinated by lighting a cigarette and hoping someone else would volunteer. When nobody did I returned to the phone and called his son, Benjamin, to inform him that his father was missing, that we had found his personal belongings, and of our current situation. I gave him our hotel numbers in both Tenosique and Palenque, as well as Alfonso and Julie's number in Palenque as contacts.

When the phone rang fifteen minutes later it startled everyone, including the curious villagers. I don't think anyone imagined that our contact with the outside world would be so punctual. Nevertheless, as I moved to pick up the phone a man ran up to us and told us that one of his companions had found Enrico's body by diving into the water below the falls. Although the connection and the turkey made it excruciatingly difficult to understand each other, somehow Julie's echoing voice was comforting. When I told her that Enrico had been found, she told me that Alfonso had a friend in the state prosecutor's office and would contact him immediately. She told me to wait for twenty or thirty minutes and she would call back. Once again I was faced with the spirit-deadening onus of responsibility and called Benjamin to tell him that his father was dead.

Within the next couple of hours, Julie called several times and finally informed us that the authorities were on their way. By then two of our rafting companions, Gina and Steve Keller, arrived and told Steve Korhner that his wife, Emilia, was taking Enrico's death very badly. Steve decided to return to the camp to comfort his wife. You, Kenzie, and I remained for phone calls and the arrival of the authorities.

What I remember most about the wait was the heat and my swollen ankles. They had swollen to the point where I could not tie the strings of my tennis shoes. At one point we picked our way very slowly down to the river in order to watch for the arrival of the authorities on the other side of the river. We were watching a dozen or more small boys from the village playing naked in the river when another child arrived and told us that someone had called us and would call us back in about ten minutes. The girls decided to wait by the river while I struggled up the hill through the rain forest passing through several clearings containing turkeys, chickens, and pigs. Exhausted, I sat on the bench in the hot sun until the phone rang again. It was Raul Hernandez, one of Enrico's closest friends.

After talking with Raul for a few minutes I hung around the jacal, mostly sitting on the ground in whatever side of the building created the most shade. I found some relief by removing my tennis shoes completely.

About four hours after Julie's last call, I was informed by a young boy that the authorities had arrived on the other side of the river. It was the public minister of Palenque, his female secretary, and another man. Afraid to cross the river in the dugout, the secretary stayed on the other side of the river with Jessica and Kenzie while Jorge poled the two men across to my side. The attitude of the two mestizo men toward the Chol people was infuriating. They addressed the people of the village in such an arrogant manner I had the urge to smack one of them in the face. They were impatient, and after demanding refreshment from one of the villagers they headed downstream using a well-worn trail above the river. They carried with them a red plastic stretcher for Enrico.

Not too long afterward, I was hailed by Jessica and Kenzie across the river and they were poled over to my side. It appeared that the secretary wanted to speak with me as I was the one who had called to notify the authorities. Having done so, I was obliged to make a formal declaration. I poled myself across the river in a dugout canoe in order to find out what was expected from me.

Forever, the landscape will be burned into my soul. On my side of the Chocol-Ha River I sat for three hours waiting for the authorities to return with Enrico. I used that time to examine the hillside scene across the river. It was in reality quite peaceful. Only portions of one or two of the village jacales were visible. The rest were hidden from my view by the rain forest and the draping bejuco vines over the water on far edge of the river. Nothing stirred except an occasional light breeze and the sound of birds. Then, suddenly, through the rain forest, I could see flashes of muted color and a few minutes later several small boys appeared on the bank across the river. Eventually, behind them, came eight Chol men carrying the red stretcher tied to and supported by two long poles among them. The small column broke into a sandy beach near the bank of the river, and I watched as the pall bearers deposited the stretcher and Enrico's body in the dugout.

As the Chol Jorge began poling the craft across the river, I looked up at the hillside on the other side and was taken by surprise: there must have been three or four hundred villagers standing in a dozen groups along the far hillside. They seemed to materialize out of the forest. It was the most emotional sight I have ever experienced in my life, almost like a Hollywood movie of a Viking funeral as the villagers gathered to pay Enrico their final respects. The scene was so beautiful it gives me goose bumps to recall it as I write.

I feel a great amount of gratitude to the Chol village of Netzahua-coyotl, to Alfonso and Julie Morales in Palenque, and especially to you and Kenzie for accompanying me to deliver Enrico out of the rain forest and into the care of his family. I am extremely proud that your mother and I produced such a mature lady.

Since you were a baby, I have dragged you around rain forests and ruins of Mesoamerica. But there was one project that you missed—El Templo Mayor of ancient Tenochtitlán.

◼ ◼ ◼

CHAPTER FOUR

THE HOUSE OF COLD

Templo Mayor Project

INAH

I returned to the Instituto Allende from Yaxchilan amid an atmosphere of gossip and change. It appeared from the rumors circulating around the campus about our work that the five months we spent in Yaxchilan were a continuous stream of drunken revelry and orgy. The first group of students had obviously returned to the little town of San Miguel with exaggerated tales. I was amused; nobody could have survived that much fun.

Nevertheless, when the Institute's new director, Larry Lyle, asked to see me in his office, I was nervous. The Mexicans have a saying, "A little town, a big hell," and I thought the requested meeting had something to do with the rumors. Instead, Larry wanted to know if I would return to the Instituto Allende and offered me the position of dean of students. I thanked him and told him that I would get back to him within a couple of weeks.

Leaving Larry's office, I went straight to the nearest telephone and called the office of the general director of INAH, Don Gaston García Cantú, and made an appointment for the following week. There was no doubt in my mind after working in Yaxchilan: if I could get a job with INAH I would leave the Instituto Allende.

I spent almost an hour in the waiting room outside the director's office in Mexico City. I was surprised that Esperanza (Hope), his secretary, remembered me. She brought me coffee and told me that as soon as the director finished an important meeting he would receive me.

Considering the circumstances—the stately building I was in, the magnificent wooden furniture in the luxurious room, the charming and sophisticated secretary, the powerful man in the next room whom I was about to ask for a job—I wasn't really nervous. Instead, I was considering the direction my life was taking. Scenes of forests and Mayan ruins flashed through my mind like HBO's "coming attractions."

I examined the face of the boy with the ball under his arm with my binoculars for several moments. I had the strange feeling that at the same time he was examining me. Whatever the case, his dark penetrating eyes made me uncomfortable, so I moved the binoculars. When I finally found the other boy in view, I was in for a shock. They were twins. I immediately searched once again for the boy with the ball, but he was no longer looking in my direction. With his back turned to me, he was walking down a path that led into the forest. He stopped once in order for his twin to catch up. Then they disappeared into the dense rain forest.

As my daydreaming continued, images of Tikal, Uaxactun, Quirigua, Copan, and Yaxchilan flashed behind my closed eyelids.

"Señor Patterson," a voice said softly.

"This is an illusion," I said to myself. "Finding a portal into Xibalba cannot be this quick or easy. It must happen in bits and pieces at intervals and over an extended period of time. In some ways, it has to be like putting together a large, elaborate jigsaw puzzle in your spare time. You find two pieces that fit together but you don't know where to put them in the greater scheme of things. You move on with your life, until on another day, a couple of more forms begin to take shape," I reasoned. "You don't follow two adolescent boys into a rain forest!"

"Señor Patterson?" I opened my eyes.

Your descent into Xibalba depends upon your focus, time, and effort. Even without interruption, it could take years.

"Señor Patterson, the professor will see you now."

I smiled as I stood up, "Gracias, Esperanza."

She opened the door to the great hall. Don Gaston sat behind his desk at the far end of the room. He seemed a mile away.

As I approached the front of his desk he rose, smiled brightly, and extended his hand. "Professor Patterson, it is a pleasure to see you again!" I relaxed completely, intuitively sensing that there was nothing dark or hidden about the man. Next, he very courteously thanked me and the students for the photographs and drawings we had made for INAH at Yaxchilan. Then we both sat down and he asked what he could do for me. I asked him for a job. He told me that although he would like to hire me, the *sindicato* (union) would not allow him. "However," he said as he picked up a phone, "I am going to send you over to talk with Professor Eduardo Matos Moctezuma at the Templo Mayor."

Don Gaston talked on the phone with a person called Tere for a few minutes and then informed me I was expected at the Templo Mayor at nine o'clock the next morning. He asked me if I knew where it was located.

"No, Professor, but don't worry! I will find it."

We shook hands again. After thanking him, I left the great hall. I made a point of offering thanks to Esperanza before skipping down the stairs and out of the building. I had a date the next morning with one of the most renowned archaeologists in Mexico! I had to tell somebody the good news. I went to tell Roberto García Moll.

Roberto received me graciously, and after listening to my enthusiastic story he insisted that I stay the night in his apartment rather than go to a hotel. Mexican hospitality is the best!

THE GREAT TEMPLE OF THE AZTECS

"There is nothing fancy about this office," I said to myself as I opened the street door and entered the building. It was bustling with bodies.

Perhaps twenty people were casually packed into a space that I calculated to be sixteen square meters. The secretary's desk was on the far side of the masses. I maneuvered my way through the throng to reach her.

"Is your name Tere?" I asked the secretary shyly.

She looked up, glanced at her watch, and then smiled, "Professor Patterson?"

With the introductions complete, she told me that Professor Matos was expecting me. Motioning toward a door, she explained that he was at the site and would return in a few minutes.

I thanked her and squirmed my way over to an empty space near a wall. From there I could observe the entire room as well as see anyone coming through one of its three doors. The people inside appeared to be going nowhere. Most of them were milling about talking to one another in groups of two or three. I tried not to be intrusive but I was always under scrutiny from someone in the room. My Spanish was not good enough to pick up on any of the rapid conversations. Several times during the next twenty minutes, the door to the street opened and more people entered the already crowded room.

Finally, a cheerful man with a big smile and an enormous beard entered the door from the ruins. He wore a straw hat and as he entered the room he pushed his glasses closer to his face with the middle two fingers of his right hand. He greeted several people before walking over to the secretary's desk. There was a brief conversation and finally the secretary lifted her arm and pointed to where I stood. The man looked in my direction, and after saying something to the secretary, he disappeared through the door behind her.

The secretary motioned for me to come to her desk. "The professor will see you now," she said, as she stood up to open the door behind her.

I walked into a small room. Inside, the bearded man stood in front of the single piece of furniture in the room, a desk. He peered at me over the top of his glasses, extended his hand, and asked, "Professor Patterson, what can I do for you?"

"Professor García Cantú sent me to you for a job," I answered.

"What kind of job? What is it that you do?"

"I draw *tepalcates* (pottery shards)," I responded.

Matos looked taken aback by my answer and then a puzzled expression appeared on his face. "Draw tepalcates?" He repeated my response like he could not believe it. As I didn't say anything, he continued. "Well then, how much do you think you should earn drawing tepalcates?" The question was tinted with sarcasm.

Now it was my turn to be taken aback. I had no idea. I thought very quickly and answered, "Why don't you make me an offer?" He looked directly into my eyes and named a figure.

I would have accepted anything. "That's fine with me. Why don't we try this for three months and if you like my work and what I produce, you raise my salary."

My declaration must have amused him for he laughed softly and then answered, "That is fine. Why don't you go out to the site and wait for a few minutes and I will send someone to give you a tour of the workplace and operations as well as introduce you to some of the project personnel."

I thanked him and after leaving his office stopped to ask his secretary for directions.

I stood against the outside wall of the building that housed Matos's office and reception area and looked below over the vast remains of the once great Aztec temple of Tenochtitlán. I tried to imagine, through the words of Bernal Diaz de Castillo, how the Spaniards must have seen the great temple and city of Tenochtitlán.

And when we saw all those cities and villages built in the water, and other great towns on dry land, and that straight and level causeway leading to Mexico, we were astounded. . . . It was all so wonderful that I do not know how to describe this first glimpse of things never heard of, seen or dreamed of before.

The pollution of dust and noise in the center of the city was distracting. I closed my eyes to concentrate harder.

So we stood looking about us, for that huge and cursed temple stood so high that from it one could see over everything very well, and we saw the three causeways which led into Mexico, . . . we saw fresh water that comes from Chapultepec which supplies the city, and we saw the bridges on the three causeways which were built at certain distances apart through which the water of the lake flowed in and out from one side to the other, and we beheld in that great lake a great multitude of canoes, some coming with supplies of food and others returning loaded with cargoes of merchandise . . . and we saw in those cities Cues (pyramids) and oratories like towers and fortresses and all gleaming white, and it was a wonderful thing to behold; then the houses with flat roofs, and on the causeways other small towers and oratories which were like fortresses.

It was hard to imagine it, and I couldn't. For a few minutes depression enveloped me: there were no lakes, no causeways, no bridges, nor any gleaming white buildings! Everything was colorless—gray, dusty, and dirty. Even as I looked out upon the ruins, my eyes were filling up with grit and tears.

I didn't have long to contemplate the site because the door leading back into the building opened and a young lady and gentleman stepped through it.

"Professor Patterson? I would like you to meet Dr. David Grove from the University of Illinois. My name is Isabel. I am an archaeologist working at the Templo Mayor and will be your guide today." Her English was impeccable. I learned later that her nickname was "Snoopy" after the dog in the comic strip by Charles Schulz.

I don't recall much of the tour. Perhaps it is because after spending a year and a half at the ruins, what I saw that first day becomes mixed with the daily encounters I had afterward. I do remember the surprise on Dr. Grove's face when I mentioned that I had been sent over to the Templo Mayor by Don Gaston García Cantú.

"That's unbelievable! Cantú is a socialist and has a reputation for hating gringos!" He shook his head.

I didn't know how to respond to his declaration, and the simple fact that I had been hired was statement enough. So, shrugging my shoulders, I replied, "Well, I don't know anything about Don Gaston's political and economic philosophies, but I'm here, aren't I?"

I soon found out that Dr. Grove was right about one thing: there were a lot of people in INAH that "hated" or were at least suspicious of gringos. The fact became manifest to me quickly and I spent the next few weeks becoming accustomed to being shunned. When Isabel introduced me to people on the team that first day they were typically the hospitable Mexicans whom I had come to love and appreciate. I suspect that neither Isabel nor they understood that I would be working with them. When they saw me at the site over the next few weeks, they were certainly curious but had dropped their mask of courtesy. Their greetings were very cool.

There were no instructions from Professor Matos, so the next day at work I wandered about the project excavations and labs looking for something to do. It seemed to me that they had everything they needed. Finally, I discovered a little niche where I might contribute.

The archaeologists were making detailed drawings of their excavations but I noticed that the individual pieces coming out of the burials and offerings were sent to the ceramic or restoration labs. During the process they were photographed and then stored on shelves. I decided that I could draw these pieces and went to Professor Matos with the idea of drawing all of these artifacts from the offerings individually for publication. He was amused and a little bit relieved. I don't think he knew what to do with this gringo that drew tepalcates. He signed my request for a 35mm camera, a tripod, and five rolls of color transparency film. Much to my surprise, the supplies arrived the very next morning.

I spent the rest of the week taking artifacts from the shelves and photographing the pieces with a five-centimeter scale placed carefully beside them. This activity provoked the two project photographers' curiosity. They hung about for some time before they approached me to find out what I was doing.

They were very stiff and arrogant, and in their chilly manner I sensed they were concerned about being contaminated with the virus of "capitalism." It wasn't just the photographers who were cold. I received the same vibrations from almost all of the younger archaeologists as well.

Occasionally during those first days, when I tired of photographing the artifacts, I took a walk through the site with the camera shooting photos of people working. But this activity only created more suspicion and mistrust.

I didn't know it at the time, but rumors had begun to circulate among the project personnel. I found out later there had been three different, simultaneous rumors. One was that I worked for the CIA as a spy and was taking photographs for the United States government. Once again the Cold War exerted its ugly influence. What the United States government might want with photographs of excavations and artifacts, they apparently didn't ask themselves. Others suggested that, being a gringo, I might be a drug dealer. I guess they put that rumor aside when they found out that I didn't drive a Ferrari to work. Instead I walked more than three miles to get to the Templo Mayor each day. But the rumor that actually broke the ice between me and the other staff was that I was a homosexual. This rumor must have found a lot of support and traveled very quickly, because out of the blue five of the female archaeologists invited me to have lunch with them. Within the next two weeks the ladies were inviting me to the movies, the theater, and for dinner, some telling me their sexual problems with their boyfriends. I still didn't have any idea why I was suddenly receiving so much attention from the ladies, but like my dad used to say, "Boy, don't look a gift horse in the mouth." I didn't ask. Later, when I became aware of the rumor, I confessed to one of the female archaeologists that I was not a homosexual. But bonds had already been established and I continued in the role of a confidant.

Early Monday morning after my first week of work, I knocked on the door of Professor Matos's office and various voices told me to come in. Most of the archaeologists were sitting around the room,

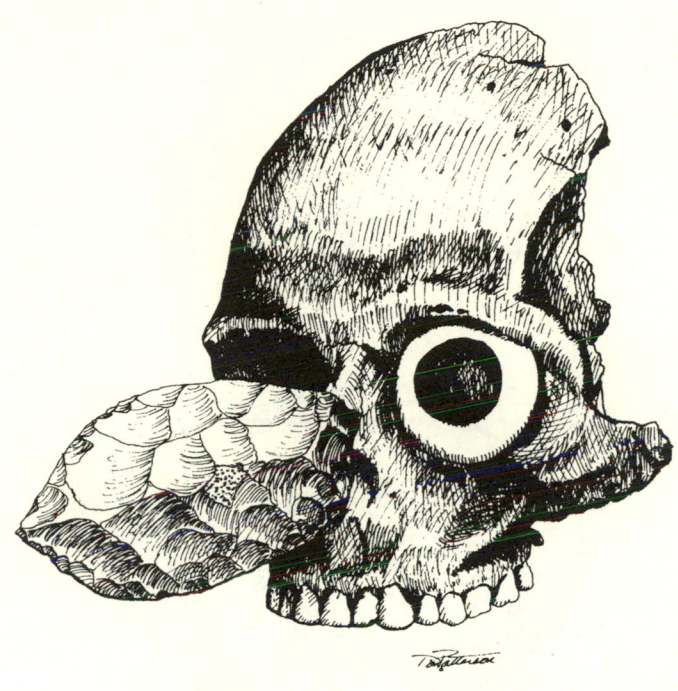

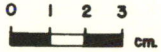

Figure 11 Templo Mayor
(drawing by author)

0 1 2 3
cm.

on the floor, drinking coffee. I entered the small space and advanced among the feet of the archaeologists until I stood directly in front of the professor's desk.

"Good morning, Professor Matos. If you have the time I would like to show you the drawings I have made. Some are the artifacts from Offering VI." I unrolled 126 pencil drawings of the artifacts complete with their scale indicated just below. Of course it was the volume of work that impressed him, not my drawing skills. The week before, nobody had seen me with a pencil in my hand.

I had noticed that the room had gotten quieter when I entered, but now the silence seemed pronounced as Matos asked, "How did you do this? I mean, how did you do so many in such a short time?"

Figure 12 Templo Mayor (drawing by author)

I tried to explain in my halting Spanish.

"It's nothing new. I got the idea from a piece of equipment called a camera Lucida that Fredric Catherwood used back in the 1840s to make some of his drawings of the Maya ruins. I put a similar system together back in San Miguel de Allende.

"My camera Lucida entails projecting slides on a mirror and then onto the bottom of a glass plate that has been placed into a cut in the top of my drafting table. All I have to do with one of two buttons is change either the distance of the projector or the focus of the lens until the five-centimeter scale on the slide matches the ruler in my hand. Then I just trace the important characteristics of each artifact."

Everybody in the room listened intently and I continued, hoping to sound a little humble in case I hadn't been before.

"Of course, this is only the beginning of the process. They are not the finished drawings. They will take more time because I have to compare them with the original artifacts, make corrections, and then model them in black ink. I will use a pointillism technique similar to that of Georges Seurat."

I noticed a blank look on the faces of several students, so I continued. "To put it another way, I will try to emulate the black-and-white drawings of pre-Hispanic artifacts by Miguel Covarrubias."

The professor complimented my work and I excused myself and left the room. I didn't get very far before I turned to knock on the door again. Again, multiple voices told me to enter. And as before, a hushed silence thickened the small room.

"Excuse me, Professor, but is there a space available here at the project for me to work on these drawings?" I felt like a fish floundering on dry land.

I was given just enough space at one end of the ceramic lab for a drafting table, a stool, and a cabinet for my equipment and the finished drawings. The small space wasn't the ideal spot for me to be working. The fluorescent lighting flickered constantly and the dust from the work of cleaning the dirt from the pottery shards with tooth brushes settled on everything in the room.

For several months I battled the air pollution in the center of Mexico City. It wasn't just my nose and eyes that were affected; I actually became accustomed to the irritation, but it ruined my drawing paper. After the paper was exposed to the air for an hour, I constantly had to clean its surface or my Rapid-o-graph pen would not function properly. There came a point when I went to Professor Matos with a request. Before making it I took him to the corner of the ceramic lab where my drafting table was located. I had intentionally left a drawing exposed to the air during the night. I moved a finger over the surface of the drawing and pointed to the drawing. My finger had drawn a light line across the dark surface. Then I held up my finger to show Eduardo the black grit. From then on, most of the finished drawings were made at home.

Apart from that, the Templo Mayor was an exciting place to be working. Every day something new was brought to light in the excavations. Especially rewarding were the artifacts coming out of the offerings that I chose to draw. The archaeologists were discovering an enormous variety of objects in these offerings: ceramic vessels and stone idols with images of Tlaloc; beads made of drilled bones and stones, including jade; Olmec heads; carved masks from the Mezcala region of Guerrero; molded copal, gold, skeletons of birds, caiman, jaguars, and so forth.

The Templo Mayor received a lot of publicity, not only in Mexico but internationally as well. Provoked by a massive media campaign and the support of the president of Mexico, visitors came by the thousands. Academics, princes, kings, presidents and congressmen, ambassadors, movie stars, and important men in the financial districts around the world came to see the *Coyolxauhqui*, whose dismembered body, weighing eight tons, lay at the bottom of the stairs to the temple of *Huitzilopochtli*.

Matos, always charming, attended the visitors like a professional talk show host, and they loved him. He did more to focus the attention of the world on the Aztec culture of Mexico than did Hernan Cortés. Hundreds of publications, films, and posters came out of the project ranging from academic treatises to coffee-table books and spots on the news and the Discovery Channel. Twenty years after my own participation in the project, it is still under way.

More important to me than shaking hands with Presidents Jose Lopez Portillo and Jimmy Carter were the numbers of lasting friendships that I made because of the project. Happily, they included many of the students that I had felt were antagonistic toward me in the beginning. But one person stands out among the many.

One day Matos came to me and asked if I would show a "Chicano" around the site. This was an unusual request. Usually the tours were given by professional guides or one of the archaeologists whose turn had come around. Whatever Matos's reasons for asking me to do this, it brought me together with Dr. David Carrasco, and after twenty years we remain in contact.

Figure 13 Moon Goddess (drawing by author)

David was teaching at the University of Colorado when he first visited the Templo Mayor. While at Boulder, Colorado, he started the Mesoamerican Archive and Research Project (MARP). A few months later and with the permission of Matos, I flew up to the university to give his project copies of all the drawings I had made while at the Templo Mayor. Through his efforts, the University of Colorado financed excavations in Mexico. Later David took the MARP project to Princeton, where he published several books on Aztec ceremonial centers and became the editor-in-chief of Oxford's Encyclopedia of

Mesoamerican Cultures. Today he occupies a chair in the department of Latin American Studies at Harvard.

My lack of confidence and uncertainty about becoming part of the "team" at the Templo Mayor, on one hand, and a desire to return to those fabulous carvings and inscriptions at Yaxchilan and the dream of a Mesoamerican documentation team, on the other, combined to make me nervous and unsettled, but I was determined to do a good job. My private dream of a documentation team slipped quietly, for a while, into the distant recess of my mind.

Documentation Team

After a year I was approaching seven hundred completed drawings, but archaeologists had pulled more than four thousand artifacts out of the offerings. I knew that eventually I could catch up; after all, even the Templo Mayor was not a bottomless pit of buried objects. I realized that in order to build a documentation team I would have to find a greater volume of artifacts and monuments to document.

The first thing I had to find out was how much work was out there. My casual inquires within INAH produced another job for me with the archaeologist Juan Yadeum and his project in Las Limas, Veracruz. It turned out to be a small job with a half dozen artifacts to draw for a small journal publication of INAH, *el Boletin*.

I didn't put a lot of effort into the search for more work, but when opportunity presented itself, I inquired. So I presented the idea of contracting work outside of INAH with Dr. Paul Schmidt from the University of Mexico (UNAM).

Paul's wife's family and my wife's family had been friends for several generations, so it was predestined that we would become friends. He came to visit me at the Templo Mayor one day and we went to lunch together. When I approached him with the idea of searching for work in the Anthropological Research Department of the university, he thought it was a great idea. I would need permission from Dr. Jaime Litvak, the chairman of the department. Paul offered to make an appointment.

I arrived thirty minutes early on the day of the appointment, so Paul showed me around his office and other facilities on his floor. The secretary then informed us that Dr. Litvak was expecting us. It didn't take long to realize there had been a mix-up. Dr. Litvak was not ready for us. In fact, for the first few moments we were invisible. He was tearing into one of the department's investigators for some sloppy work involving Carbon 14. The person sat in a high-backed chair with his back to us, and all we could see was the back of his head. He never turned around.

When Dr. Litvak noticed us, he spoke to Paul.

"You should come back later!"

I felt very uncomfortable as we retreated from the office. In order to pass the time while we waited for our turn with Dr. Litvak, Paul told me he wanted to introduce me to the department's famous *telpalcatero* (ceramic specialist), Evelyn Rattray.

When we entered Evelyn's research lab, we could see that she also had another visitor. It was Dr. Clemency Coggins from the Peabody, an expert on Maya ceramics. She was visiting Mexico with Dr. Tatiana Proskouriakoff, also from the Peabody. When Dr. Coggins found out that I had been working in Yaxchilan during the last field season, she asked if we had uncovered any ceramic pots with hieroglyphs. We had, so she asked if she and Tatiana could see them. I told her that I would call Roberto García Moll and see if I could arrange an appointment for them. Our conversation was interrupted by the notice that Dr Litvak would see us.

This time when we entered his office, the chairs in front of his desk were empty. I have to admit that Dr. Litvak intimidated me. It wasn't just because of the previous scene that had taken place in his office; he intimidated me physically as well as mentally. Physically, he was squat, with a thick build, a very solid man. But it wasn't until I sat down in the chair and faced him at his level that I lost my concentration and my preplanned plea for work. It was as if his brilliant mind had begun to devour the rest of his body. His neck had already been consumed!

But Dr. Litvak was direct and to the point. His directness settled my nervous stomach. He was an executive through and through so it didn't take more than ten minutes to resolve my request for working with his department. I walked out of his office with his blessing. However, I didn't get the opportunity to take advantage of his permission, because within two weeks after my visit to the university I was on my way to Oaxaca. But for the moment I was having a great day.

After leaving the university I stopped at Roberto's office in the Museum of Anthropology and History. He gave his permission to show Drs. Coggins and Proskouriakoff the ceramics that had come out of the tomb in front of Templo 33 in Yaxchilan. We set a tentative date for seven thirty that evening. I left a message for Dr. Coggins at her hotel and took the metro to the Templo Mayor.

At first I thought that all the great Mayanists were converging upon the city, since immediately upon my arrival at the Templo Mayor, Matos introduced me to the aged archaeologist Alberto Ruiz. Alberto Ruiz was, among other things, the discoverer of the tomb of Pacal in the Temple of Inscriptions at Palenque. What a day I was having!

It turned out that the scholars had all come together to honor Tatiana Proskouriakoff, who was taking her last trip through Mesoamerica in order to say good-bye to old friends.

Dr. Proskouriakoff didn't go with us to Roberto's office. Tired and overcome with emotion she chose to stay in her hotel. So Dr. Coggins and I went to the basement of the museum to talk with Roberto.

Roberto graciously showed Dr. Coggins the ceramics that had come from Yaxchilan the previous field season. Though I noticed he was somewhat distracted during the conversations, I didn't find out what was bothering him until the next day.

Dr. Coggin's stride from the museum to her hotel was breathtaking. She is a giant, not only as a Mayanist but as a person as well. Her long legs stretched out like a thoroughbred's. I was out of breath by the time we reached her hotel in the Zona Rosa.

I found out the next day that Roberto was upset. He asked me why Dr. Proskouriakoff had not come to the museum as planned. He was unconvinced when I explained that she had been very tired. Instead he made a statement that I didn't understand.

"They are trying to keep me away from her!"

Who were "they"? Was this institutional paranoia or were "they" the Lords of Xibalba to which he referred?

It wasn't until years later while reading Michael Coe's *Breaking the Maya Code* that I guessed that it might have been Roberto's interest and support for the new generation of epigraphers that stood in the way of his meeting Dr. Proskouriakoff.

LIVING IN CHILANGOLANDIA (MEXICO CITY)

Roberto let me stay with him for a couple of weeks while I looked around for an apartment. It was interesting to be around Roberto. He had a fantastic record collection and was one of the few archaeologists I knew who had a library containing books on literature and philosophy. Most archaeologists' libraries, no matter the size, were narrowly stuffed with their technical books and journals. He always invited me to the meetings he had in the evenings with other INAH authorities. I enjoyed living there so much that it was difficult to gather up enough motivation to look for an apartment of my own. It was then that I learned the Mexican expression for lack of motivation, "*Qué hueva!*"

When I finally got it together, the first place I found was a loaner. A young couple I had met in San Miguel had an apartment in the Colonia Doctores. They were leaving for England for most of the summer and told me that I could "apartment sit" for them for a month. It was a wonderful gesture on their part and an opportunity for me. It was close enough that until I got paid I could walk to the Templo Mayor from there. Also it was close to two other areas where I was interested in finding an apartment, the Colonia Roma and the Colonia Condesa. Meanwhile, the loaned apartment had a couple of drawbacks.

The first was its location right across the street from the main boxing ring in the city. This translated, after the evening's events out in the street, into what I called "instant replays." Sometimes it got very loud, and one night shots were fired. Several times the noise of the street even drowned out the sound of the blind trumpet player who usually sat in a doorway under my window. He was the second drawback. I don't know whether he was really blind, but surely he was deaf. As he probably made most of his money after the boxing events, he played his loudest, if not his best, after 11 p.m. A blinking neon sign outside my window reminded me of a description in a Raymond Chandler novel or a scene from an old Bogart picture.

I didn't spend much time in the neighborhood. I had to muster a lot of courage just to leave the apartment at night and walk two doors down the street to a bakery. As a matter of fact, I tried to get out of the neighborhood whenever I could.

Only two weeks into my job, Roberto invited me to a lecture he was giving in the auditorium of the Museum of Anthropology and History. Since it allowed me to leave the apartment in daylight and return after dark in a taxi, I accepted his invitation.

When I arrived, the auditorium was packed and there was very little standing room from where one could hear his lecture on Yaxchilan. I squirmed my way into a mass of persons standing in an aisle and made it about a quarter of the way toward the lectern.

About halfway through his lecture, Roberto showed a slide of the stelae carved on the stalactite in front of Temple 33 in Yaxchilan. Then he surprised me with a wonderful gesture. He showed my drawing and, giving me credit, then complimented me in front of a large portion of INAH's academic community, and other important people in the areas of anthropology and history of Mexico City. Of course, there wasn't any applause. Even the people standing in the aisle around me ignored me. For some reason I didn't feel shunned. I reasoned that I was only one person in a city of ten million.

After the lecture I approached Roberto in order to congratulate and thank him and along the way bumped into Professor Eduardo Matos, who was heading in the same direction. Everyone congregated in the foyer in the entry to the magnificent museum and you couldn't help bumping into somebody. After we shook hands with Roberto, he took Eduardo aside and began talking to him in earnest. It was embarrassingly uncomfortable because I could hear little bits and pieces of their conversation and it was about me. Basically, Roberto was working on Matos to raise my salary. I began to suspect that Roberto knew that Matos would be in the auditorium that night and that was why he showed my drawing during his lecture. At the end of my first three months, Eduardo kept his word and gave me a 30 percent increase in my salary. I went shopping for a mattress.

About a week before I had to move from the loaned apartment, someone came to visit me at the Templo Mayor. He was Iñigo de Martino Solano, one of my students in the Yaxchilan Project, who had returned from Los Angeles to live in Mexico. He had been hired to design theater sets for Bellas Artes (the National School of Fine Arts) in Mexico City, and he needed an apartment, too, so we began looking for one together. We found one on Colima Street in the Colonia Roma. In the positive column, it was cheap. The rent had been frozen by the government at fifty dollars a month. It had seven rooms, including two bedrooms and two baths. It was just two blocks from the central offices of INAH on Cordoba.

In the negative column, the apartment was unfurnished, and until I got my raise we slept in our sleeping bags on the floor. During the first winter we heated up the apartment with the fireplace, burning wood and paper that we collected from the empty lots in the neighborhood. The apartment was on the first floor, and at times during the day the noise from the street was irritating. We lived directly below the apartment of a noisy and scandalous pair of transvestites and a Brazilian stripper. The activities of the pair and their frequent guests could be heard in our place below. Fortunately, they were forced to vacate the apartment after a rowdy night when someone threw a chair through a window and onto the street.

Iñigo had everything going for him: he was talented, he worked in one of the most beautiful buildings in the city, and, last but not least, he was the nephew of one of the most distinguished men in the government, Dr. Fernando Solano.

One evening, one of Iñigo's cousins came by the apartment with some "breaking news." The president, José Lopez Portillo, was about to pick one of two men for the cabinet post of Secretary of Public Education. It would be either Dr. Fernando Solano or Professor Gaston García Cantú. The next day I mentioned the possibility to Roberto without telling him the source of the rumor.

He looked at me with an expression of disbelief and said, "You had better hope that this is not the case. If Don Gaston leaves INAH, we will have to begin politicking all over again."

I wasn't comfortable with the inclusiveness of his statement. The word "we" sounded like too many people.

The day after that encounter I met with Roberto again. He had a new look of admiration on his face as he said, "You were right! I just talked with Don Gaston and he told me. How did you know this? Are you sure you don't work for the CIA?"

Fortunately for us, nobody had to politic. Don Gaston bowed out of the president's offer and Dr. Fernando Solano became the Secretary of Public Education. I can't remember if I ever told Roberto the source of my information.

In 1978, Mexico City's population numbers were very close to those of New York City. But where New York was built upward, Mexico City spread out like an uncontrolled virus for seemingly endless miles. Since I didn't have a car, I limited my travels to where I could go on the Metro. It cost one peso and it was, for me and the majority of the other 999,999 plebes, the choice for transportation in Mexico City. It took me to work and back, to the theater, ballet, movies, restaurants, airport, and bus terminal. Night or day, during a twelve-year period, I never had a bad experience on the Metro. During rush hour the city policed the stations and separated the women into other cars from the men. It was such an easy way around the city that I often thought that there should be an article for tourists called "Mexico by Metro."

ENAH

Somehow my name reached the administration of the National School of Anthropology and History (ENAH). When they called me I was taken completely by surprise. They offered me a job.

For a semester I taught a course entitled, "Technical Drawing for the Archaeologist." When the class started, I had twenty-two students. After I explained what was required and expected of them, only eleven arrived for the second class. By the third class there were nine.

Since several of the nine students worked at the Templo Mayor, we held the classes there. The students were prepared for me to begin the technical part of the course. They came to the first class with graph paper, triangles, scale rulers, T-squares, and calipers. Several of the students brought slide rules. But I didn't start there. I started as if it were a beginning life-drawing course at the Rhode Island School of Design. I told them to buy five kilos of butcher paper and bring drawing boards. They thought I was nuts, and they were probably right, but I had a reason.

Over the previous several months, I had observed the students excavating at the site. All of them participated in the documentation process by making technical drawings. All of them could accurately detail the position, location, and size of the objects in the offerings. What most of them couldn't do was to make a bone look like the bone and a pot look like the pot. So we put aside the calipers, slide rulers, meters, T-squares, triangles, and such and began to draw freehand.

We practiced for hours making contour drawings with the objects and materials that surrounded us at the Templo Mayor. We talked about the concepts of motion and gesture and to demonstrate them we went to the zoo to draw animals, people, and trees.

I think almost every student enjoyed the class. One of the students, Pilar Luna, came to me one day and told me she was sorry but she had to drop out of the course. She had been offered a job building the Department of Underwater Archaeology of INAH. Although I was happy for her good fortune, I was sorry to see her leave. Of all the students in the class, she concentrated the hardest and made the most improvement in her drawing and observation skills.

The very first day I set the rule that no one would be admitted to the class more than five minutes late. For the first three weeks of the class, attendance was high as well as punctual. After that, class attendance for several of the students was very sporadic, but I noticed that the students who worked at the Templo Mayor never missed a class. Those who came to the class from work, home, or school were the ones who missed classes most frequently. It was understandably difficult for them. Every one of them had to work long hours and spend a lot of time crossing the city from one place to another. I was patient with their absences. But the only way to learn to draw is to draw; the more you draw the better you get, and this didn't have to take place in the classroom.

What I had a problem with was the final exam. Only three students showed up. I was shocked, but went ahead and gave the exam. For the next four weeks I posted a new exam date both at the Templo Mayor and on the bulletin boards of ENAH. No one showed up.

Finally, the day came when the three students who had taken the exam approached me. They needed their grades turned in to the office. After apologizing to the three students, I went to the main office of ENAH and turned in my grades. Immediately the bad grades were questioned by one of the administrators. What kind of teacher gave such low grades to two-thirds of his students? Didn't I understand that these students were "socialists"? Didn't I realize that they had to work?

I puzzled over the administrator's second question, unable to see what socialism had to do with the course I was teaching. "Perhaps I should have taught the technical class from a Marxist point of view?" I asked myself. After several minutes of explaining that I had given them ample opportunity to make up the exam, I could see that it didn't matter to the administrator. Finally, in complete exasperation I told the lady that the grades were going to stand and would not be changed.

Two weeks later I received a telephone call from Roberto García Moll. Evidently, the school had called him and asked who could teach the class the next semester. He told them only two persons that he knew were qualified to teach the class, Ramon Carrasco and Don Patterson. Since they didn't call me, Ramon must have taught the class.

For weeks I had contemplated the possibility of attending ENAH for a degree in archaeology. I found myself in very much the same position as six of the students in my class. In order to attend the school I would have to supply my room and board as well as to buy the books and materials. In short, I would have to work as well as study. Then my archaeologist buddy from the University of Arizona, Ben Brown, suggested that I contact a friend of his at the U.S. Embassy who was in charge of scholarships. Ben gave me his friend's card and I made an appointment. Unfortunately, I could not get a scholarship from the embassy to attend school in Mexico. Their job was to provide scholarships for Mexican nationals who wanted to study in the United States. For the next few days I was depressed and disappointed. Then, out of the blue, I ran into a friend whom I hadn't seen for several years and he gave me some advice that helped me make an important decision and alleviated my depression.

I was going to be late for work! This had never happened before and I was anxious about the gridlock in which the taxi was caught. I was irritably reproaching the driver for his choice of routes to the Templo Mayor when I saw a familiar face in a heated discussion with a lady on the sidewalk not two meters from my taxi window.

I rolled down the window, "Tom? Tom! Tom Trow!"

Both Tom and the lady were surprised. Because of the gridlock we were able to arrange a meeting later that evening.

I was excited all day at the prospect of meeting Tom that night. Tom was the state archaeologist of Minnesota, but several years ago he had applied for work in the dean's office at the University of Minnesota. I was curious whether he got the job.

We met at my apartment that evening and then went out for dinner. During the course of our conversation I broached the subject of getting a degree in archaeology, mentioning my recent disappointment at my ineligibility for a scholarship through the embassy. To my surprise, Tom began to discuss the advantages of working in archaeology as a technician as opposed to an investigator. My idea of creating a Mesoamerican documentation team fit nicely into his advice. Less than a week later I made the decision to remain a technician. Still, one of Tom's arguments didn't pan out. He thought that as a technician I would be outside the realm of the bitter political infighting so often encountered in academic and governmental institutions.

Figure 14 Monte Alban (photo by Eric Geothals)

Chapter Five

The House of Bats

Monte Alban Project

The Proposal

Monte Alban was the first project I coordinated for the general director's office of the National Institute of Anthropology and History. I was in Oaxaca from March 1, 1980, until March 2, 1981. During that time we documented the carved monuments of Monte Alban, Dianzu, and Yagul, Oaxaca. After a few more years of labor, the work at Monte Alban evolved into a reference book. In 1986 two editions of *Los Monumentos Escultoricos de Monte Alban* were printed, one in Spanish and one in German, but more important, the project gave me the opportunity to observe some of the innermost political intrigues of INAH. There were clues from the very beginning.

A young archaeologist, Paco Hinnojosa, and I were returning to the Templo Mayor from lunch. As usual we were laughing. We always had a great time at lunch. In fact, Paco is one of the nicer elements of my tale. On that particular day we were a little late and when we arrived at the site, Eduardo Matos, in the distance, was aggressively motioning us toward himself and another man. As we approached, Matos made a gesture that clearly indicated that it was my presence that was needed, so Paco, without a word, turned off our common path and headed for his place in the excavation. I was still smiling when I walked up to the two men.

"Don, where have you been? We have been trying to locate you for almost an hour. I would like to present you to Professor Manuel Esparza, the state director of INAH in Oaxaca." We shook hands and

Matos continued. "Manuel is here to see you on behalf of Don Gaston for some project at Monte Alban and has been waiting here to take you to lunch."

"Unfortunately, Paco and I are just returning from lunch." I directed my reply to Eduardo. Then I turned and extended a hand to the other man. I continued quickly, "Still, it would be a great pleasure to accompany Professor Esparza. We can discuss the project while you eat," I said, shaking his hand.

I can't recall all of the details of my conversation with Professor Esparza that day, but I do remember it wasn't exactly cordial. While he ate he described the political problems that he was having with the governor of Oaxaca. He was still talking about them when his dessert arrived.

After listening for the better part of an hour, I lost my patience and interrupted him. "Excuse me, Professor, but I am not interested in the political problems behind this archaeological project. As a foreigner, I will not and cannot get involved in these problems. My only interest is in the work that is expected of me at the ruins and I still do not understand what is required of me."

My gringo directness made him uncomfortable and he lashed out venomously.

"I did not want you for this job! I had someone else in mind for this project and only came here because you were recommended by Don Gaston! Perhaps you cannot do it," he suggested rather hopefully.

"Professor, how do we know that, since I don't even know what you need or Don Gaston wants?"

"Then why don't you ask him?" he replied caustically.

"I will."

I don't know what happened, but immediately after my reply, the mask of fury on his face softened and he continued.

"You should talk with the archaeologists Angel García Cook or Roberto García Moll. They are the ones who suggested this project."

There was nothing notable in the remainder of our conversation except politeness. When we left the restaurant, Manuel Esparza and I shook hands at the closest corner and we parted company.

As I walked back to the excavations at the Templo Mayor, I indulged myself in mindless speculation. Was Manuel Esparza going to return to Don Gaston's office and inform him that I was not the person for the job? Had my gringo directness got in the way of my goals? How would Don Gaston react? I didn't want to let him down so I had to take some affirmative action. First I would consult with Eduardo Matos. I didn't know Angel García Cook, but after talking with Matos my next stop would be Roberto's office.

When I returned to the site I looked for Matos to explain what had happened at the restaurant. He was nowhere to be found.

Roberto, at his office in the Direction of Pre-Hispanic Monuments, explained in less than fifteen minutes the problem as well as a solution proposed by Angel and himself.

Down in Oaxaca, Manuel had built a large metal roof support to protect the carved stones located in Structure J, the observatory at Monte Alban. The governor protested the aesthetics. Roberto showed me a photo. Considering my recent encounter with Manuel Esparza, it was hard to be objective. The governor was right. It was the ugliest thing I had ever seen.

The archaeologists' concerns went beyond the carved stone in the observatory; they wanted to protect all of the carved stones at the site. Therefore, they developed a three-part solution. The first was to document in detail all of the carved stones at the site. I was to be in charge of this first phase of work. The next step was for an artisan to make good copies of the originals to replace them at the site. The final phase would be the construction of a museum and storage space for the original carved stones.

Roberto told me what needed to be done, and gave me some ideas about how I might start. He shrugged off my report of the bad vibrations I felt at my meeting with Manuel Esparza. His attitude was that if Don Gaston had recommended me, Manuel had no choice but to accept my appointment. At the same time, he cautioned me to be careful in my dealings with the state director of INAH.

The next day as I entered the office of Don Gaston's secretary, I was greeted cheerfully. "Good morning, Don!" My anxieties dissolved. Esperanza and I were now on a first-name basis.

If Don Gaston had any misgivings about my ability to perform the task, he didn't show it. On the contrary, he greeted me with enthusiasm and told me that there was an airplane ticket and money waiting for me in the office of his administrative secretary, Eduardo Villa. I spent the next several days in Oaxaca collecting bibliographies and visiting Monte Alban with Dr. Marcus Winter, the archaeologist in charge of the site.

I returned to Mexico City four days later with a proposed budget to work at Monte Alban for one year. I took the proposal to Roberto for his scrutiny. He made a couple of changes and told me that it was ready for submission to the general direction. My proposal was accepted and I was about to begin coordination of my first project for the National Institute of Anthropology and History.

PROBLEMS AND THE PRESS

At the end of the first month I began to have problems. The first problem started when I delivered the notes for the month's expenses to the administrator at the regional offices of INAH. Everything was meticulously gone through, verified, checked, and approved by the accountant, until we came to my personal expenses.

According to the system used by INAH, I was allocated 400 pesos per day for my personal expenses. I found out later that this allocation was based on a table agreed upon by the authorities of INAH and the workers union. When I presented my notes for these expenses I had only spent half the allocated amount. The administrator demanded that I bring him receipts for the other half. I argued that I couldn't bring him more receipts because I had no more, although I had expected, and indeed was prepared, to return the other half in cash. Having explained my position, I placed the cash balance on his desk. He refused to take it and insisted that I bring receipts for the money instead.

My position was that INAH and the taxpayers should be happy that I was able to reduce the cost of the project from 12,000 pesos per month to 6,000 pesos per month. He argued that that was not how he was accustomed to handling the accounting and that it created "bookkeeping problems" for him. He insisted that I go out and find him the equivalent receipts. This sounded like a bureaucratic problem, so I asked who had the final authority on these matters. He told me that the authority responsible for all accounting matters was the administrative secretary of INAH. I suggested that he call the administrative secretary. He refused, so I did. The matter was settled by Eduardo Villa, the administrative secretary of INAH, and the accountant received the cash balance. But the regional administrator was never very friendly after that.

Within two weeks of returning to Oaxaca, the problem of creating a team was resolved. I ran an advertisement in one of the local papers and about a dozen persons applied for a position. After making a couple of changes due to errors in my judgment, I finally ended up with five of them: Beto, Eugenio, Porfirio, Manuel, and José Luis.

Beto Hernandez was a very small young man from the village of Santa Cruz Xoxocotlán. He was a good choice, as through the years he showed loyalty, an ability to think anthropologically, and an amazing resilience to whatever environment we entered. He was the most dependable person on the team and became my right arm in the field. During the Monte Alban project, he clearly demonstrated that he was the best of all of us at making rubbings.

Eugenio Candiani, of Italian descent, was a draftsman and rock drummer. While some of the Candianis owned and operated my favorite bookstore in Oaxaca, Eugenio's immediate family managed to have the reputation for being mafioso.

Porfirio Vazquez was a young and extremely polite topographer and draftsman. He talked in such a deep voice that the other team members often tried to mimic him.

Manuel Hernandez was the mischievous son of one of the maintenance men at Monte Alban. His father asked if I would hire him. He told me that if his son didn't have a job he would just drink and get into trouble. His frankness and concern for his son moved me, so I hired Manuel, whom everyone called *Gusano* (worm).

José Luis Tiznado was an artist from Guadalajara who joined the team later than the others. He was a wealth of cynical humor and had a great amount of talent.

Quickly we fell into our daily work habits.

The alarm went off at 4 a.m. each morning, and by four thirty I picked up the team members along a prearranged route to the market. Our breakfast, at the market, consisted of a *pan de yerma* (regional bread) dipped in a soup bowl of hot chocolate. After breakfast we drove the blue Volkswagen Safari up the winding narrow road in to the site. Usually, we arrived on top of the mountain in time to see the sun rise. We took an hour off for lunch and finished working by 2 p.m. each day.

We commenced documenting the carved stones in the observatory. Back in Mexico City, Roberto had previously suggested that we begin our labor on this building. As this was the structure that had caused the conflict between the governor and Manuel Esparza, I guessed that Roberto wanted to demonstrate to the governor that INAH was working to resolve the problem. But whatever dialogue was going on in the celestial palaces of power above our heads, it wasn't going too well. Our first hint of the press's attitude and their criticism of INAH appeared in the two local newspapers. They continued every day for a week. I was beginning to think that the governor controlled the local press.

When the articles started I wasn't bothered too much. If they didn't bring me any prestige, at least the commercial establishments where I bought supplies recognized me as a person of some distinction. Some of them even thought it was funny and joked with me about the conflict. Others were more serious and engaged in discussions concerning the site. After listening, most of them expressed their approval of INAH's solution. Finally, something happened at the state level that knocked our project off the front page of the local papers and brought some temporary relief to us: the tragedy of Juan Ruiz.

According to the local press, Juan Ruiz was an ex-soldier who was allegedly involved in the drug trade in Oaxaca. He was accused of drug smuggling by the Federales in the press, as well as of killing both his wife and his mother-in-law. In the paper the next day, Juan Ruiz's children were interviewed. According to the reporter, the children claimed that the father was not at home the day their mother and grandmother died. Indeed, they were both fine when the Federales entered their home but were found dead after the police left. Even for Oaxaca, this was scandalous. Bodies were exhumed and rope burns were allegedly found on the arms and wrists of the corpses, tending to substantiate the kids' story. At one point during the week, Juan Ruiz made serious threats and accusations about the governor to the press. One persistent rumor was that the governor had been the general who had killed Luis Cabañas, the revolutionary in the state of Guerrero a few years before. The general had received the governorship of Oaxaca as a reward for this service. Rumor and gossip filled the streets of Oaxaca. Most of them glorified Juan Ruiz. Months later I even heard a *corrido* (ballad) written about his exploits. I began to see that *la raza* (the race) turned those who opposed the government into folkloric heroes. Secretly I thanked Juan Ruiz for taking the pressure of the governor and the press off our project. But the fickle press and clandestine individuals, some of whom claimed association with the governor, were back at us the following week.

It started on a Monday morning with a cartoon of me holding a carved stone from Monte Alban above my head and the reconstructed words of a popular song, "Hay una piedra en mi camino . . . y mi destino es robar y robar" (There is a stone in my way . . . and my destiny is to steal and steal). I was being accused of stealing the nation's carved monuments!

For the next three days other articles appeared. While very personal, they invariably got my name wrong. I was called John Peterson, Don Johnson, and "the archaeologist from INAH." At the site, unidentified persons tried to separate the other team members from me by asking them, "Por qué estás trabajando con un pinche gringo?" (Why are you working with a dumb American?). Another person, more aggressive, pulled our control strings from the walls we were drawing. Still, I kept calm. Then, Thursday morning a young and bright-looking couple from

Mexico City approached me. They introduced themselves as reporters for *Uno Más Uno*, a national newspaper. They wanted to borrow my camera to take pictures and write a story of the conflict. I began to lose my cool.

"Mira jóvenes, es possible que soy un gringo loco, pero no soy pendejo!" (Look, kids, I may be a crazy gringo, but I'm not stupid!)

Beto, the small Zapotec team member, standing close by, began to laugh. His laughter made us all relax and the two reporters ended up apologizing for their intrusion. They said that they were on vacation and had not brought a camera with them. But when they heard the gossip back in Oaxaca they came up to see for themselves what was going on. I apologized for my reaction to their request and suggested that if they wanted an interview it would be better to go to INAH's regional offices.

That afternoon I called Esperanza and made an appointment to see Don Gaston the following day. The next morning I took the first flight to Mexico City.

Don Gaston listened intently while I explained what had happened in Oaxaca. He told me that he wasn't concerned about the local newspaper articles, but if the national newspaper *Uno Más Uno* was interested and people were getting physical, these were disturbing matters. He asked me if I was happy with the work and wished to continue. I told him that I was, but perhaps it was better to substitute a Mexican national because my nationality was being used like a political football. He smiled and told me that he had a meeting scheduled with President José Luis Portillo on Sunday and for me to return to his office the following Monday morning for a solution.

I spent the weekend being entertained by Paco. He did everything possible to lift my spirits, including a party and inviting me out to eat.

On Monday morning, Don Gaston handed me a return ticket to Oaxaca and told me that everything was going to be just fine. "The president has found a way for the governor to save face." He then sent me to another office for a credential. I was then officially assigned to the general director's office.

My return to Oaxaca was a new beginning. It was like magic. Never again did we have any bad press or harassment and interference from the citizens at Monte Alban. But, like the Credence song from the movie *The Big Chill*, there was a bad moon rising.

Unlike the song, I didn't see it coming.

Los Judiciales

I wanted aerial photographs of Monte Alban, and I made the mistake of going to the director of the state offices of INAH to ask a favor. I told Manuel Esparza of my desire for such photographs and asked if he would use his position to request a helicopter flight from the judicial police. His response was negative. Manuel told me that the Monte Alban project was not worth his wasting a political favor. He then implied that "good people" don't associate with such a notorious, gun-toting, murderous arm of the government.

At first I was depressed, but as I drove away from the INAH offices I made a decision.

I would make the request myself.

The waiting room of the state Narcotics Division was occupied by four ladies sitting behind desks with ancient typewriters in front of them and piles of papers on either side. I waited for forty-five minutes before a man came through the door of another room and announced that *El Comandante* (the commander) Orduñez would see me.

I followed him into the room where he motioned me to take a chair at one end of a long table. The room was occupied by several men. All of them carried guns. Some of them looked suspiciously like gringos. One of them wore a green beret. Men were rapidly moving through an open door to the street. They carried metal ammo boxes as they went through the door. I could see from my position in the room that they were loading the boxes into the trunk of a car. At one point I saw a man lift a small-caliber rifle with a large scope out of the trunk. He wrapped it in a blanket and then relocated it.

On the wall, at the far end of the table, was a large map of the state of Oaxaca. Dozens of little flags were pinned to the map in areas that appeared to be valleys or canyons. A young, small, slender man with a moustache and carrying a clipboard approached and sat down in a chair directly in front of me.

"I am Licenciado Orduñez. How may I help you?"

I explained that I worked for the National Institute of Anthropology and History and my project was at Monte Alban. Then I requested his assistance with a helicopter flight over the site.

Instead of answering my request, he asked, "Why isn't the state director of INAH here making this request?"

I told him that I didn't work for the state director but rather was in Oaxaca by orders of the general director of INAH, Professor Gaston García Cantú.

"Nevertheless, I would think that the correct protocol would be for the state director," he stopped and looked at his clipboard and then continued, ". . . Professor Manuel Esparza, to make this request personally."

I explained, word for word, the conversation that I had with Esparza, including the reason for his refusal, and then added the punch line, "Also, I think he was nervous because of the reputation of the *Judiciales.*" He laughed and then asked me for a favor. He wanted me to make an appointment with Esparza for him. Put on the spot, I agreed to try.

There were several seconds of silence, and I felt that the audience with the commander was over. I had not achieved my goal. I gathered up the courage and asked, "¿Y el vuelo? Hay pedos o no hay pedos?" (And the flight? Are there or are there not any problems?) Everyone in the room laughed loudly. I found out later that the word "pedos" had two meanings. Not only did it mean problems, it also meant farts.

When the commander finished laughing he put a hand on my knee and told me that there were no "pedos" and that I could have as many flights as I wanted. He then suggested that I be at the airport at 10 a.m. the next morning. I thanked him and left the room through the door to the street, still puzzled by their laughter.

I had no idea why Orduñez wanted to meet with Esparza but I felt it was my duty to notify the director as soon as possible. Since it was almost dark, I went to the professor's house. I knew he wasn't going to be pleased.

When I informed the director he went berserk. Oddly enough, his rage had nothing to do with the lack of protocol but rather his fear. During the stammering, incoherent tirade, he repeated several times his reluctance to meet with "this type of people." I left him muttering to himself, after apologetically pointing out that I was only delivering a message from the commander.

As I passed the state offices of INAH on my way to the airport the next morning, by sheer coincidence I saw the commander, accompanied by three men, getting out of a car. I slowed down and waved. Orduñez motioned me over to the curb. He leaned over the door of the Safari and extended his hand in greeting. He was smiling from ear to ear.

"Thanks for arranging the meeting. I should be through in about thirty minutes. All I need is permission from the director for the use of the theater at Santo Domingo to show a film to the kids. It is part of our antidrug campaign. Wait for me in the hangar of the small building on the right side of the main terminal and I will introduce you to the pilot."

For several blocks I couldn't suppress my laughter, imagining rather gleefully Manuel Esparza's sleepless night.

A huge hangar took up most of the space in the building. In it were two helicopters and several mechanics. The man with the green beret was there, this time with a red bandana tied around his neck. He was cleaning something metal in his hand with a rag. I assumed that he was a mechanic. Another man, nicely dressed and wearing a shoulder holster, approached me and asked me what I was doing there. After I explained that I was waiting on Orduñez, he left me standing and circled about the hangar, obviously explaining my presence to the others.

Twenty minutes later Orduñez arrived, accompanied by a young man wearing dark sunglasses and a flight suit who carried a white helmet in his hands. We shook hands for the second time that morning, and after introducing me to the pilot, Orduñez informed me that they had succeeded in obtaining the permission they needed for the use of the theater. He chuckled several times during his statement. I forced myself not to do the same. In fact, I remained quiet while Orduñez gave instructions for the men in the hangar to roll one of the helicopters outside.

We hovered for several minutes just a few meters off the ground while the pilot talked to the tower through the microphone attached to his helmet. At one point, the pilot looked over at me and asked if I had a cigarette. I reached in my front shirt pocket and removed a pack of Marlboros. As I opened the lid and flicked my wrist to dislodge a smoke, I nearly pissed my pants. There was a tightly rolled joint in the pack. "Jesus Christ," I thought. "How did that get in there?" I looked quickly at the pilot but his attention was focused on the control tower. Trembling slightly, I fumbled a cigarette from the pack and nervously closed it. He thanked me for the smoke when I handed it to him and we began to ascend.

For the first few minutes of the flight I was a nervous wreck. Was someone trying to frame me? It didn't seem likely. The more likely reason was that I had picked up someone else's pack of cigarettes from the table the evening before at the restaurant where I had eaten. Paranoid, and with a dry mouth that made me feel like I had been trying to swallow cotton, I asked the pilot about his job.

He told me that he loved to fly, and had been working for the government for nearly five years. For most of that time he was stationed in the state of Sinaloa. But when his brother was killed in a crash there, the government transferred him to Oaxaca. I asked him how his brother had been killed. He explained that drug growers had strung metal cables across a canyon where they were planting marijuana and his brother had run into it with his helicopter and died in the crash.

He displayed great enthusiasm for his work. At one point he bragged, "They still plant marijuana and *amapola* (poppies) in Sinaloa, but because of our successful campaign, they no longer are able to harvest it."

By the time we reached the ruins we were chatting amiably and I forgot the jolt of the joint in my pack of cigarettes. The pilot asked me for instructions, but I didn't have any experience taking photographs from a helicopter, so I told him to fly close to the buildings and I would just shoot as we flew by. Once or twice I asked him to fly by a particular structure and hover. He had obviously flown for a photographer before because he kept the sun behind our backs most of the time. Occasionally, I could see sun spots through the lens reflecting on the glass bubble of the helicopter. So I asked if I could take the door off. He said he was sorry but we couldn't take the door off in flight.

After shooting a roll of film I suggested that we could return to the base. On the return flight he again requested a cigarette. I reached in my pocket, hesitated for a moment, and then handed him the pack. He opened it up, took out a cigarette, and passed the pack back to me. If he saw the joint inside he didn't say anything. I watched his face closely for some sign or expression. There was none.

I encountered the young pilot several times in Oaxaca after that flight. He always greeted me pleasantly, to the displeasure of some of my friends. "How do you know people like that?" was a typical question thrown at me. Obviously, others shared the opinion of Manuel Esparza about the judicial police.

Months later, in December, I encountered El Comandante. It was during the fiesta of *Los Rábanos* (the radishes), and I was sitting at a table under the arches in the main plaza. Because of the fiesta, the tables were filling up fast as more people came to town for the parade and fireworks. Suddenly, there was El Comandante Orduñez standing in front of me.

"¿Puedo sentarme?" (May I sit down?), he asked.

"Of course, Señor Comandante, please do!" I replied as I began to rise. We shook hands and then chatted amiably for several minutes. He asked if I was still working at Monte Alban and if the flight had produced the results I wanted. Then, much to my surprise, he said that he was aware that I had resolved my problems with both the governor and Manuel Esparza. I guessed he read the local newspapers. Still, all that had taken place several months ago. When I told him how it had been resolved, he nodded his head approvingly and said, "My respects, you used *el dedazo* (the finger) very effectively." Though I did not know what he meant at the time, I later learned that el dedazo refers to an authority giving a direct order to a subordinate. When the authority is the president of Mexico, the order is always obeyed.

The commander told me that recently they had been very busy at his office and that he had come to the plaza for a few minutes to relax. I recalled the armed men in his office loading their vehicles. I didn't want an explanation of what "busy work" he was involved in, so instead of inquiring, I invited him to drink a beer. He accepted and before it arrived another figure joined our table.

This time it was a young lady, obviously a gringa. By now the only two chairs left under the arches were the two at our table, so I invited her to sit down. She looked relieved. I had watched her briefly just before she joined us. Her hair was drawn back into a bushy ponytail. Her gaunt face was tanned and her body very slender, even frail. She looked tired and used up. Her thin cotton dress couldn't have possibly kept the chilly air off her body. When she thankfully accepted my invitation to sit down and I had a chance to look at her eyes, I was startled. The white parts of her eyes were covered with thin red lines and reminded me of a road map. I introduced her to Licenciado Orduñez, who had risen from his chair to greet her. No matter what devils beleaguer them, Mexicans are always polite and courteous. At that point our beers arrived.

The girl didn't speak any Spanish, so, after taking a sip of my beer, I politely inquired in English where she was from. She said that she had just arrived from the coast. When I asked where along the coast, she replied *Zipolite*. I immediately knew why her eyes were so red. Zipolite was a beach on the coast of Oaxaca known as a hippie colony. I invited her for a beer but she declined the offer. Instead she looked over both shoulders and then leaned forward and asked if I knew where she could find some grass.

I came very close to spitting the beer in my mouth over the entire table. I looked at Orduñez who had begun to laugh. First she looked startled and then puzzled as she looked at one of us and then the other. Orduñez surprised us both as he inquired in perfect English, "Lady, do you have any idea who you are talking to?" He didn't wait for an answer. "I am the commander of the Federal Narcotics Bureau in the state of Oaxaca."

We were both shocked. I was shocked because I had never heard Ordúñez speak English and she was shocked for the obvious reason.

The girl's hands dropped from the table onto her lap and she just sat there for a few moments without moving. Then, without a word, she slowly pushed her chair back from the table, stood up, and without a backward glance, began walking away from our table.

Ordúñez could hardly stop laughing. When he did, it was to take a sip from his beer. Finally, returning to Spanish, he said, "I have waited a long time to be able to do that!" Then he laughed some more. He was still chuckling as he finished his beer and excused himself from the table.

I never saw El Comandante again, though years later, while visiting a distant cousin of my wife at the Hacienda Sauceda in the state of Guanajuato, I met a helicopter pilot who had worked with Ordúñez in Sinaloa. It is a small world.

THE BATTLE OF THE BUDGET

Now they were put inside Bat House,

with bats alone inside the house, a

house of snatch-bats, monstrous

beasts, their snouts like knives, the

instruments of death.

—Popol Vuh

Six months into the project everything apparently was going well. The team was producing much faster than I had originally calculated. We had finished with about 75 percent of the work at Monte Alban and had spent only a quarter of the budget. I calculated that by the time we finished we would still have nearly half of the funds. It occurred to me that

Figure 15 Monte Alban (photo by Eric Geothals)

these surplus monies could be used as an incentive for INAH to publish the work and at the same time repair the "bad blood" between Professor Manuel Esparza and me. So I went to the director with a proposal.

First, I explained the good news about the progress the team had made at Monte Alban. Then I threw out the idea that with the surplus funds we could publish a catalog of the carved monuments at the site in the small publication section of the Oaxaca regional center of INAH.

To my great relief, he liked the idea. He even seemed enthusiastic and began to discuss the possibilities of the publication. Then he threw the proverbial wrench into the machinery.

"We can ask Dr. Kent Flannery or Dr. Joyce Marcus to write the introduction!"

I found myself in an ethical and academic dilemma. On one hand, to have the work associated with such renowned Mesoamerican scholars as Kent Flannery or Joyce Marcus was tempting. It would certainly be an academic feather in my cap in the United States. On the other hand, this was an INAH project coming from two INAH scholars in the Direction of Pre-Hispanic Monuments of INAH; Angel García Cook and Roberto García Moll. I made up my mind.

"Professor, although I have great respect for Kent Flannery and Joyce Marcus, this *is* an INAH project. Wouldn't it be better if someone from INAH wrote the introduction?"

I could see that he was displeased with my response. He then began to mutter something, as if talking to himself, about Alfonso Caso creating this overwhelming bureaucracy of an institution where nothing of real value ever got done.

It was obvious that he was not going to make a decision in that moment, so I excused myself after asking him to think about my proposal.

The next morning a young archaeologist from the regional office approached me at Monte Alban. Nelly Robles, outside of the project members, was one of the few friends I had made in the Oaxaca offices. I could tell she was uncomfortable. She had a small piece of paper in her hand and began to apologize even before she handed it to me.

"This was not my idea. It came from Esparza."

I began to read the memorandum. It was a serious blow for any chance of publishing our work.

Paraphrasing, it stated that after talking to Don Gaston García Cantú by telephone it had been decided to use the surplus funds of the project for work that needed to be done at other sites in the state of Oaxaca. I was to put myself under the orders of the archaeologist Nelly Robles.

At the bottom of the memo I could see that copies were sent to various authorities including Don Gaston.

After reading the memorandum I looked at Nelly. She was obviously terrified. I consciously tried to tone down the expression on my face.

"Don't worry, Nelly. I know you are not to blame for this. With your permission I will handle this myself." I winked at her and added ". . . boss." She forced a weak smile and I put my arm around her shoulder. "Remember my philosophy, when you are depressed, spend some money. Let me invite you to dinner tonight."

I waited an hour after Nelly left and then jumped in the Safari and headed for the regional offices of INAH. Without knocking I entered the office of the director with the memorandum in my hand.

"Why did you do this?" There was no anger in my voice, only directness.

"We decided that your work is not worth the expense of a publication," he replied.

The "we" was like a nail driven into a coffin. I turned and left the office with the spirit-deadening onus of finality lying heavy upon my shoulders.

Tormented with the idea that our work was inferior, I mulled over the problem. I even put the memorandum in a small frame and placed it on my bedside table so that I saw it every morning and evening. Then something happened. A small voice coming from a crevice in the recesses of my brain spoke to me. "You are a mouse that longs to be a rat."

For the next two weeks I battled with myself, trying to mount enough courage to act. Finally, I reached a decision and I purchased a ticket for a flight to Mexico City.

I walked into the office of the administrative secretary of INAH. I handed him the memorandum and said, "Eduardo, I am not in agreement with this."

He read the memo and then said, "Wait here, I will be right back." I didn't have long to wait.

In less than five minutes Eduardo returned to his office with Don

Gaston. As he passed behind his desk, Eduardo handed the memo back to me. Don Gaston sat in a chair directly beside me. Turning to face me, he leaned forward and placed both of his hands on my knees.

"Don, I want you to know that we are very happy with your work at Monte Alban. What is your problem?"

I handed him the memo and repeated what I had said to Eduardo.

Don Gaston read the memo and then said, "This is a lie. I never talked to Manuel Esparza concerning this."

Relieved, I quickly told the professor what had happened. When I finished, the professor turned to Eduardo, seated behind his desk, and said, "Get me pinche Esparza on the telephone!" It was the only time I ever heard Don Gaston use a word that might be considered vulgar. Then he turned back to me.

"Don't worry, Don. You keep up the good work and I assure you that the Institute is going to publish your work." He then excused himself and returned to the privacy of his office and his conversation with Esparza.

After he left, Eduardo, with a big smile on his face, asked me, "Are you happy now, Don?"

I thought for several moments before answering him.

"Actually I am not."

Eduardo was taken aback by my answer, so I continued.

"Whatever Don Gaston is saying to Esparza is not going to make my life any easier in Oaxaca. Remember, Oaxaca has the reputation of being the land of the 'chinga quedito.' Since all of the funding for the project is under Manuel's control, I guarantee you that my life is going to be a bitch. Do you understand what I am saying? It may take a week to get money for a pencil!"

Eduardo laughed and said, "Don't worry; this is easy to take care of. When you get back to Oaxaca, open a checking account and send me the account number. I will send the necessary funds." Then, almost as an afterthought, he asked me, "Do you know that this is the first time that Don Gaston has ever come to my office?" He seemed pleased by the thought.

I returned to Oaxaca the following day feeling not only as good as a rat, but better. The work would be published, and the funding for the project was going to come directly to me. I approached Dr. Winters about writing the archaeological history of Monte Alban for the publication and he agreed. I was in good spirits.

I stayed away from the INAH offices for the next two weeks. Then a message came to me from the regional office. I was to call Eduardo Villa. I made the call from one of the secretary's phones on the first floor.

The conversation was less than three minutes. He requested that I try to smooth the ruffled feathers of Esparza by doing him a favor. Eduardo suggested that I might offer to do a small job, apart from my work at Monte Alban, for the regional center. Something inside told me to watch out, but I respected Eduardo and thought that his suggestion might be coming from Don Gaston, so I agreed.

After hanging up, I went up the stairs to Manuel's office. This was not going to be easy. I kept thinking of a saying that a friend back in San Miguel de Allende had told me: "Screw me once, shame on you. Screw me twice, shame on me."

Manuel didn't look happy to see me, but ignoring his stern countenance I jumped right in with my proposal.

"Professor, I realize that our relationship hasn't gone too well but I would like to make a peace offering. As you know, our work at Monte Alban is progressing very quickly and I would like to do something for the regional center. Is there anything that you have pending that our team could do for you?"

Surprisingly, his face displayed a smile.

"Actually there is something you could do for us. There is a village, not far from the city of Oaxaca, that has seven or eight carved stones that we have been unable to document. The name of the village is Zachilla. The work shouldn't take your team more than half a day. I will send Nelly Robles along with you. Have Nelly tell me when you have come to an agreement on the date and I will write a letter of introduction to the *Comisario* (commissary) of the village for you."

As I left the director's office, I kept thinking to myself, "This is too easy." Remembering the director's smile, I was uneasy. Still, I found

Nelly and made arrangements with her to take the team the coming Saturday to Zachilla.

Early Saturday morning I picked up Nelly. She not only had Manuel's introduction letter with her, but had procured a list and the last known locations of the carved stones we were to document. I found her efficiency very refreshing. Along my normal route I picked up the rest of the team.

They were surprised to find out that we were not heading to Monte Alban, but only Beto made a comment.

"Are you sure you want to go to Zachilla?" he asked in a voice full of concern.

"Is there a problem, Beto?" I asked.

"There is a saying we have in my village about Zachilla. They (the people) have a reputation for being very *cabrón* (bastards)."

"What is this saying of yours, Beto?"

"Si las mujeres no quieren, los burros no entran!" (If the women don't want them, not even the burros enter.)

"You're kidding me, of course. In any event, we have a letter of introduction to the community from Esparza." Still, Beto had planted the seeds of doubt, and there was a lingering thread of anxiety that continued to haunt me the rest of the journey.

Zachilla is only fifteen or twenty kilometers from the city of Oaxaca, and we reached the main plaza of the village quickly.

A quarter of the plaza was a market, and it being Saturday, about forty women in their colorful traditional Zapotec clothing were fussing over their goods. The smells of a spicy meat called *cecina* and roasted chocolate beans were very strong. Many large trees in the plaza surrounded a small gazebo. It looked more like a park than the typical Mexican plaza. I immediately located a carved stone sticking upright out of the ground near the market.

When we left the Safari I had stuck two four-inch brushes in my back pocket and grabbed a trowel. Beto and I made for the stone in the plaza while Nelly took the other members of the team to locate the carved stones reportedly located in the church and school.

We could see both from where we stood.

Beto and I walked over to the stone, and he began cleaning the upper surface with a brush to remove the dirt and dust. Meanwhile, I discovered that the carving disappeared beneath the soil. With the help of the trowel I began to carefully remove the earth in a small trench at the base of the stone in order to relieve the remainder of the carving.

Suddenly a man appeared behind us.

"What are you doing?" he asked.

I explained that we were here on behalf of the National Institute of Anthropology and History to draw and photograph the carved stones in the community. He responded immediately, quoting the words of Benito Juárez.

"Entre los individuos y las naciones, el respecto al derecho ajeno es la paz." (Between individuals and nations, the respect for basic rights is peace.)

"I couldn't agree more," I answered with a smile. "We have a letter from the state director of INAH to the comisario for permission to do this," I explained as I handed him the letter.

He received the letter and stared at it for several minutes. I noticed that his eyes didn't move back and forth across the page and I suspected that he couldn't read. He finally handed the letter back to me and said, "Nevertheless, you must show this document to the comisario."

I asked where we could find the comisario this early in the morning and he answered tersely and somewhat sarcastically, "At his house."

I apologized for our thoughtlessness, and then asked for directions to the comisario's house. Leaving the two brushes and the trowel on the ground, Beto and I walked back to the gazebo in the middle of the plaza. When we reached it we could see Nelly and the rest of the team crossing the street in our direction, so we waited until they arrived.

I explained to Nelly what had happened and she offered to take the letter to the comisario's house. Meanwhile, the rest of the team and I waited patiently, sitting and/or standing on the steps of the gazebo.

Presently, two Zapotec women passed, the younger of the two tenderly helping the older woman walk across the plaza. The elderly woman used a homemade cane. She appeared to be in her late eighties. As they passed in front of me they stopped. The older woman turned slowly and looked directly up into my face and spoke.

"Just wait and see. You are going to die in Zachilla. We are going to ring the bells of the church. When the men arrive from the fields you are going to die." Then she turned, and with the help of her friend and cane she slowly hobbled away.

I stood there, watching them go, with an amused smile on my face. I wasn't sure that I had understood the lady. I kept thinking that she could have easily been my grandmother. I was still pondering what had happened when Beto coughed. When I turned in his direction his natural good-humor face was a mask of deep concern.

"What's wrong, Beto?"

"The situation is critical, Professor!"

"What?" I asked with both surprise and great attention.

"Take a look around us."

I did as Beto had suggested. The women had left the shelter of the market and were standing around or near the carved stone. They formed a formidable mass, but they had broken up into many groups and appeared to be arguing. Many of them stooped down to pick up rocks. Some were even shaking their fists in the air. It didn't take a genius to realize that we were the subject of their rage.

I must not have been breathing because when "Jesus *Cristo!*" left my lips it came out in a hiss. Porfirio, usually very quiet, spoke for all of us, "And I don't want to be Maria Magdalena!" And then he tilted his head in the direction of the Safari.

I looked at him and asked, "What about the tools?"

There wasn't a molecule of shame in his voice when he replied, almost in a whisper, "Professor, forget the stupid tools. Let's get the hell out of here!"

Loud voices reached us, and as I turned in the direction of the mob I saw that the man who had originally talked to us was arguing with the women. He stooped down and picked up the two brushes and the trowel. Although the voices reached us, the ongoing dialogue was in Zapotec and I had no idea what they were saying to each other. Suddenly, the man turned on his heels and walked across the street to a rather large colonial building. I suspected that the building had something to do with the local government. I watched as he and our tools disappeared inside.

My attention refocused on the mob as the volume of the debate lifted. A man I had not seen before stood in front of the stone, speaking in a loud voice and waving his arms in the air. He was obviously trying to get the ladies' attention.

At that moment Nelly appeared beside me and explained that the man was the comisario. She had found him at home with a hangover. There had been a fiesta the night before, and although he lived only a block away it had taken a long time to wake him up and then to convince him to come to the plaza. Nelly didn't need an explanation of what had occurred during her absence. You could see the deep concern on her face.

While we were watching the drama in front of us, the comisario threw up his arms in disgust and departed the scene in the same manner as the man before him.

During my conversation with Nelly, Beto had moved closer to the rabid women and returned with disturbing information. The Zapotec ladies were accusing the mestizo comisario of selling the village's carved monuments to "el gringo." As I was the only gringo in the plaza at that moment, the situation became very personal. I figured that if it were personal I would face it head-on.

When I asked Porfirio to get our rubbing supplies from the Safari, he looked at me as if I had lost all my marbles. He didn't move so I continued.

"I have an idea that might just allow us to settle this affair and even let us finish what we came to this village to do. Porfirio, bring me two pieces of the colored wax, some tape, and a sheet of the polished cotton. Cut the polished cotton a little larger than the carved stone at the Safari. Whatever you do, don't bring the scissors. I don't want the scissors anywhere near those women! Beto and I are going to make a rubbing of the stone!"

Still a reluctant believer, Porfirio hesitated for a moment. Then, after a stern look from me, he left in the direction of the vehicle. I turned to Nelly.

"I know it is Saturday, but do you think you can find the principal or a teacher from the school? If you do, tell him or her that we urgently need them at the plaza."

There wasn't a lot of confidence in our approach to the stone. As we wove our way through the women toward the stone, an ominous, yet convenient, silence settled over the crowd.

As Beto and I attached the polished cotton to the carved surface of the stone, the women closed ranks around us. There was soft buzz of whispering. They were very curious as Beto and I began to rub the colored wax over the cloth. Slowly, and I hoped magically, details of the carving began to take shape on the surface of the cloth. We worked rapidly and when the upper half of the carving of the stone appeared, I stood up. We were completely encircled.

"Ladies, may I have your attention please?"

I raised my right arm and motioned them closer, repeating my request. "That's right, please come closer so that all of you can hear and see what we are doing." Then I waxed eloquent.

I told them that we were not there to take the stones from their community but only to make rubbings like the one Don Beto was finishing. If they approved, we also wanted to make drawings and take photographs of them. I then gave them reasons for doing this.

I told them that scholars from all over the world were interested in their culture . . . blah, blah, blah. I told them that these rubbings, drawings, and photographs would be studied so that the history of their people would be known throughout the world . . . blah, blah, blah.

At some point in my oration Beto stood up, and I knew that the rubbing was finished. As the women were still silent, I continued.

I told them the benefits such knowledge would bring to their community. I told them it would bring them great pride and a glorious satisfaction to have pictures of their village's carved stones on the

classroom walls of schools throughout the communities of mankind
... blah, blah, blah.

At this point I was relieved to see that Nelly had returned in the company of a young man. A great idea occurred to me as they approached
the crowd. I was pleased with myself for my speech, and as I looked out
over the throng with a huge smile, I extended my hands in a gesture of
peace and what I thought would be the final solution.

"Furthermore, and with your permission, we will make two rubbings of all the stones and these copies will remain in your village for
the school. Just think, your children will have these rubbings in their
classrooms every day to remind them of their roots!" I looked over at
Nelly and the young man and my smile widened even more.

Then something happened that deflated my enlarged and self-
inflated bubble.

One of the women, standing directly behind the stone, reached
over the top of it and removed the rubbing. She didn't tear it away. In
fact, I remember the act as if it happened in slow motion. Standing only
a couple of feet from me, and with the rubbing dangling in her hand,
she looked me directly in the eyes and asked in Spanish, "Why do our
children need a copy if they have the original?"

Her sincerity was not in question. I stood there, dumbfounded. I
didn't have an answer. Yet, I felt the need to reply was lingering silently
in the very air I breathed and hovering over the entire crowd.

Instead, I reached over and gently tugged at the rubbing in her hand.
I tried to muster a pleading expression on my face. She allowed me to
take the rubbing from her and I began to roll it up as I walked slowly
through the crowd toward Nelly.

As I handed the rubbing to the young man who stood beside her,
I said in a voice just loud enough to be heard by everyone, "Professor,
it is obvious that the gentle people of the community do not want us to
continue our work here. Nevertheless, please accept this rubbing as a
means of apology on behalf of the National Institute of Anthropology
and History for any misunderstanding that our team may have created
here in the community of Zachilla."

Without waiting for a response, I turned and walked slowly toward the building the comisario and the other man had entered earlier. There was no need to motion to my companions; they followed me out of the plaza and across the street.

As we neared the building I could see the comisario and the other man peering out the door. They seemed reluctant to open the large door any farther. Our entire team slithered sideways, one by one, in order to gain sanctuary.

After Nelly presented us to the comisario, he shook his head and said, "When will INAH ever learn!" I did not respond to his curious statement, although it implied that something similar had happened here before. Instead, I asked him if we were going to be able to leave his community alive.

He told us that we would be fine if we kept together, stayed away from the stone, and went directly to our vehicle. I thanked him for his effort and we did exactly as he suggested.

Although it was still before noon, I dropped off the crew and told them I would pick them up Monday morning. Nelly and I continued to the INAH offices.

When I entered Esparza's office he looked up and then at his watch. "Did you finish so soon?" he asked smugly.

As I related what had transpired in Zachilla, he began to smile. By the time I finished he was chuckling.

"That was nothing. Last year I had to send soldiers to retrieve an archaeologist whom the women of the village had locked in the tomb of 7 Flower!"

I could hardly believe my ears. "You mean to tell me that you knew this and sent me to Zachilla? We might have been killed!"

He laughed until I reached across his desk and grabbed the phone. Esparza looked at me quizzically as I dialed. Luckily, Eduardo Villa was in his office.

"Well, Eduardo I did as you requested," I said. While I explained to Eduardo what had happened that morning, Esparza sat there with his mouth open and stared at me in disbelief.

". . . and your director of INAH here in Oaxaca sent me to this village knowing full well the possible consequences!"

Eduardo suggested that I calm down. "Where is Manuel right now?"

"He is sitting right in front of me at his desk."

I heard a noise that sounded like a controlled giggle coming over the line. Then Eduardo said, "Leave his office and I will get back to you later this afternoon." He hung up and I handed the phone to Esparza. I didn't wait to see his expression when he discovered that no one was on the other end of the telephone. I turned my back and left.

Later that afternoon I received a message from the INAH offices: I was to pick up Roberto García Moll at the airport Monday morning.

Roberto's flight didn't arrive until late in the morning so I first picked up the crew and took them to Monte Alban. They asked me what had happened on Saturday after I had dropped them off. I repeated what had taken place in Esparza's office and told them that later that morning I had to go to the airport and pick up Roberto García Moll. They asked who Roberto was and why was he coming to Oaxaca. After explaining it to them, I suggested that there was a chance that I would be relieved as coordinator of the project.

They stood quietly for a moment and then Beto spoke up. "If you get fired, I am going to quit!" Everyone responded the same.

I was deeply moved by their loyalty, but I suggested that that would be a shame because they were very close to finishing the project. They didn't respond so I changed the conversation to the tasks remaining.

The first thing Roberto said to me when he arrived was, "Well you have really done it! Esparza is out of here." He didn't elaborate and I didn't ask for further clarification. Roberto had been sent by Don Gaston as a "hatchet man." The state was going to have a new INAH director.

As we approached the city, Roberto told me to take him to the INAH office building and he would meet me later that afternoon at the town square. I returned to Monte Alban with the good news: nobody had to quit.

Figure 16 Dianzu (photo by author)

Figure 17 Monte Alban (photo by author)

The project at Monte Alban continued without interference, and we had enough time and funds to document the carved monuments at the archaeological sites of Dianzu and Yagul before leaving Oaxaca.

LIVING IN OAXACA

Within a week of arriving in Oaxaca I rented a small, skimpily furnished house in San Felipe de las Aguas. The place drew me like a magnet. Less than a kilometer from the back of the University of Oaxaca campus, it was a friendly, small, and villagelike community, near the pine-forested slopes above the city. My first acquaintance in the village was a local policeman.

Juan, like his four companions, wasn't supplied with a uniform or a gun. The community was small enough that uniforms and guns were not necessary. Everyone in the village knew everyone else. Since I was a newcomer, Juan showed up at my door the second day I was there. I don't know if he was sent by the local authorities or provoked by his own curiosity, but he came to investigate my presence. After a twenty-minute interview, apparently satisfied that I posed no threat, he gave me introductory tours of what he thought were the important places and people of the community. I must have shaken hands with fifty people. After showing me the plaza and the church and introducing me to the local governmental officials, he pointed out two rather subterranean aspects of the community.

The first was the double-bungalow residence of the Federal Police. Juan cautioned me to stay away from these unsavory people. The second was a small house with a faded green door. Juan's instructions were quite simple and accompanied by demonstration. We took an empty pop bottle and knocked on the door. The door opened just wide enough for a brown forearm and extended hand to appear, into which we placed the bottle. A few minutes later the door opened again and the hand returned the bottle full of "Moonshine" mescal. Juan encouraged me to put ten pesos in the empty hand. Needless to say, Juan kept the bottle. It was the price I paid for the tour. Later, I took advantage of the green door on a number of occasions during my stay in the village.

After two months I changed houses.

My second residence in the community was an exceptionally beautiful, single-story, ranch-style house with an enormous garden. It belonged to a retired geologist who spent most of his time in Cuernavaca. The house sat on the corner of the main road leading up the hill and into the village from the city, and the walled-in property extended the full width of the block. The house was U-shaped, and between the two extensions was a covered veranda where I spent a lot of time working, reading, and admiring the extensive garden. The house had three bedrooms but my access was limited to just one of them. The owner's possessions occupied the other two bedrooms. The geologist would appear from time to time and spend a weekend. We got along very nicely so there was no inconvenience for me. The project used my living room as both a studio and office.

During my stay in San Felipe, I read D. H. Lawrence's book *Mornings in Mexico*. I was fascinated that Lawrence mentioned San Felipe in the book. Especially interesting to me was his description of an encounter with the owner of a small establishment that sold fruit juice. Lawrence, thirsty after a long hike up the hill from Oaxaca, stopped at the establishment to buy some fruit juice. Seeing banana plants close by, he asked the proprietor to sell him some bananas. The proprietor told Lawrence that he had no bananas. The answer infuriated Lawrence and he described the owner as a "dumbbell." The use of "dumbbell" by Lawrence for some reason angered me.

Curious, I decided to play gumshoe and see if I could locate the by now aged juice seller in the village. I realized it would be a difficult task. On the one hand, the proprietor was more than likely dead. On the other hand, how do you locate the offspring of a dumbbell? Was the affliction passed on genetically?

Over a two-month period, I spent an hour on several Sundays with people in the village. I started with people who sold fruit juice. I tried to find establishments near banana groves. Only one came close to fitting the description. After ordering an orange juice and spending a few minutes in polite conversation, I asked the proprietor if I could buy bananas. He sold me some bananas. I reasoned that if the man was a relative of the dumbbell, the affliction was not carried by the genes.

Playing detective was fun and it gave me the opportunity to make small talk with a number of people in the village. Word spread very quickly that the gringo was eating a lot of bananas. Several of the villagers stopped me on the street and gave me directions to the stores and establishment that sold bananas. One lady said that she knew where there was a very nice banana grove and insisted on taking me to it. The grove was sandwiched between two houses. We inquired at both houses and no one seemed to know who the owner of the grove was. The lady became very sad and apologized for not being able to help me. As we started walking back to the center of the village, she suddenly became very excited. "Here comes Don Nacho! He knows everyone in town and will be able to tell us who owns the bananas!"

Don Nacho was an elderly gentleman. He led a burro whose head and ears were the only features visible underneath an enormous load of corn stalks. After introducing me to Don Nacho, she began to explain.

"Our friend eats a lot of bananas and I thought that perhaps he could buy them from the owner of the grove down the street cheaper than in the stores. Do you know who owns the bananas?"

"I do not know their names, Doña Lupe. I think they must live in Oaxaca for I have seen a family loading bananas into a car from time to time."

We thanked Don Nacho for his information and continued our little walk back to the plaza. Doña Lupe once again apologized for not being able to help me. In reality, she had helped me more than she knew. The experience was beginning to confirm a growing suspicion that the dumbbell was none other that D. H. Lawrence. Had he even asked the proprietor of the juice stand who was the owner of the bananas? I stopped looking for the Dumbbell of San Felipe de las Aguas and recovered from my preoccupation with Lawrence. Still, I managed to have another encounter with the writer several weeks later.

Arriving at Monte Alban at the crack of dawn, I had driven the team and equipment into the site that day. I parked the Safari out of sight of the tourists, behind and on the west side of the extensive South Platform where we were working. Around 10 a.m. I had to return to the city for some supplies. As I rounded the corner of the platform and entered the plaza, I was struck by something very odd. The stairs descending the south structure of the main plaza were full of hippies. I was so amazed at the sight that I almost ran over a man who was shouting and waving a megaphone directly in front of me. I slammed on the brakes and in the few seconds it took to realize that the man was shouting in English, I took in the scene behind him. There were two large trucks, one with a boom rising several meters in the air blocking my exit from the site. At the end of the extended boom a man sat in a chair pointing a camera at the hippies. There were dozens of people mulling around the vehicles.

"What the hell do you think you are doing?" a voice blasted into my left ear.

I turned my head toward the man with the megaphone. His thin lips were tightly pressed together and his jaw was clamped down so tight that I could see from the movement of his cheekbones that he was gnashing his teeth.

"I work here," I replied.

The man lost some of his tension and his shoulders dropped as he simultaneously let out a long sigh with a question attached, "Why didn't someone inform us that you would be working here today?" He kept shaking his head.

"I don't know what to tell you. I wasn't informed of your presence today, either." I wasn't sure he heard what I said because he was looking over the top at my head and frantically moving his arms, reminding me of someone trying to direct a jet landing on an aircraft carrier. When he lowered his arms, I continued.

"What are you doing?"

He looked at me and, obviously exasperated, replied, "Trying to make a movie about D. H. Lawrence!" I didn't mention that I thought Lawrence was a dumbbell.

Normally, San Felipe was a quiet, peaceful, and thoroughly tranquil village. But early one Saturday evening just before sunset, two small-caliber pistol shots were fired from somewhere behind the back wall of my garden. Following the shots I heard the sound of angry voices. The nearest house on the other side of the street from the wall belonged to Eugenio Candiani's family. I had been in the house just once, where I met Eugenio's older brother and his wife as well as a younger brother and sister. The sister was about fourteen and the brother perhaps a year younger. I never met the parents. Eugenio never talked about his family but the rumors that did come to me always portrayed the family as mafioso.

I was convinced that the shots had been fired near the house of Eugenio, and after waiting several minutes I crossed the garden and peered over the back wall. No one was moving up or down the street, so I shrugged my shoulders and returned to the veranda to read. About thirty minutes later the tranquil dark was again shattered by gunfire.

Unfortunately, the wall was too high and I could not see the light from the muzzle flashes as the shots were being fired.

This time the shots were being made by a variety of arms: small- and large-caliber pistols, shotguns, and the ominous sound of semiautomatic rifles. It wasn't continuous but sporadic, as if two groups were moving stealthily back and forth in battle. This time I didn't let my curiosity get the best of my judgment and I stayed where I was on the veranda. The shooting had been going for about fifteen minutes before the police arrived.

Two police cars showed up with their lights blinking but without sirens. They pulled up behind my garden wall, leaving their flashing lights on. Encouraged by their arrival, I stood up and walked over to the wall close to their cars. During this time the sporadic sound of one or more guns continued from the other side of the garden. During silences I listened closely to hear what the police were doing or saying on the other side of the wall. Much to my surprise, there was no sound at all. Not even the sound of a car door opening. The situation remained the same for another thirty minutes: silence from the police and the occasional shots coming from the direction of Eugenio's house. Finally there was only the sound of silence. This lasted for some time, and then someone opened the door of the police car closest to the back wall. Then the sound of muted voices came over the wall, too softly whispered to hear what was being said. I decided to slink back to the veranda and wait for clarification. Perhaps an hour later, I heard the voices coming from near the still-flashing lights of the police cars and shortly thereafter the sound of cars doors opening and closing. The police cars moved forward and the flashing lights disappeared around the corner. For some reason I was relieved that they did not turn right to Eugenio's house. Nevertheless, I worried most of the next day. I was very concerned about my employee.

Much to my relief, Eugenio showed up early Monday morning for work. He jumped the back wall of the garden and walked across the yard to the veranda where I was drinking my first cup of coffee. I didn't need to ask; almost immediately Eugenio began his description of Saturday night.

According to Eugenio, he had been shooting baskets through the hoop attached to the garage door of his house. Since the garage came right up to the edge of the street, he had been dribbling and shooting his baskets from the gravel service of the street. Three judiciales on their way to their bungalow passed by and told him that he could not play in the street. He argued that he had been playing there for years and refused to comply with their order. Angered by his apparently belligerent attitude, one of the judiciales grabbed his basketball and refused to return it. As the men began to walk away with the ball, Eugenio's little sister fired two shots through the open window of the house at the departing police. One of the shots hit a judicial in the lower leg. Angered even more, they threw out vengeful threats as they retreated with their wounded companion up the street. Thirty minutes later they returned and opened fire on the house.

Eugenio and his little sister, by themselves in the house, returned the fire with the small pistol and a shotgun. At the beginning of the battle Eugenio called the police. Evidently the police, after things quieted down, interviewed the judiciales and then, with Eugenio's approval, entered the house to listen to their side of the episode. After questioning Eugenio and his sister, they left.

Amazed by Eugenio's story, I began to ask questions. Why didn't the police take you to jail? Why didn't they confiscate the guns? Would the judiciales return at a later time to seek revenge? Eugenio only sneered and clicked his tongue on the roof of his mouth and said, "Estos pendejos no quieren pedos con los Candiani!" (These stupid people don't want problems with the Candianis). It was the only time that Eugenio ever suggested that his family was above the law. It made me suspect that there was some truth to the rumors I had been hearing about them.

My third and final residence in Oaxaca was only two blocks from the main plaza of the city. The move was provoked by the geologists' return for a prolonged stay. I rented a small apartment in an old Colonial house owned by some friends. One part of the house was a restaurant called El Sol y La Luna, where I first met my new roommate, a German gypsy flamenco guitar player with the unlikely name of Wolfgang Fink. Everyone called him Lobo.

Lobo was more than just a musician. He was also a composer. Technically, he had the fastest right hand I had ever seen in a guitar player. He practiced eight hours a day and played in the restaurant every evening for his food and his share of the rent. It was one of my most wonderful experiences in Oaxaca.

One weekend near the end of my stay in Oaxaca, I asked Lobo if he would like to go over to the coast for a couple of days. He expressed his desire to go but lacked funds for the flight. We cut a deal. I would pay his airfare and hotel and he would provide our meals. It worked out great and he didn't have to spend a cent.

The first night in Puerto Escondido, he played a couple of his compositions on his guitar and the owner of the restaurant plied us with food. Of course the restaurateur was happy. His place completely filled every time Lobo played.

When Lobo left Oaxaca, he went to San Miguel de Allende where he lived with my wife and me for a while. He played at Mama Mia's for several years and finally hooked up with a fiddle player as crazy as himself. Over the last few years, they have made ten CD recordings, the last three or four on Atlantic Records.

🔳 🔳 🔳   LETTER CONTINUED   🔳 🔳 🔳

By some miracle, I returned from Oaxaca to the Federal District with the five men, documentation team intact. We didn't have an office and the team didn't have a place to stay. Paco's and my apartment doubled as the team's work space and dormitory. Luckily, our apartment was less than three blocks from the main administration offices of INAH and less than four blocks from the Direction of Pre-Hispanic Monuments and the Department of Museums.

After turning over my report to Don Gaston and Eduardo Villa, we began the initial discussion of a Monte Alban publication. Eduardo suggested that apart from INAH's in-house publication department, I get at least two different printing companies' estimates for the job. He also suggested that we hire a commercial artist to help design the catalog. He had someone in mind and showed me a sample of his work on the recently published book by INAH, *Corazón de Copil*.

While I busied myself with contacting the commercial designer and reputable publishers and began the laborious task of writing, the rest of the crew took on the tedious burden of organizing and indexing the documentation materials for the publisher.

In between my traumatic typing battles, taking out the wastepaper basket that I filled several times a day, and coordinating the work for the catalog's publication, I relaxed by visiting friends.

This was easy enough to do, as almost all my friends were employees of INAH. Most of them had offices near the apartment. Although they were not all archaeologists, this was the group I associated with the most. We usually ate breakfast or lunch together at some nearby restaurant.

Paco's and my apartment became a center for numerous gatherings, formal as well as informal. The formal meetings centered on Mesoamerica in general, personal projects, philosophy, and professional ethics, and now and then a little gossip filtered in. Surprisingly, very little *grilla* (bad-mouthing) of either the institution or its employees took place. If we complained at all, it was generally about the amount of gossip and grilla that permeated the institution. Moreover, I can't remember an angry phrase or word ever being uttered in the apartment. I guess we got along well and didn't get tired of one another because most of us had projects that took us away from the city, and each other, for long periods of time. Oddly enough, it was a comfortable, as well as an exciting, period in my life. It lasted for two months.

Then, Eduardo Villa sent word for me to come to his office.

◼ ◼ ◼

CHAPTER SIX

THE HOUSE OF SNAKES

Chichén Itzá Project

A new king will awaken there

[Chichén Itzá], along with thousands

of resurrected beings of a past

creation: the petrified feathered

serpent will breathe with life again

and wreck havoc on the creatures

of this creation.

—Paul Sullivan, *Unfinished Conversations:*
Mayas and Foreigners between Two Wars

FROM OAXACAN ZAPOTECS TO YUCATEC MAYAS

Eduardo was not as formal with his meetings as Don Gaston. He could have been. True, he was not meeting all the time with the president of Mexico or his cabinet members, but he received the directors and coordinators, not only from within INAH but from various arms of the government. He was just too approachable to be formal. His secretary would call or get a message to me to see if I could come at a given time. But more often than not, someone within the halls, offices, and corridors of INAH would tell me that Eduardo wanted me to stop by his office during the day. If I needed to discuss some matter with Eduardo, I would just present myself to his secretary, without an appointment, and sooner or later he would receive me. He always took my phone calls, no matter the hour, and he always made me feel like I was a team player.

Some time later, a young Belgian photographer that I hired told me why he respected Eduardo Villa: "He is an up-front guy and always gives me *la neta* (the bottom line)."

I spent less than thirty minutes on that particular day in Eduardo's office. He informed me that I was on my way to the Yucatán. I was to bring back a proposal and estimate for documenting the carved stones at Chichén Itzá.

The truth of the matter was that I was disappointed. I had hoped that I could return to Yaxchilan with Roberto. I even had one of my team members drawing pots that Roberto had found in Yaxchilan the season before. I was hoping that if we did a good job on these drawings, Roberto would request our team for his project next field season. I didn't mention this to Eduardo because it was obvious that orders had come to him from above—i.e., God, president, Don Gaston, Eduardo, and then to me. As a result, I stepped out of the air-conditioned plane the next day and into an oven!

It was May, and Mérida was the infernal furnace of Satan's imaginative fury. The blast of hot air could neither be inhaled nor swallowed, so I held my breath until I reached the airport terminal building. When I finally got to the comfort of the terminal, I realized that the relief was only temporary. I would be out the other side of the terminal within a few minutes, as soon as I picked up my luggage. When I left the airport I headed straight for the INAH offices.

In 1981, the archaeologist Norberto Gonzalez Crespo was the director of INAH's regional offices. Compared to Manuel Esparza, he was a god. It was immediately apparent that he was a no-bullshit guy.

Norberto immediately offered me any assistance that I might need and put me in contact with Dr. Peter Schmidt, the archaeologist in charge of Chichén Itzá.

Peter was robust but not tall. He was usually smiling and carried around an infectious enthusiasm for the Maya, which he injected in all of our discussions. He always displayed a sense of good humor, even when he was serious. Peter cordially invited me to his house later that afternoon and introduced me to his lovely wife, his crocodile, and his wonderful library. Most important of all, he introduced me to *Architectural Notes and Plans*, some of Karl Ruppert's work at Chichén Itzá.

When Peter drove me to Chichén Itzá the next morning to look over the site, he brought the book along. It was a road map of the close to eight square kilometers of the heavily forested site. At one point Peter enthusiastically explained, "Imagine, after working all week long for the Carnegie Institute, Ruppert did this work with his students on their free time, Saturday afternoons and Sundays!"

During the two-hour trip from Mérida to Chichén, Peter gave me a good background of the archaeological history of the site. Once we arrived at Chichén Itzá, Dr. Schmidt gave me a tour of the site which we traversed via its central axis, from north to south. As only a small part of the site had been excavated, there were many more mounds overgrown with vegetation. Several times we got lost. We made a rough calculation of ten thousand carved stones. It turned out that this figure was less than 30 percent of the total that were finally documented. Nevertheless, Dr. Schmidt had only one day to dedicate to the project, and I was very grateful.

We returned late in the evening to the INAH offices and much to my surprise there were various people still working. I rapidly developed a positive image about the southeastern employees of INAH working in the Yucatán.

Peter took me to dinner that evening and as we returned to my hotel we ran into an acquaintance of his, a former helicopter gunner in Vietnam, accompanied by a young photographer from Belgium. They had just arrived in Mérida after walking through the forest using the

208 ▦ CHAPTER SIX

ancient *Sacbe* (Yucatec Maya for "white road") heading west out of the Classic Mayan city of Cobá, Quintanaroo. The hike had taken them a week. They both looked ripped and ragged from their journey but invited us across the small plaza to their hotel room.

During our conversation that evening I became impressed with the youthful enthusiasm and stamina of the photographer. I asked Eric Goethals if he would be interested in taking photographs and working with me at Chichén Itzá. He was, so I asked him to bring me some samples of his work in Mexico City when he returned.

I left for the Federal District the next morning.

I spent the next several days working on a proposal and budget for documenting the carved stones at Chichén, as well as catching up on the work for the publication of Monte Alban.

The graphic designer, hired by Eduardo, had begun to put together the catalog for Monte Alban, with the elements handed over to him by the team. We took this preliminary "dummy" to several printing companies to get an idea of the cost of the publication. We were surprised to discover that INAH's "in-house" estimate was almost three times greater than the highest quote outside the institution. I asked the graphic designer why, and he replied that he didn't know. He then suggested that we should ask Eduardo to check on this for us. Before this happened I was called into Eduardo's office and told that my proposal for Chichén Itzá had been accepted and to prepare the team for leaving for the site. Luckily, Eric Goethals showed up at my apartment that same afternoon with his résumé and samples of his work. I explained what the project required of him and asked him to meet me in my apartment early the next morning with a list of equipment and supplies. If he could defend his proposed budget with me, we would go directly to Eduardo's office with it.

Reading and going over Eric's proposal was one of the most concentrated learning experiences of my life. Piece by piece we went over the photographic and lighting equipment and accessories. I was amazed at Eric's technical knowledge and field experience in his medium. He was a twenty-one-year-old pro. I was finally beginning to realize how wonderful the world of photodocumentation could be. His proposal for photographing large numbers of carved stones at night both challenged and exhilarated me. If his proposal were accepted by INAH, we would be working at the site two shifts every day! The initial cost of equipment was going to be a major factor in my superior's decision concerning his involvement in the project. His budget for equipment and supplies was tens of thousands of dollars!

I watched Eduardo's expressions during Eric's presentation of his proposal. Eduardo, who probably knew more about photographic equipment than I, asked only a few questions. He then told Eric that INAH would contact him when a decision was made.

I will never forget the look on the young photographer's face a week later when I handed him a check for several thousand dollars and a round-trip airline ticket to New York City. After the reality of the situation dawned upon him, he expressed his greatest concern: "How will I get all of the equipment and supplies back through Mexican customs?"

"Don't worry about it. Leave those kinds of problems to the INAH executives. They authorized your proposal so I am sure they will notify customs. When you arrive in New York call and let me know when and where you can be reached and I will fill you in on all the details of your return. Look at your ticket. You'll be in New York tomorrow morning. You have one week! Don't spend INAH's money on 7th Avenue!" He looked puzzled so I hummed a line or two of Simon and Garfunkel's "The Boxer" and he laughed.

"Do you think I am going to have enough time for that?" he asked.

While Eric was gone I received a telephone call from Eduardo. The team would be leaving for Mérida in two days. He wished me luck and said to call Angel García Cook, the director of Pre-Hispanic Monuments, and notify him of the status of the Monte Alban publication.

I called Angel the day I left for Chichén Itzá. After describing the status of the publication he told me that the introduction to the catalog should be written by Roberto García Moll. I agreed completely.

Working in Chichén Itzá with the Divine Ahau

I deliberately sought the man out after reading J. Eric Thompson's *Maya Archaeology*. In later conversations Don Eugenio May revealed he had worked with other renowned Mayanists such as Sylvanus Morley, George Valiant, and Karl Ruppert, to name but a few. On the other hand, he denied any relationship to the infamous General May of Santa Cruz.

I was bonded from the moment that I first laid eyes upon the little man. It was inside the sixteenth-century chapel in Piste, Yucatán. He couldn't have been much over five feet tall and so slight of build I thought he was too fragile for the work I had in mind. Boy, was I wrong! Also, I had been told he was eighty-three years old. But there was youth in his eyes, and when I suggested that there might be a job for him, he grinned from ear to ear and butted his closed fists together in front of his chest. It was a gesture that reeked of total dedication, enthusiasm, and delight. I couldn't resist hiring him. It turned out to be one of the best decisions I made during the project. Having worked the better part of his life at the site, he knew the location of every mound in the twenty-two square kilometers that encompassed the great center of Chichén.

All sixty-four Mayans I hired, from three villages around Chichén Itzá, treated Don Eugenio with great respect and referred to him as *El Abuelo* (the grandfather). Because of their respect for the man, if there were any internal confrontations or jealousies within the Mayans, they never manifested themselves to the rest of the team during the fieldwork.

Armed with the Kilmartin-O'Neill map, made by the Carnegie Institute in the late 1920s and early 1930s, and Karl Ruppert's *Architectural Notes and Plans*, we began to systematically document the carved stones of the site. We worked two shifts every day except Sunday for almost a year and a half.

The day shift included the restorer, the topographer, six artists, and Maya men from the surrounding villages, who worked from five in the morning until two in the afternoon except Saturdays. On Saturdays we all worked until noon.

Figure 18 Restoration (photo by Eric Geothals)

Figure 19 Restoration (photo by Eric Geothals)

This part of the thirteen-member technical team ate breakfast and lunch in a jacal with Doña Simonia, the wife of INAH's chief maintenance administrator for the site. Except for the occasional *cucaracha* floating in the soup, the food was, as in Yaxchilan, monotonous.

After breakfast the team would disperse to their respective areas within the site where Don Eugenio had already formed the different work crews. We finished lunch by three o'clock, and on the forty-five-minute trip back to our base in Valladolid we stopped at the *cenote* Dzinup (one of the natural sinkholes in the area) every day for an underground swim. If we spent an hour or more swimming, we usually ran into members of the second shift on their way to work.

Figure 20 Photographic Team (photo by author)

Eric ran the night shift. His team consisted of an assistant photographer and three to five Maya workmen. Eric and his assistant would arrive at Chichén Itzá every day between 5 and 5:30 p.m. They would set up the generator and photographic equipment in the remaining daylight and begin photographing after dark. They would begin packing up their equipment and supplies an hour before daybreak. All of the carved stones found in the distinct areas of rubble around the uncovered platforms and construction were photographed in this manner.

The carved stones that were integrated into standing architecture were, for the most part, photographed during the day. Thanks to Eric's magnificent equipment, many of the larger friezes were photographed in stereo. Many times, on the taller structures such as the large ball court and the Castillo, we erected scaffolding in order to give Eric an altitude level with the carved stones that he was photographing.

One thing I recall about the topography of Chichén Itzá is that it's relatively flat. Compared to other sites I had worked at, there was very little climbing or walking down steep slopes. There were a few exceptions, like the great depression in the southeastern quadrant of the map made by Killmartin and O'Neill where a pre-Hispanic well was located. But the general rule of thumb was that if the ground started to rise abruptly, there was either the beginning of a platform or a *sacbe* (white road) under your feet. Being relatively flat was only a minor blessing. Because of the heat, any expended energy resulted in immediate sweating. It took weeks to acclimate.

After physically walking over almost every square inch of the site covered by the Carnegie map, I began to visualize a pattern. The major constructions at Chichén Itzá were built upon islandlike platforms with spokelike sacbes connecting them and a sea of forest surrounding them. These island platforms had at least three methods of access to potable water. They either had one of the two cenotes close at hand or dug a well down to the level of the aquifers in a natural depression. They created another source of potable water by directing the flow of rainwater on their platforms into specially adapted *chultuns* (artificial storage units dug into the bedrock) for storage. During the next several years we almost doubled the number of chultuns previously located by the Carnegie Institute. Although not all of the chultuns were constructed for water storage, many had easily recognizable drainage ditches carved into the bedrock that channeled the water from the terraces and platforms. During the final season, the job of the project topographer, Porfirio Vazquez, with the aid of Victor Ik Tun, one of Don Eugenio's assistants, was to photograph, measure, and draw the chultuns that we had located earlier.

I had just returned to Chichén from Mexico City, accompanied by a young archaeologist, Luis Felipe Nieto. During the flight from the Federal District to Mérida, I mentioned the chultuns to the young man and that I was anxious to know how the work was progressing. Upon arriving at Chichén, Roxana, the restorer, told us where Porfirio and Victor had started working that morning, so we set off in the direction of the chultun that she had pointed to on the map.

When we arrived at the indicated chultun, no one was in sight. But since I wanted to explain the different uses of the underground storage to Luis Felipe, I lifted the stone cover from the chultun and we knelt down on our knees to peer inside. It took several minutes before our eyes adjusted to the dark.

"Look at the boot-shaped facing stones that have been used for lining the interior of the storage unit," I began.

I was about to explain the structural reasons for using this type of stone for the facing when Luis Felipe exclaimed excitedly, "Look! What is that moving on top of the rubble in the center of the chultun?"

It was a fat rattlesnake about a meter long. "Jesus! I wonder if it was down there while the guys were documenting this chultun?"

We moved on to the next chultun, which, although hidden from our view, was located on a small platform only fifty meters or so southwest of the first. When we arrived, there was a tell-tale pole sticking up out of the opening that we used as a ladder. There was also a dark column of smoke and swarming wasps rising above it. We could hear voices coming from within the chultun.

I called out, "Hello. Porfirio? Victor?" I didn't want to get to close to the opening because of the wasps.

After dislodging the wasps from their cool, dark residence, it took about an hour for Porfirio and Victor to finish their measurements and a first-draft sketch on millimeter graph paper of the chultun. While they worked, they disclosed that they had finished the first chultun about twenty minutes prior to our arrival, and although they had descended into the chultun they had not heard or seen any snakes. Nevertheless, we reasoned that the rattler had been there all along, waiting safely in the cool crevices of the rubble under their feet.

When we arrived at the next chultun, the air above the opening filled with dozens of bats surrounding Victor as he descended. Luis Felipe stood there shaking his head.

"What are you thinking about?" I asked with a slight chuckle.

"I am thinking that I prefer the archaeology in the high plateau!" he responded straight-faced and without hesitation.

The dry remnant forests surrounding the platforms of Chichén Itzá were different from those clinging to and draping over the ruins of Tikal in the Peten of Guatemala and Yaxchilan of East Chiapas. One difference was that whereas most of the forests surrounding Tikal and Yaxchilan were hundreds of years old, the forest and soils surrounding the island platforms had been worked continuously for centuries. In fact, as late as 1986, the vegetation between the platforms and sacbes, and even on many of the smaller platforms and lower mounds, was still being burned at the end of every dry season in preparation for planting. The smoke from the various fires seeped outward through the forest like low-flying cirrus clouds. Sometimes it hugged the ground so tightly that you couldn't see your feet. At this time breathing was difficult. The vegetation in these areas was, for the most part, shorter, smaller in diameter, denser, and thornier, and consequently the Mayas living nearby had their own way of dealing with it.

They had a unique technique for what I call "tunneling through the forest" to get from one platform to another. After I realized the scale and speed of this, I began to examine their methods, techniques, and rhythms of work.

None of the Mayas I worked with were very tall, and, with my meager height of five feet nine inches I towered above them. Scale became something more than a ruler as I had to stoop over and follow behind them with a lowered head. Aside from humbling me, it gave me a bird's-eye view of what their world looked like.

They always carried four essentials: a machete, a koa (a short and thick-bladed hand-scythe), a net bag that contained their lunch and a whet stone, and a *guaje* (hollow gourd) for their water. For tunneling they worked as a three-member team with the tallest in front, who assumed the responsibility of direction.

As Don Eugenio May was one of the few Maya who understood the topographic map of Kilmartin and O'Neill (he helped to make it!), we would point the workmen to a cardinal reference, such as east, southeast, or southwest, and in spite of obstacles such as distance, crevasses, boulders, large trees, roots, and thorns, they would tunnel directly to the next location we wanted to document. They never missed! The only prerequisite they had prior to beginning was they could not cut any vegetation that had a diameter of more than five or six centimeters. The person in front of the tunneling process would concentrate on the higher vegetation, while the second person cut through the midsection of the tunnel. The person in the rear took care of the vegetation closest to the ground. The progress was so efficient that one could walk behind them like a cautious deer, taking two forward steps then pausing.

Once the tunnel came to the edge of a platform, a larger group of men were brought through it to begin clearing the area for measuring, mapping, and drawing the structural vestiges and carved stones. Over a period of a week or more, the fifty to sixty Mayas traversing a tunnel twice a day created a rather comic illusion of traveling by subway in Mexico City.

At some point during the clearing of a platform for documentation, Eric would arrive to coordinate the removal of any branches or foliage that might adversely affect his photography of a particular carved lintel, doorjamb, or frieze. The only vegetation that gave us fits was the plant the local Maya referred to as *pica pica*. It was an excellent onomatopoeia for the irritating plant.

The first time Don Eugenio warned me about the pica pica was at the beginning of the rainy season and the plant brought to mind the nettles of the Pacific Northwest of the United States. On the underside of its broad leaves were thousands of tiny, light-colored fussy spines. Most of the year the plant could be avoided, as it was easy to identify. But from March until the beginning of the rains the plant dried up until the dry shriveled leaves were light, crisp, slightly diaphanous, and delicately unstable. Visually, they became lost in a collage of ocher-colored vegetation surrounding them. The slightest breeze or stirring of a nearby twig that touched the plant would dislodge the fuzz, spreading it through the air. The fuzz particles acted like modern smart cruise missiles that couldn't be avoided. Invariably they landed on our skin and clothes. The small, airborne spines of the plant "picapicated" through the clothes. They felt like hundreds of needles pricking the skin. We tried to avoid scratching as it activated the penetration, leaving a tiny, bright red sore on the skin. Showers and lots of soap got rid of them from the skin, but we didn't dare use the same pair of jeans two days in a row. Our clothes had to be washed daily.

There was at least one truly magnificent species of tree in Chichén Itzá that the Maya call *Pich*. They grew so large that I suspect they were the oldest trees in the nearby woods. The pich had roots, some bigger around than my body, which spread out on top of the ground like spokes on a bicycle wheel and foliage that created an enormous area of shade across all below them. Sometimes the shade extended over fifty meters. Unfortunately, even these resplendent trees within the site appeared to be doomed to extinction. A dozen or more artisans were exploiting the roots of these to make wood carvings that they sold to the tourists. I made several vain attempts to stop this practice.

At first I talked to the local artisans about conserving the environment as a means of protecting their economic future. With Victor Ik Tun's help on Sundays, we carved a couple of small Maya figures they called *Aluxes* (Atlanteans) out of the local bedrock, then made molds and poured a mixture of concrete and *sascabe* (local lime mortar). We offered these materials and methods as an alternative to their carvings made from the roots of the pich. When this failed I wrote a letter to INAH's National Consejo of archaeology describing what was happening to the pich trees. Weeks later, on a trip to Mexico City, I encountered Roberto García Moll with a copy of my letter in his hand.

His only comment as he sternly shook the letter in his hand was, "Nobody in this institution has any balls!" I knew that the battle to preserve the pich trees in Chichén Itzá was lost.

Concern for the environment was hardly a priority anywhere in Mexico at the time. Roberto was one of the few archaeologists I knew during this period who ever demonstrated concern. It became even clearer that this was not the case when the contract to build a new tourist reception area at Chichén Itzá was awarded. The contractor—I can only guess in order to save money—had his laborers cut hundreds of trees from the surrounding forest to use as supports for pouring his roofs.

The fauna did not appear to be as abundant as in Yaxchilan and Tikal. One reason was the dryness of the forest floor. It was hard to keep from making noise as we walked through it, thus giving the animals ample warning of our approach. I also suspected that there was intensive hunting in the area due to the amount of game meat on the menus in the local restaurants.

On one occasion while working in the northern part of the site, we startled a deer. Although I couldn't understand the rapid-fire discussions among the Maya workmen, the excitement in the voices was obvious. Throughout the day there were other clues about what might happen. The workmen usually spoke slowly and clearly around me. It gave them great pleasure for me to learn their language. But that day they spoke rapidly to each other, many times they enjoined in whispered conversations. When questions of work brought us together they averted their faces and avoided all eye contact. As the hour approached for the termination of work, their excitement built and there was a mad rush for their bicycles at 2 p.m.

The next morning, while the technical team was having breakfast, the workmen sent a messenger with an offering: the heart and liver of what was perhaps the last deer in Chichén Itzá. They knew very well my position in regards to what they had done, so they made me an offering I couldn't refuse.

Snakes were certainly not as abundant as in Yaxchilan, but Eric managed to photograph a few of them at night. Once during the early morning we found a three-meter-long boa appropriately coiled in the mouth of one of the stone serpent heads in the main plaza. We took it home as a pet for several days, but it alarmed our cook and cleaning lady so we eventually returned it to the forest where it belonged.

Upon another occasion while walking through an open area of the woods, Don Eugenio swung his right arm forcefully into my chest, pointed to the ground at our feet and yelled, "Cuatro Narices!" (four noses). It was a member of the bothrops family like the Nauyaca of Yaxchilan, Chiapas. Don Eugenio killed it with his machete before I could stop him.

Then, near the end of the six-year project, Policarpo, one of the Maya from Piste, was bitten by a small rattlesnake. He walked three kilometers back to the main plaza and then had to be driven to the hospital in Mérida.

After he recovered from his ordeal, he told me that he continually had *sueños extraños* (strange dreams) during the two-hour drive. The hallucinatory effect of snake venom had been recounted to me by several people who had been bitten. My photojournalist friend Andy, who had worked in Yaxchilan with me, had actually injected himself several days in a row with small amounts of rattlesnake venom. He reckoned that by doing this he could build up immunity to their bite. On the third day he managed to inject himself with an overdose, and he hallucinated for several hours.

Years later I was reminded of these experiences while reading *Blood of the Kings,* by Mary Ann Miller and Linda Schele. They proposed that the classic Maya nobles at Yaxchilan provoked their "visions" by the loss of blood during their rituals. While not denying the ritual of blood letting, I found it hard to conceive how they could control the amount of blood loss (oxygen) to produce a hallucination. Checking the theory of these authors with several doctor friends, I discovered that the key to hallucinating through blood loss was the word "massive." There was general agreement that hallucinations can occur with *massive* blood loss. However, the slightest mistake by the Maya in their calculation could result in death. I could not find any reference on the carved monuments in the Classic Maya world that read, "He let blood. He died." Rather than the letting of blood as the esteemed writers suggest in their book, I suspect that it was, like Andy and Policarpo discovered, the controlled intake of snake poison that provoked the visions, hence the "Vision Serpent" that we had found carved on various monuments at Yaxchilan.

DIESEL FUMES AND MAYARAMA

Almost every problem I ever encountered while working for INAH was intensified by underlying personality differences, even when there was a professional question on the table. Ironically, one of the few exceptions was a confrontation between the documentation team of INAH and the bus drivers of a large tour company called Mayarama. There was nothing professional about it.

Our drafting tables were set up in a small building located near the southwest corner of the pyramid known as the Castillo, next to the narrow highway that curved as it passed through Chichén Itzá between Mérida and the Caribbean coast.

The building consisted of four rooms, including a bathroom and a covered terrace. The north room acted as the ticketing office for visitors to the site. The INAH maintenance staff utilized the south room as a *bodega* (storeroom) for everything from supplies and equipment to artifacts. The regional office of INAH gave us the center room, bathroom, and terrace as a workspace. The center room was small and lacked sufficient light to work on detailed drawings so we used it to store our materials and equipment. We placed our drafting tables outside and did most of our work on the covered terrace. We screened the area in order to protect us from the mosquitoes and other *bichos* (bugs). Since it was near the entry to the site, the numerous tourists who visited the site often scrutinized us as we did them.

Although there were no-parking signs on both sides of the highway because of the curve, the tourists who arrived early by car parked next to a barbed-wire fence along the easement of the highway and west of the main entrance. There were never more than two or three cars parked along the easement, and by 11 a.m. they were gone. At nine o'clock, the INAH caretakers opened the gate and cars arriving afterward parked inside the fence. INAH had built a couple of additional parking areas for the tour buses. One was about thirty meters east of the entryway and the other about equal distance to the west. The tourist buses, coming from either Mérida or Cancun, usually arrived around 11 a.m. stayed for a couple of hours and left.

One day when I returned to the terrace where Roxanna and several of the team were working at the drafting tables, there was an empty tourist bus with the motor running parked on the easement next to our work area.

"Professor, will you talk to the driver of the bus? The diesel fumes are so bad we cannot breathe. We tried to talk with him but he just ignored us."

"Of course. You probably offended him. Watch my charm and learn."

The bus driver had been watching us as we talked. Now his gaze followed me as I approached. When I was no more than a couple of meters from him, he turned his head and stared straight ahead at the great plaza of Chichén Itzá.

"Good morning, sir," I said as I extended my hand in friendship. He looked vacantly at my face but ignored my hand.

"My name is Don Patterson and I am part of a team from INAH working here at Chichén Itzá. You are probably not aware of it, but the fumes from your bus are making it very difficult for my companions to work. As you can see, the fumes are going through the mosquito screen and becoming trapped inside by the roof of the terrace. Could you please turn your motor off?"

"No."

"Why not?"

"I have to keep the air conditioning going so that the bus will be comfortable when the tourists return."

I looked at the windows above the huge letters that read "Mayarama." Almost half of the windows on that side were open.

I forgot my charm and answered sarcastically, "Shouldn't you close some of the open windows? You are letting most of that comfortable air escape." Since there was no reply, I continued.

"Didn't INAH build you a parking lot for the buses?" No reply.

"Why don't you park your bus in the parking area like the rest of the buses? You can keep the motor running without choking my companions."

The driver folded his arms across his chest in a gesture of defiance and responded, "I can't do that because the tourists are accustomed to getting on and off the bus here."

I realized that he was just being *necio* (stubborn), but I could not refrain from pointing out, "How can the tourists be accustomed to getting on and off the bus here if this is their first trip to Chichén Itzá? Do these tourists return regularly?"

He chose to ignore my question with sullen silence and determined defiance, so I shrugged my shoulders and returned to the work area. In spite of the choking diesel fumes, there were smiles on all of the faces.

"We were watching, Professor. What was it you were saying about charm?"

The bus left about thirty minutes later and we considered the affair finished. Much to our surprise, the next day there were two Mayarama buses parked along the easement with their motors running! Needless to say, the fumes doubled. The forces of opposition were beginning to gather. Their attitude toward us was a complete lack of respect as well as a declaration of chemical and biological warfare.

We developed guerrilla-type tactics.

Early on the morning of the third day of the conflict, we placed dozens of softball-sized rocks in the area of the easement occupied by the buses of Mayarama the day before. This worked for two days. Unfortunately, the following day our small army of volunteers was working in other places at the site. During our absence the enemy forces responded by moving the rocks up against the fence and once again occupying the terrain along the easement.

So we battled back and forth a few times with the stones. But it soon became apparent that we were losing the battle. They had a reserve of strength we did not. We were tired and hot after hours of work in the sun while they had nothing to do while waiting for their passengers but move the stones in our absence and then take refuge in their air-conditioned buses. We had almost decided that our only recourse was to rearrange our work schedules so that from eleven to one thirty nobody would be working in the terrace, when Eric brought us some hope.

"Don, where do you want me to stack these scaffolds? I am not going to need them for a week or so." His knowing smile infected the entire team. There were thirty-two meters of heavy metal scaffolding in sixty-four different sections! During that week we cheerfully but smugly worked on the terrace without being gassed. But we had underestimated the determination of the drivers, and they were right back when we moved the scaffolding for work in a remote area of the site.

In a last-ditch attempt to not give in and adjust our schedules to their stubborn posture, I made contact with the appropriate authorities.

I talked to the two highway patrol officers who occasionally stayed in the same hotel as our team. After humorously explaining the circumstances, showing them the presence of the no-parking signs, they eagerly accepted their duty to insure that buses did not park on that very dangerous section of the highway. However, their uniformed authority and influence was short-lived. Evidently, the police officers were facing interests that were more powerful than a couple of drivers of Mayarama. One Sunday, in my absence, the patrol officers told team members that they had been given instructions by their superior not to intervene. In the end, we adjusted our work schedule to Mayarama's.

The Tomb of the Nine Lords of the Night

Dr. Schmidt sought me out at the site. Normally very calm and jovial, he appeared nervous, agitated, and serious as he took me aside from the team in a moment of confidence. Ironically, we were standing in the middle of an unexcavated small ball court just northeast of the buildings known as the Market, surely a place of sacrifice in Chichén Itzá's pre-Hispanic past.

"The director of Pre-Hispanic Monuments, Angel García Cook, called the regional director, Norberto, about your project in Chichén Itzá." There was a moment of silence. "They are out to get you," he added before I could assimilate his statements and form any questions. Finally I responded.

"What did Angel say about the project? What are the criteria for his concern?"

"I really can't tell you. I was in the office when the call came in, so I didn't hear the details. But from the one-sided conversation, I could tell that Norberto was defending you. It is my impression that they want you to stop the project immediately!"

"Thanks for informing me, Peter. I have to go to Mexico City the day after tomorrow so I will try to find out what is going on."

I arrived in the Federal District, went straight to the apartment, and called Eduardo Villa. He was not in his office and his secretary informed me that he would not return until the next morning. So I sat around the apartment thinking about how Peter had told me about the situation. Was he being a bit theatrical? Was someone out to stop the project? There must be a motive, so I had to ask myself why? Around ten o'clock that night I received a phone call.

Although the voice on the other end of the telephone line did not identify himself, I knew it was the archaeologist Ramon Carrasco.

"Don, I just read a copy of a letter that was sitting on the desk of Angel García Cook. It is addressed to Norberto Gonzalez Crespo. There are copies going to all of the big guns of INAH: Don Gaston García Cantú, Eduardo Villa Kamel, Otto Schondube, and Joaquin Garcia Barcenas, among others. The document says that your project has not met even the minimum requirements for an archaeological study and that it should be suspended immediately."

"Really?" I lifted my voice at the end making it a question.

"Listen, I know you have a good relationship with Don Gaston and Eduardo Villa, so you might recommend me to become the director of this project as a possible solution for this problem with the Consejo."

"Huh? Well, thanks for the offer but first give me a chance to talk with Eduardo Villa in the morning to see if I can find out the details of the Consejo's objections and I will get back to you."

The next morning I was in Eduardo's office when he arrived. I explained what Peter had told me in Chichén as well as the content of the telephone conversation with Ramon Carrasco the night before.

"I have not received this document and until I do there is nothing that we can do about it. Stay close to your phone and I will call you if and when the document arrives."

I returned to the apartment and waited. It was late afternoon before Eduardo called and told me to come to his office.

Eduardo passed the document to me across his desk. The content was more or less as my night caller had paraphrased to me over the phone. Although the document was only a couple of short paragraphs, the author referred to me as "Doctor" Patterson, questioned my authority for the project, wanted to know to what department I was assigned, and suggested that an archaeologist be put in charge of my project. I noticed that a copy was also sent to me.

When I finished reading the document, Eduardo said, "Well, I will answer this letter from an administrative point of view. I am sure that the motive behind this is to get their hands on the funding you are receiving for their friends' projects. But since they are sending you a copy, you have the opportunity to defend yourself, right?" He handed me a small booklet. It contained the rules and regulations for projects in INAH. I took it back to the apartment to read. Late that night I wrote a letter directed to Angel García Cook with copies to all who had received the original. I personally delivered copies to the persons whose offices I knew, and sent the rest through INAH's normal mailing channels.

Eduardo read my response and laughed. Esperanza, Don Gaston's personal secretary, read my response and asked, "Are you guys still fighting?" And when I arrived later in the afternoon at the driveway for the building that housed Pre-Hispanic Monuments and the office of Angel García Cook, I ran into Roberto García Moll.

"Good afternoon, Doctor." I emphasized the word "doctor" knowing full well that if he hadn't had a hand in writing the letter, he had at least read it.

"This is not Angel's fault. It's because your last name is not Mexican."

"What? Roberto, give me a break," I replied with a dispassionate sigh. "You had better take a look at the last names of almost everybody who received Angel's letter." And I began reading the last names from the letter. "Let's see what we have here. Hmm. There is a Contu, Kamel, Barcenas, Cook, and a Crespo. Jesus, there is even a German— Otto Schondube! In fact, I don't see a purely Mexican name in the entire letter!"

I thought for a second and then added, "And in my response, there is even a Moll."

"You are stepping on the *gremio* (field) of the archaeologists," he stated defensively.

"I am sorry, Roberto. But my work is technical. Besides, when I need an archaeologist to excavate, I have always hired an archaeologist. If you 'investigators' would train the technicians to do their jobs, you would have more time to investigate!"

While waiting for some kind of decision from the authorities, I went to the Templo Mayor site to cry on the shoulder of Eduardo Matos. After I told him what was happening, he made just one wistful comment.

"I don't understand why these people don't leave us alone. We could get more work done."

To this day I do not know how the situation was resolved. All I know is that the next day Eduardo told me to get my butt back to the Yucatán. Evidently, the members of the establishment who wanted a piece of the funding I was receiving could not defend their position adequately. Whatever the reason, I returned to Chichén Itzá. Still, I had upset some very powerful people at INAH, people with a lot more ability and purpose than what I had encountered in the direction and administration of INAH offices in Oaxaca. It was going to cost our documentation team down the road. But at the time I felt safe and secure under the protection of Don Gaston, so I did not feel nervous when Angel García Cook called me to his office several weeks later.

"It appears that they have discovered a tomb in Comacalco, Tabasco, with remnants of nine stucco figures on the interior walls. If you have the time I would like some of your team to photograph and draw these figures."

"Of course we will, Professor. Two of my team members are here in Mexico with me right now. We were planning to return to Chichén Itzá in the morning, but we can change our flight destination to Villa Hermosa instead. It may be several weeks before I can return to Mexico with the graphic documentation of the tomb. Will that be a problem?"

"No. In fact, you can leave your drawings and undeveloped film with the archaeologist in charge of the site. However, I understand they have found hundreds of ceramic tiles with drawings and possible glyphs at the site. These tiles will eventually need documenting."

Comacalco was an interesting site for the student interested in restoration. There must have been five or six different restoration solutions based on as many different criteria. When the archaeologist showed us the tomb, I was taken by surprise. For some reason, I had left Angel's office with the idea that the tomb was a recent discovery. It had actually been discovered by Franz Bloom earlier in the century and was none other than the tomb he called the Nine Lords of the Night.

LIVING IN THE YUCATÁN PENINSULA

Valladolid was a small and semirural community. It could even be described as a sleepy little town, back in 1982. It was hard to believe that during Mexico's colonial period it was one of the three largest towns on the Yucatán Peninsula. Still, it was one of the larger communities on the narrow paved road between Mérida and Cancún. There were two or three hotels in the town, mostly used by salesmen, highway patrol officers, and the few tourists who traveled through the northern Yucatán by car. It had a half-dozen good restaurants, although we preferred to shop in the traditional market, hire a cook, and eat at home. It also had a movie theater and a couple of pool halls, which we patronized often. The only other attraction in the community was a cenote.

The friendliness of its residents made up for its lack of entertainment and belied the reputation it had attained in the nineteenth century's caste wars. In 1848, when it was still called by its Mayan name, *Zaci* (Yucatec Mayan for "white vulture"), the community was attacked, sacked, and the wealthy Spaniards massacred by the revolting Maya warriors.

The team occupied most of the rooms in one of the hotels. The hotel had a swimming pool that only Jessica and her friends used. We also rented a house to use as a dormitory, dining room, and office. In general, we made good friends with the community. But there was one bit of excitement that could have turned into something scandalous.

BAILING THE TEAM OUT OF JAIL

Roberto Turnbull and I were returning from the local pool hall late Sunday afternoon when we ran into Hollywood Harry McKnight. He was excited, agitated, a little drunk, and in his slurred and bad Spanish he proclaimed, "Estamos en la cárcel!" (We are in jail!), as he hurried toward us.

Roberto and I looked at each other, not sure of what he was trying to tell us.

"Calm down, Harry. Who is in jail?" I asked in English.

Harry began listing off a litany of names that included members of the technical team and some of the Maya workmen from the village of Piste. His slurred English wasn't much better than his Spanish. As we were in the street only a block from the hotel, I headed straight for the receptionist. Not trusting Harry's current state of coherence, I wanted to confirm what Roberto and I understood: that practically all of my team was in jail.

Valladolid was a small town, and knowing that gossip traveled faster than technology I had the receptionist at the hotel fill me in on the particulars.

"Yes, they are in jail!" she began. "They were drinking and about twenty minutes ago had a minor accident denting the left rear fender and breaking a tail light of a local resident's car. However, a few of them had been belligerent with the driver of the other car so he called the police. Somebody had talked back to a cop and they were taken to jail."

She then looked across the counter at Harry and added with the beginning of a smile, "Oh yes, they are also looking for a tall, blonde gringo."

I turned slowly to look at Harry. He couldn't meet my gaze but looked at his feet and mumbled, "I ran when the police arrived and told us we were going to jail."

It seemed to me that this was a good time for guilt, so I asked, "What do you mean, you ran? You abandoned your friends?" Then as an after-thought I added, "Who was driving?"

Harry didn't answer so I turned to Roberto. "Let's go find out what is happening."

As the three of us walked across the main plaza toward the municipal police station, Harry became very repentant and remorseful. Repeatedly he told us that he was going to "give himself up" to the authorities.

As we walked through the front door of the office of the municipality, it was obvious the situation was providing excitement in the small community. It seemed like everyone in the governmental offices was peering out their doors. Feeling very self-conscious, I nevertheless noted that they were all smiling. That was a good sign.

The local *comandante* (police chief) was serious but not threatening. And, almost word for word, he repeated the hotel receptionist's tale. I was apologetic and told him that whatever damages had occurred they would be taken care of. Harry, in English, kept interrupting our conversation by trying to get me to tell the police chief that he was guilty and should be locked up with his friends.

The comandante didn't speak English, and since I ignored Harry so did the chief, who said he would make an appointment with the driver of the other car on Monday morning so that we could come to an agreement on fixing his car.

"What is going to happen to my employees?"

"Let them spend the night in jail. We have removed their belts so that they can't hurt themselves or each other. I also had the shoes removed from the belligerent ones. You can come for them in the morning around nine o'clock."

Harry was still insisting on his right to be jailed, so I asked the comandante, "What shall we do with this one?" pointing at Harry.

"What do you mean?"

"He was with the others but ran when your policemen arrested them. Now he feels remorse and wants to turn himself in."

The comandante laughed loudly. "Take him home and put him in bed. The others are so drunk that they probably don't even know that he is not with them."

I thanked the police chief, and Roberto and I coaxed Harry from the police station. On the way back to the hotel, Harry continued insisting that he should be in jail. I tried to cajole him by singing a few bars of Arlo Guthrie's song "Alice's Restaurant."

Early the next morning, the non-criminal members of my team and I returned to the police station to pick up our companions. They were brought in single file and stood shamefully with their heads bowed in a line in the middle of the room. I knew that everyone, including the police chief, expected me to say something, so I began by walking very slowly in front of the convicts, appraising each one like a military officer at a parade inspection. I hesitated a few moments longer in front of each person who was holding his shoes and successfully suppressing a grin. Then I tore into them for representing the rest of the team and INAH in such a bad light. And in a moment of inspiration, I told them that starting the next morning I would get them up at 4 a.m. instead of four thirty to begin our work. Too late I realized I had just punished myself!

On Monday afternoon I met with the owner of the other car and told him that I would personally pay for any damages done to his vehicle. He was satisfied with that, and immediately thereafter we left the police station and shared a cup of coffee and some interesting conversation in one of the local restaurants. He even paid for the coffee.

Weeks later I was in the INAH administration building on Cordoba Street in Mexico City picking up monies for salaries. The clerk mentioned that it was a lot of money for a bunch of drunken convicts. I was not pleased and realized that almost nothing escaped the chisme and grilla within the institution.

A Birthday Party and a Prayer for Rain

We celebrated Don Eugenio's eighty-fifth birthday at Chichén Itzá with a surprise party. By some miracle it actually surprised him, in spite of the fact that it took two weeks of frantic activity and dozens of people, including his friends, who were involved in the preparation. Never was a secret kept so well.

The first complications in the process occurred when we decided to barbeque some goats and roast a pig for his party.

It took almost a full day of traveling north on the peninsula to acquire the goats. I suspect the extended journey and distance was made in order to include a visit with our guide's family.

The pig was a different story. There were pigs everywhere. One of the traditional domestic meats on the Maya table for Yucatán fiestas was called *Cochinita Pibil*. The preparation of anything Pibil was known by most of the cooks in the Yucatán. In fact, nine-tenths of everything we consumed, breakfast or lunch, in Doña Simonea's jacal was Pibil. With pigs to be found everywhere I didn't foresee the problem we were going to have acquiring a pig.

After work one Saturday Victor, Socio, Hapon hap, my six-year-old daughter Jessica, and I headed east out of Chichén in the Safari. As Jessica was attending a school in a small Maya village, her communication skills, I reasoned, would be of great value to me that day. The objective of the trip was to buy a pig and I thought it was time that my daughter learned something of what my father called "horse trading." Somewhere after we passed the turnoff to the cave of Balancanche, we left the narrow pavement and headed north for several kilometers on a dirt road.

Eventually, we arrived at a small hamlet. Since there were no streets, we parked the Safari at the edge of the village where the track ended and walked to the nearest hut to inquire as to the whereabouts of pigs for sale. The huts were widely dispersed between sections of the forest, and we walked for about thirty minutes down a trail that led past several residences where we stopped to make further inquires. Following instructions, we came upon a small clearing that contained a hut, three small children, two turkeys, several pigs, and a happy woman.

Yes, she would sell us a pig. The price depended upon the size. So after consulting with the group and calculating the number of people who would be partaking of the Cochinita Pibil, we decided upon a big one. My Maya companions graciously allowed Jessica to inform the lady of our choice. This both surprised and pleased the lady, who began to make a big deal out of Jessica.

When I put the requested amount of pesos in the lady's hand, the already happy lady actually beamed. As the cynical thought that I had paid too much for the pig began to dawn upon me, I had no choice but to smile myself. I turned back to face my stoic but grim-looking companions. We stood there quietly for several moments until my daughter's voice broke the silence.

"Papi, where is Don Eugenio's pig?" Jessica changed into English.

"Huh?"

I looked around the small clearing. There were pigs there all right, just not Don Eugenio's pig. Mysteriously the pig had disappeared. I tried to convince myself that the damn pig didn't really know what was in store for him.

I turned back to face Victor. "¿Ahora qué? ¿Qué vamos hacer? ¿Dónde está nuestra puerco?" (Now what? What are we going to do? Where is our pig?)

Victor, smiling broadly, answered my most important question, "Vamos a pescar un puerco." (We are going to fish a pig.)

"¿Pescar un puerco? ¿Pescar un puerco?"

I tried to visualize "fishing a pig," but never having had the experience it was beyond my comprehension. Finally I understood: we had to catch it. God bless supermarkets and butcher stores!

The "fishing" trip lasted an hour. It would have taken longer, but fortunately we found that the area of search was limited by a stone wall that wandered through the forest, enclosing about two acres. Much to the amusement of the giggling children and happy mother, the chase took us through the clearing several times. Nevertheless, bitten, bruised, and scratched, we finally managed to trap the stubborn squealing pig between the stone wall and some thorny shrubs. Jessica, standing on the wall near the climax of the chase, was so upset by the affair that she began to cry and spoke in three different languages in the same sentence.

Yet, in spite of the difficulties the results were far more important than the effort.

Don Eugenio's reactions will remain with me for the rest of my life. Tears filled his eyes as dozens of companions, as well as friends coming from as far away as Mérida to celebrate his birthday, began to congratulate him. But two hours after the party began he couldn't stand up. I was concerned about the reaction of his wife when we returned Don Eugenio in his inebriated condition to his jacal in Piste later that afternoon. Much to my surprise, she appeared pleased and couldn't control her giggling as we carefully placed him in his hammock. The next day he confessed that he had not taken a drink of alcohol for almost twenty years.

Don Eugenio demonstrated his appreciation by inviting Marisela and me to an important Maya ritual, *La Oración de la Lluvia* (the prayer for rain). The invitation came when a friend of ours, Juan Yadeum, an INAH archaeologist working at the Maya site of Toniná in Chiapas, was visiting with us.

As I have already indicated, I first met Don Eugenio in the small sixteenth-century chapel in Piste. Prior to working for the project he had been the church sexton. But the growing community was building a new church less than fifty meters from the old chapel. With support from the laborers from Piste, the rest of the team and I designed, and with the help of a local carpenter and mason, contributed an altar for the new church as a measure of our appreciation. I don't know Don Eugenio's theological understanding of the church, but he was apparently civic minded and supported the local belief systems. One of those local beliefs was that if the prayers of the Catholic priest didn't bring the needed rain, it was time to mount an altar in the rain forest.

A small clearing measuring less than four meters across was cleared of all vegetation except two small trees on the east and west side of the altar. The main altar was made from slim poles from secondary growth tied together with small bejuco vines. A thatched roof covered and protected the offering. Cooked chicken, turkey, and a thick corn broth called *pasol* had been offered as gifts to the gods by members of the community. The gifts covered most of the makeshift altar table.

Facing west, and on that side of the altar, was a small portrait of the Virgin of Guadalupe and a clear quartz crystal. On the ground, under the table altar, sat a half-dozen young boys. On the east and west sides of the altar sat two men with water gourds and wooden machetes. I found out later that the water gourds had been filled with water from the sacred cenote at Chichén Itzá. The final player in the ritual was the priest. Including Juan, Marisela, and me, there were only a dozen spectators.

Marisela's presence caused a bit of a stir just before the ceremony began. Evidently, women were not encouraged to attend these rituals. But whatever Don Eugenio told the priest, he finally knelt down on the west side of the altar and began the ceremony by praying and offering the communities' gifts to the four cardinal points. Then he did the same with the quartz crystal.

The priest then began to concentrate on the god of the east. As he prayed, the young boys underneath the altar began to croak like a chorus of toads crying for the rain. At the same time the man on the east side of the altar began to hit the sapling beside him with his wooden machete. This caused the leaves and branches to tremble as if the wind were arriving from the east. He punctuated the likeness of wind by blowing across the hole in the top of his gourd. If the young boys became quiet, he tossed water from the gourd on them. They giggled and took up the chorus once again.

Evidently, the wind passed over the altar with its gifts and the man on the west side of it began hitting the sapling nearest him and blowing across the top of his gourd. By this time it took several douses of water to keep the lads croaking. The ritual took the better part of an hour. On the way back to Piste, Don Eugenio explained that the ceremony sometimes needed to be repeated for several days before it rained.

Underestimating the efficiency of the Maya gods that evening, Juan, Marisela, and I went for a walk in the ruins of Chichén Itzá. We were drenched by the time we reached the Safari.

Figure 21 Don Eugenio May (photo by author)

THE DEATH OF THE AHAU

Less than a year after the rain ceremony, I was in Mexico City when Dr. Peter Schmidt called me with the news. Don Eugenio was dying.

According to Peter, Don Eugenio had called Victor Ik Tun to his side one morning and told Victor that he was too tired to continue working and was turning the site over to him. Later that day Peter went to Don Eugenio's jacal and found him very sick. Peter took him to a clinic in Mérida were he stayed a couple of days. He then told Peter that his old bones were tired and he wanted to return home to die.

I took the first flight to Mérida, hoping that I would not arrive too late.

Beto and I entered the jacal quietly. Don Eugenio's immediate family was standing around his hammock. The two men in the room were obviously drunk. Don Eugenio's frail little wife was sitting beside him, tenderly trying to administer water to him through a plastic straw. I was shocked. His body was devoid of muscle and fatty tissue. His skin, as white as an angel's robe, was drawn so tight that I could make out the contour of his bones. Except for the color of his skin and the lingering light in his eyes, he could have been an Egyptian mummy.

Beto and I sat on the two stools that had obviously been prepared for us near the front side of his hammock. Don Eugenio's bony right arm lay across his naked and collapsed chest. His left arm extended along the left side of his body near the edge of the hammock.

I looked across the hammock at his wife. She looked at me for a moment, slowly shook her head, and then dipped the straw into a Coke bottle for more water. As she released her finger from the top of the straw the water ran down upon his thin lips. Some of it went into his mouth. Don Eugenio didn't swallow.

My lower lip began to quiver and I could feel the water building up in the corners of my eyes. I was embarrassed and consciously tried to stop the tears from flowing down my face. It didn't work.

Suddenly, Don Eugenio's left arm fell off the hammock onto my legs. It was as light as a bird wing but it startled me and I immediately looked at his face. Although he couldn't move his head, his eyes were looking directly into mine.

I softly took his hand in both of mine and tried to smile. "Im puksicqal ech" (you are my heart), I murmured in bad Maya.

His lips moved very slightly as air passed through them. He was trying to say something. Puzzled, I leaned closer and looked across at his wife. She leaned over his head placing her ear close to his mouth.

When she straightened up she said something like, "Tin bin t-in na ob."

I wasn't sure of the meaning. It could be translated, "I am going to a better house" or perhaps "I am going to his house." Before I could ask, she continued speaking. I was unable to understand her, but when she finished one of the men explained in Spanish. "She thanks you on behalf of El Abuelo and his family for coming but it is time for you to leave." I slowly, tenderly, and reluctantly replaced Don Eugenio's arm back by his side on the hammock and then stood up. Beto followed my example and as I looked down upon the wasted form for the last time, I noticed that he was staring at his technical equipment hanging from a nail on one of the support poles for his hammock. His equipment was, in fact, a net bag, a machete, a koa, and a water gourd.

As we passed through the door into the front yard, one of Don Eugenio's relatives followed us. He was barely able to walk but he rudely thrust into my hands a koa and water gourd.

"These belong to El Abuelo. He wanted you to have them."

Before I had a chance to thank him, he continued angrily, "He has done a terrible thing. He has placed the stones in the hands of a member of another house. We have been shamed in the community."

Without further explanation, he turned and reentered the house.

Near the gate was a bucket of water, and I stopped to splash water over my face. Beto said nothing but I could tell he was sympathetic to my sorrow. During the two-kilometer drive from Piste to Chichén Itzá we didn't speak, but as we neared the entrance I turned to Beto and asked, "Where is Victor working?"

I arrived through the forest tunnel where the workmen were quietly standing around sharpening their machetes. Sharpening machetes was an activity that not only served to make their physical work easier but often was done when they got bored or tired. From the sorrowful expressions emanating from their faces today, I interpreted the sharpening as a mindless task.

Victor was sad, and although I wanted desperately to ask him about the scene that took place outside Don Eugenio's jacal I realized that this was not the right moment. Instead I told him that it wouldn't be very long before Don Eugenio left us and I was concerned about what would happen to his aged wife. We decided that we could help by delivering several pickup truckloads of kindling to her house so that she wouldn't have to worry about firewood for a long time. Before we finished our discussion, a messenger came and informed us that Don Eugenio was dead. We stopped work for the day.

For me the death of Don Eugenio May was the end of an era in Maya archaeology of the Yucatán. Ironically, his death also coincided with the coming of a different era back in the highlands of Mexico, in the once-great Aztec capital, Tenochtitlán.

TRANSFER OF POWER

For some strange reason I was unaware of events taking place around me. I would like to think it was innocence or concentration on my project in Chichén Itzá, not stupidity. Then, sometime during the late summer or early fall of 1982, Eduardo Villa called me to his office. As always, he was direct and to the point.

"Don Gaston has asked me to give you the following message. He cannot assure the continuation of the documentation team during the next presidential administration. Therefore, he has asked me to present you with two options. One, we can raise the contract salaries for the team for the rest of the year, or, two, we can award the documentation team *plazas* (tenure). The second option will secure you guys jobs during the next administration but nothing more. Who knows if the team concept will be continued by the new director?"

He then added with a wry smile, "You have made some powerful enemies."

He waited for an immediate response, but I was not ready.

"Eduardo, give me twenty-four hours to digest these options. My first reaction is that I don't think I would make a very good bureaucrat. However, there are other people's considerations to take into account. I would like to talk with the team members before making a decision."

"You can have more than twenty-four hours for a decision. We don't have to worry about this for a couple of months."

Leaving Eduardo's office it finally dawned upon me that my dream of the documentation team might never get out of its infancy. I suddenly realized that Don Gaston was going to leave INAH, and in doing so raise the big question, what was going to happen to the team? He had given his unconditional support. Also, Eduardo's last statement did not escape me. I had not made everyone in the institution happy. As I walked the twelve blocks to our office on Colima, I mulled over what I could do to keep the team intact, finish the work at Chichén Itzá, and continue to produce for the next six years.

With some hesitation, and in at least two cases reluctance, the team opted for tenure. It was understandable that Roberto Turnbull and Antonio Lopez were reluctant. They wanted to return to their painting. But the rest of the team, Roxana Peña Haas, Beto, Porfirio, and Jesus Real, for example, were in favor of the tenure. Jesus was also an artist but his oldest child had a rare hormone deficiency and the medicine was very expensive. Working for the government, Jesus's access to the needed medication was easier and much cheaper. Naturally, the bureaucracy nailed us.

The first step was the union. This took several weeks. They called us in one by one and gave us a verbal test. I don't know what the others were asked, but my questions were those of a high school student. What pigments were dangerous? What colors tend to recede? What colors tend to advance? None of the questions had anything to do with the work the team was doing. It was like trying to stick the proverbial square peg in a round hole.

After miraculously passing our union exam and acquiring tenure, the next step was for Eduardo to have the team transferred from the General Direction to the Department of Pre-Hispanic Monuments. Angel García Cook was waiting for me with open arms.

By now it was late November and his office was a mess. One could tell at a glance he was beginning to abandon his post as director of the department. There were boxes of books and folders already packed, but there was disarray on his desk, which he had to shuffle through. Finally, he found the official document ascribing the team to the Department of Pre-Hispanic Monuments. I signed the document as received, and with a huge smile on his angelic face, he announced, "Ah-ha, now you work for me!" His delight at the thought was so obvious that it made me wince. Almost magically he produced the photographs and preliminary drawings of the ceramic tiles from Comacalco. His smirk could only be interpreted as, "Now I gotcha!" But he voiced matter-of-factly, "I expect these will be done without delay."

"Great, Professor. I will get right on this as soon as you give me a detailed list of these photographs and drawings."

"Of course," he said, as he took them to the outer office and laid them on his secretary's desk. Neither he nor I imagined that the work could be finished before he left as head of the department. The whole thing was political sarcasm and I couldn't keep my mouth shut.

"Professor, what are your plans for the next six years?"

"I am going to return to a project of mine in the state of Puebla."

"Oh? You have a project in San Miguel Canoa?"

The secretary stopped typing and looked up quickly.

San Miguel Canoa was a little village in the state of Puebla that had a reputation of being a nasty place where any interference from anyone outside the community could be disastrous, even life threatening, a place described in the Mexican movie industry where "the church of the village has the power to decide the life of its inhabitants." In fact, in 1968 several youths were dragged through the streets and then hung by the villagers, based solely upon the church and community's suspicions of their youthful intentions. Needless to say, Angel was not amused.

December was fast approaching. I had put the nix on the publication of the Monte Alban project because of the inflated cost through INAH's in-house publishing department and because the work at Chichén Itzá had consumed so much time that I had waited too long to be able to take it to another publishing company before the end of the present government. The graphic designer had done a wonderful job. The format and presentation were superb. Notwithstanding, with the possibility of the documentation team's disappearance, the book sat on the back burner as I decided to make a video of the team's work and accomplishments for the next administration.

For the remaining days and weeks of Don Gaston's direction, I utilized every spare moment away from the Chichén Itzá project with the video concept. In my search for help, I made acquaintances, and in some cases friendships, with many young Mexicans working with the visual media throughout the city. Unfortunately, I never had the opportunity to thank Don Gaston before he left. Even though I followed his subsequent statements in articles of national newspapers, I will regret for the rest of my life not personally thanking him.

▣ ▣ ▣ LETTER CONTINUED ▣ ▣ ▣

Traveling between Chichén Itzá and the valley of San Miguel is always rewarding. There is so much to take in and absorb on each trip. There are many routes, some longer, some shorter, and each special. I have made this journey several times and by several means. I have driven it in Safaris and pickups. I once drove in a huge four-wheel-drive International jeep with a house—complete with bath, kitchen, bedroom, etc.—attached to it. I have ridden the distance by rail and bus a time or two. I have flown on commercial flights between the *altiplano* and the Yucatán Peninsula. And one time I hitched a ride from the Yucatán to Mexico City by inquiring at the control tower in the Mérida International Airport for any private flights heading in my direction. No matter what my mode of travel, I tried to search out those light ribbons of secondary dirt roads that disappear into places where I had never been before and that I yearned to travel. Ironically, one of those roads brought me back to San Miguel.

▣ ▣ ▣

Chapter Seven

The House of Dogs

Pilot Project

The Friends

Luis Felipe Nieto and I met for the first time in 1978 in the north bus terminal of Mexico City. We were both waiting for transportation to San Miguel via a second-class bus. It was strange—though I already knew members of his family, we had never crossed paths. We soon learned that each spent the week in Mexico City and returned to San Miguel on the weekends.

After competing successfully in international martial arts, Luis Felipe had decided to make a career of archaeology and was attending the National School of Anthropology and History (ENAH). I was working at the Templo Mayor for Eduardo Matos. Luis Felipe and I sat together on the four-hour bus ride, talking about the sites along the Río Laja drainage and in the valley of San Miguel. It was a brief encounter and I rarely saw Luis Felipe after that chance meeting.

Several years after our bus ride, Luis Felipe and I met again. He came to the apartment during the early winter of 1983 and proposed that my documentation team move to San Miguel and direct a settlement pattern study along the central portion of the Río Laja. He wanted to write his professional thesis on the area.

His timing could not have been better. Things were not going well for the documentation team. It had become very apparent that we performed best in the field, far away from the civilized world of Mexico City and the never-ending intrusion of the bureaucracy. Our inability to adjust to the distractions of the urban life of the capital, and our failure to keep from butting heads with the bureaucracy and cope with reduced funding, caused the team to unravel.

I had met the new director of INAH, Dr. Enrique Florescano. Although qualified, he faced a series of problems different from those of his predecessor. His biggest problem was financial. The new president of Mexico, José Lopez Portillo, who had promised to defend the peso like a dog, could not. There was little money in the government coffers and cultural investment was not a high priority. The funding that INAH did receive filtered slowly down through the administrative bureaucracy to projects and investigators in greatly reduced amounts. For example, the Chichén Itzá funding dropped from 6,492,497.18 pesos in 1982 to 80,000 pesos in 1983. Not only that, the entire year's funding was handed to me in November and had to be spent and accounted for by mid-December. Naturally, our project suffered. Instead of working at the site two shifts per day, year-round, we worked one shift with a partial team for less than two months.

For the field team, adjusting to Mexico City was a pain in the ass. Having lived in close proximity to one another for several years, the team began to see each other less and less outside of our "unionized" hours of work. Of course, the *chilango* (from Mexico City) team members returned to live with their families. Some of them lived far across town and from the very beginning they arrived late to work. Someone ratted on them to the union police. As a result, the union installed a time clock, which in turn lowered the morale of the team even more. They felt insulted. What rights did these inefficient and lazy union members have to check our time? It didn't make sense and seemed unfair. The team had been getting up and leaving for work at 4:30 a.m. for such a long time that I was sympathetic, but their exaggerated criticism of authority in the administration put me in an uncomfortable position.

With team morale low, we began to develop bad habits and consequently problems of efficiency, and Luis Felipe's proposal to join him in a project in San Miguel was opportune, but there were two initial barriers that I had to overcome.

In order to make a temporary work transfer from Pre-Hispanic Monuments to the Regional Center of Guanajuato, I needed the regional director to make a formal request for my team's presence in the state. At the same time, I had to lobby Ing. Joaquín García Barcenas, my immediate superior, arguing that the team could continue with the Chichén project and handle the Settlement Pattern project in Guanajuato simultaneously.

With the help of personnel from the Department of Museums of INAH and documentation team members, we hung an exhibition of the ongoing work in Chichén Itzá in the Bellas Artes in San Miguel. Luis Felipe Nieto invited the regional director of INAH, Rosa María Sánchez de Taggle. It was a success. The director of Bellas Artes at the time, Carmen Masip, said it was one of the better exhibitions they had presented. More important, Rosa María wrote the letter to the director of Pre-Hispanic Monuments requesting the team's presence in Guanajuato. But in addition to the documentation of the pre-Hispanic sites in the valley, the group in San Miguel also would inherit the task of documenting the historic centers of the colonial cities in the northeastern portion of the state, including San Miguel de Allende, Dolores Hidalgo, and Pozos.

I don't really know the motives behind the decision to allow my team a temporary transfer to Guanajuato, but two possibilities come to mind: (1) my boss had the confidence that I could handle both projects at the same time; and/or (2) he was happy to transfer me out of his department. In any case, the team established itself in San Miguel in the house that Marisela and I rented at Jesús 21, the same house where we had glued pottery shards together from the excavations at the Instituto Allende ten years earlier. The team took over two rooms, as well as the kitchen and most of the patio space under the arches.

THE VALLEY OF SAN MIGUEL DE ALLENDE

About twenty million years ago, during the Miocene, a huge cataclysm caused by block platting and volcanism began, and continued for ten million years. During this period these forces expelled upward gases and ashes, as well as solid and molten liquid materials. When the process terminated, it left the region from the Gulf of Mexico to the

Pacific Ocean formed as we see it today. In the state of Guanajuato, in the very center of this cataclysmic event, where the resultant Central Mesa of Mexico comes up against Mexico's Neo Volcanic Axis, a series of valleys was formed. The few rivers that cross these small valleys, on the southern tip of the Central Mesa, drain into an enormous region that covers portions of various states and is known today as *El Bajío*.

Today I live on the southeast edge of one of these valleys. My house sits upon the slope of an ancient fault line, a product of the cataclysm during the Miocene epoch of the Cenozoic Era. The view from the upper terrace, out over the Historic Center of San Miguel de Allende, is to the west. During the glorious sunsets of late winter, I spend half an hour each evening studying the valley.

Sometimes the sunset spreads its light over the normally blue and purple mountains and mesas to the north like gold leafing. When it does, it is hard to tell where the heavens begin and the earth ends. I am often tempted by these anomalies to pronounce that they are, in fact, portals that lead from Xibalba to the celestial world. Every topographic feature of the valley can find its analogy in the urbanization and architecture of Mesoamerica.

From the western horizon, the landscape steps downward from the mountains along horizontal lines in a series of deceivingly gently sloped platformlike mesas toward the rivers. Through the millennia, the eroded soils from these mountains formed huge platforms that gradually descend into the center of the valley basin, where they built up a vast flat area of rich alluvial soil, like the great plazas of Teotihuacán. Down in the center of the drainage, on the east side of the river, ancients built their most extensive settlements. On gentle slopes near the alluvial soils of the river and its tributaries, they planted corn, beans, and squash. While the sky and mountains, like pyramids and temples of old, hold promises of spiritual relief, it is the platformlike mesas and plazalike floodplains near the river below that draw my attention. Here, over one thousand years ago, man left his cultural vestiges and subsequent scars on the environment. Yet each year there are fewer and fewer of them both. During the sixteenth century, Spanish explorers gave the name San Miguel to the major river that cuts through the heart of this valley. Why and when the name was changed I don't know, but today it is called El Río Laja.

THE SETTLEMENT PATTERN STUDY

The initial work of our archaeological documentation began by selecting a rectangular area of approximately one thousand square kilometers for our study that covered the entire valley from east to west. Next, we began to gather all of the available bibliographic material, as well as purchase topographic maps and aerial photographs that covered the area of our settlement pattern study.

Luis Felipe spent forty hours studying the aerial photographs and locating the potential areas that looked promising as pre-Hispanic sites. Meanwhile, along with organizing the material of the Chichén Itzá project, the rest of the team worked on enlarging portions of the topographic maps.

The topographic maps we purchased were at a scale of 1:50,000 with ten-meter contour lines. They were well detailed and helped us locate the approximate position of the alleged sites Luis Felipe had found with the aerial photographs. Utilizing an overhead projector, we blew up the areas that Luis Felipe found interesting to two different scales: one set at 1:10,000 and another set at 1:2,000. Once we hit the outback areas, we took the two map sets to the field with us.

Acquisition of modern technology was beyond our finances. Our equipment reflected our budget. It was definitely third-world technology.

From his own pocket Luis Felipe bought the aerial photographs of the area and a Brunton compass. We even used his personal camera. INAH provided the meager remainder of our equipment and supplies, such as paper, film, pencils, erasers, 100-meter measuring tape, and a blue Volkswagen Safari. It was the same blue Safari that Emilio Bejarrano and I had driven to Tikal and passed the portal of Xibalba on our way back from Guatemala seven years earlier. With these supplies and equipment, over the next three months we canvassed nearly one thousand square kilometers and found close to one hundred pre-Hispanic sites.

Taking the aerial photos, a portable stereo viewer, INEGI topographic maps, our enlarged-scale topographic maps, compass, and drawing supplies, we set out each day for the countryside. Some parts of the valley allowed us to leave for the country early and return to San Miguel each evening. In other areas, like the Cañada de la Virgen, Luis Felipe and I camped for several nights. But first we struck out down in the valley and along the major tributaries of the Río Laja.

Part of the fieldwork took place during the early months of the rainy season, and we found crossing the rivers the most difficult part of the journey. With the exception of one or two sites, the Safari took us to within a few meters of our final destination. We tried to teach Balbina Martínez, another archaeology student, to drive. Somehow, on a dirt road with nothing but flat grassland for fifty meters on either side of the road, she would scare the shit out of us.

Still, the three of us, Luis Felipe, Balbina, and I, established a work pattern.

Once we located a site, Luis Felipe and I used the compass to triangulate its position on the government topographic map. We then measured the platforms, terraces, and/or foundations with a 100-meter tape measure. When we finished, I drew the volumes of the suspected architectural elements on the preliminary field map at a scale of 1:2,000. Meanwhile, Balbina collected samples of cultural material found on the surface and later plotted their collection area on our preliminary map. In some cases we were able to do several sites each day. It wasn't long before we began to see a simple pattern that helped us to discover more sites along the alluvial soils.

Wherever we found a present-day community, or *ranchería* as they are called in the valley, there was sure to be at least one pre-Hispanic settlement nearby. In other words, the present-day farmers were utilizing the very same alluvial soils that their predecessors had a thousand years earlier! As well, nearly every ranchería had an eighteenth-century chapel, while another few were built around the structure of colonial haciendas. This was convenient and facilitated our documentation of the colonial heritage as we could accomplish it simultaneously with the pre-Hispanic.

Another interesting pattern was the location of lithic materials used by the ancients for tools and construction materials. Invariably, we found modern extractions of these materials where we also found evidence of pre-Hispanic exploitation.

Our survey completed, we began to analyze the data. The first result was that the density of the sites with standing architecture in this northern frontier valley of Mesoamerica was nearly one every ten square kilometers. We presumed that the site density would surely be greater as one traveled south toward the heartland of Mesoamerica. If this was true, then Mesoamerica contained potentially more archaeological sites than previously suggested. We considered this to be an important factor when reviewing the responsibility of INAH for the protection, conservation, and research of the sites.

THE PROPOSAL FOR A NATIONAL ARCHAEOLOGICAL ATLAS

When Dr. Enrique Florescano, the general director of INAH, arrived at the house on Calle Jesús, we were ready for him. The director of INAH's regional office, Rosa María Sanchez de Taggle, had informed us two days before by telephone of his unexpected visit.

Fortunately, we had a lot of graphic resources produced by our settlement pattern study, such as drawings, maps, aerial photographs, photographs, and so forth, and with the help of a dozen students who were actualizing their social service obligations and requirements we hastily prepared a presentation for Dr. Florescano. We agreed that due to my unruly and vulgar Spanish, Luis Felipe would make the presentation, which, compared to the possibilities of the complex computer programs of today, was primitive. We installed several painting easels under the arches and along the east side of the patio of my house. Using the easels as our stands, we taped our graphics to thick mat boards in a logical sequence.

The day arrived and Rosa María appeared at the house with the general director and two intelligent and sophisticated ladies, María José, known by all as "Chapis," and Fridel, known as "Wow!" by the masculine occupants of the lower corridors of the main offices of INAH in Mexico City.

Along with our presentation of methods and techniques used in the settlement pattern study, we argued that INAH needed to know three facts: (1) how many sites there were in the country, (2) where were they located, and (3) what condition they were in. Until then, the institution could not fulfill its obligations to the nation to protect, conserve, investigate, and publicize the national patrimony. Pointing out that due to the density of approximately one pre-Hispanic settlement per ten square kilometers that we had found in this allegedly frontier zone of Mesoamerica, we theorized that the density near the center of this civilization should be greater. If this were the case, then the total number of sites in Mexico with standing architecture must be staggering. We recommended that INAH undertake a National Archaeological Atlas, and further suggested that due to the deterioration of the economic conditions in the country, it would probably be impossible for INAH to fulfill its obligations for all of them.

Dr. Florescano surprised everyone present by declaring that it was the best project he had seen thus far in his inspection of the country. Swelling with pride, we were totally surprised by his next statement: he offered the team the directorship of the National Registry.

I wasn't sure that I had understood him correctly. Luis Felipe and I stood there for several moments just looking at each other, and then Luis Felipe answered, "Doctor, we appreciate your faith in our abilities, but we are a field team. We do not possess the academic, social, or diplomatic qualities and skills that the direction of the National Registry requires."

Dr. Florescano shook his head for several minutes as if unable to believe what he had just heard. On the other hand, you could see the respect and admiration in his expression and gestures for the rest of the presentation. It was obviously time for our next move, which was to fly over the study area.

As we drove out of San Miguel in the direction of the dirt airfield,

Dr. Florescano received a firsthand introduction to the conditions faced by the team. As we bounced along in the old blue Safari, the Plexiglas top began to jump over our heads. I leaned forward and touched the director on the shoulder. "Doctor, if you could hold the top down with your right hand, it won't fly off."

The director did as I suggested for several minutes and then, looking over his shoulder in the direction of Rosa María, said, "These guys need a better vehicle."

When we reached the airstrip, the pilot, Armando Lance, asked us for help pushing the plane out of the hangar. This amused Dr. Florescano as he pushed on the right wing of the plane. He told his assistants that it was too bad we didn't have a camera.

Since there is no control tower at San Miguel's little dirt airfield, we left the ground with no data other than the wind sock in the middle of the runway. As we headed southwest the conversation turned to the Archaeological Atlas. I was seated in front with Armando, Luis Felipe and Dr. Florescano were seated directly behind us, and Chapis and Fridel behind them. Dr. Florescano asked Luis Felipe whom we would recommend to organize the project on a national level. Luis Felipe did not hesitate with his reply: "I think Enrique Nalda has enough experience in settlement pattern studies to do a good job." I was looking over my shoulder at that moment and caught Chapis in the act of sticking out her tongue at me. I could only guess that she wanted the position that Luis Felipe had just recommended for Enrique Nalda.

Dr. Florescano was surprised by the size of the ceremonial center at the Cañada de la Virgen on the "frontier" of Mesoamerica, and I am sure this helped to influence his later decision to go forward with the National Archaeological Atlas. I think he also realized that Mexico had a greater number of sites than INAH imagined.

Heading north over the valley, Dr. Florescano began to ask Armando Lance about his family. Armando motioned for me to take over the controls. The pilot turned around and, laying his arm across the back of his seat, began to tell the passengers of his family's holdings in Guanajuato. Taking this as a cue, I headed the plane north over the Guanajuato mountain ranges so that Armando could show them the family hacienda, San Joaquin de las Trancas, near Dolores Hidalgo.

Suddenly it dawned on them that Armando was completely absorbed in his tale and was obviously not watching where we were going. Chapis was the first to voice concern. "Excuse me, but who is flying the plane?" she managed to squeak out. As Armando didn't bother to turn around to check, it was obvious who was flying the plane. They would have been more concerned had they known that Armando was in the process of giving me my third flying lesson. I had practiced at the little airfield getting the same plane off the ground but I had never landed the damn thing before. I tried to divert my own anxieties by trying not to hit a mountain.

By the time we landed, the director had made up his mind about two things: (1) to go ahead with the Archaeological Atlas—and he requested that we present our project to the two department heads of Colonial and Pre-Hispanic Monuments respectively, at INAH; and (2) to never get into a plane with me again. The result of the two meetings set up the structure for a National Archaeological Atlas using a modified version of our Pilot Project as the basis for the national model.

THE ALLENDE HOUSE

The other unexpected result of our team's labors during this period was acquiring the consent and support of the federal, state, and local governments to restore the old Allende home and adapt it as a museum in Ignacio Allende's honor. This was one of the few times I ever became involved with a Colonial Monument for INAH.

Rosa María was promoting her own project called *El Corredor Museográfico de la Independencia* (the Museum Corridor of Independence) with the state government. The Allende house fit nicely into her program.

The Allende house was purchased by the state government during the late 1970s when Dr. Luis Ducoing was governor of Guanajuato. When the team took over, it had been abandoned for nine years. Rosa María had several meetings with the governor, supported by

Dr. Florescano, before we could move the INAH offices from our home on Jesús to the Allende house, but finally it happened.

Apart from political and diplomatic issues, there was the awful condition of the house; after such a long abandonment the house had some serious problems.

The second-floor roof leaked. The most obvious result was the destruction of the beautiful French-style decorative murals that had been painted on canvas during the Porfiriato era in the nineteenth century. Once these were removed it became apparent that the ceiling beams underneath the murals were in need of replacement. Termites had gotten fat off the neglect.

We had to work around the trenches on the ground floor that crossed the main patio and continued back into the stable area. There were huge holes in several of the first-floor interior walls.

The governor of the state of Guanajuato inaugurated the museum on Allende's birthday, January 21, 1985. The museum is still being enjoyed by thousands of visitors each year.

▦ ▦ ▦   LETTER CONTINUED   ▦ ▦ ▦

Several factors influenced my decision to give up my tenure in INAH.

The first was economic. By the end of 1986, I was earning more pesos per month than I had ever earned before; in fact, I jokingly referred to our family as millionaires. However, at 720 pesos per dollar exchange rate, a governmental announcement of 100 percent inflation over the preceding four years, and with the peso's devaluation accelerating, my salary was no longer sufficient to purchase the computer, cameras, and other high-tech equipment pertinent to my field of Archaeological Documentation. The tens of thousands of pesos I earned each month, converted to dollars, came to the equivalent of US$250. And the same economic conditions fared by our family and work companions were being felt by the entire nation.

On top of this, it did not look like INAH would be able to continue funding the Chichén project. The competition for funds was going to be horrific.

Another factor that influenced my decision to leave INAH was a growing political awareness that Roberto García Moll was going to be the institution's next general director. I had several nightmares during the winter of 1986 and 1987 and all of them involved confrontations with Roberto. Looking back, they were silly dreams. For example, in one of the dreams I found my wrists and ankles chained to a stone wall in a scene reminiscent of Alexander Dumas's *The Count of Monte Cristo*.

> The dungeon was dark but I could make out the shadowy robed figure of a man kneeling in front of me. As he leaned toward me and passed me a bowl of putrid smelling gruel I saw the smirk on the face. It was Roberto.

> However one may want to interpret the dream, one thing was for certain: if Roberto became INAH's general director, I wouldn't get any support.

There was also our family to consider. I had spent so much time in the field that, for the first time in my life, I was beginning to suffer from homesickness. Added to this factor, I had an opportunity to participate in an unrealized economic niche in San Miguel's tourist industry.

So in February of 1987 I resigned. Seven years passed before I returned to the world of archaeology and the site at the Cañada de la Virgen.

▦ ▦ ▦

CHAPTER EIGHT

THE HOUSE OF KNIVES

Cañada de la Virgen Project

WINTER 1995–1996

I stood there and listened to the twins lie to their grandmother and knew instantly the great deceit of the Lords of Xibalba. The boys hadn't overcome the Lords of the Night as they were bragging. The ballgame had been a ruse. It kept the boys distracted. The Lords had deceived them. They planned from the very beginning to allow the boys to escape. Unaware in their haste to get away, the boys had shown the exit portal to the Lords of the Night and they were flowing out of it and upon the middle world even as the boys told their grandmother their tale. Deception and deceit . . . Deception and deceit.

I awoke from my dream slowly. I didn't want to let go of it. But the mere mental struggle of holding on caused the current images to slip from my grasp. Almost immediately, I found myself in the Colonia Roma staring at a policeman guarding the doorway of Cordoba 47. The doorway was the entrance of the General Direction of INAH.

There had to be a message for me in this dream.

Had the deceitful Lords of Xibalba turned loose their demons on the very institution that was established, at least in part, to inves-tigate them? The Lords were clever enough and had observed the institution's weaknesses for decades. Knowing of the envy, greed, and arrogance that inflicted all peoples of the middle world,

*they had chosen this institution to begin their conquest. Void of
transparency, hidden behind the shield of bureaucracy, the Lords
let loose their powerful and extremely viral weapons: grilla and
chisme, cemented together by the ruse of nationalism with an
outlandish individualism.*

In the late fall of 1995, I received a telephone call from Luis Felipe.
I had just returned to San Miguel de Allende for a few days from the
Pacific slope and coast of Michoacán.

"How would you like to excavate the site at the Cañada de la Virgen?"
Even over the phone he couldn't keep the excitement out of his voice. I
responded with enthusiasm that matched his.

"Of course I would! Is there a chance?"

"I can't make any promises, but it looks like our new mayor, Lic.
Jaime Fernández, is interested in the regional project. He has been consulting with the Hotel Association of San Miguel and Jesús Cobian, a city
council member and the owner of the ranch where the Cañada site is
located. They have approached me, and if I can get permission from the
Consejo of INAH and the county government, the hotel association may
help fund at least the preliminary cleaning and mapping of the site."

"How much funding are they willing to contribute?"

"That depends on the report of what we find during the preliminary
phase. I have been promised thirty thousand pesos to begin the first
phase. Is it enough?"

"Maybe, if you are just planning to clear the underbrush off and
map the main structure utilizing a compass and measuring tape. It is
not enough to clean and map the entire site with sophisticated mapping
equipment." Then I continued with the question, "Why is the Hotel
Association interested in helping to fund the project?"

"Obviously, if San Miguel has something else to offer tourists, everyone will benefit. If a tourist spends just one more night in one of their
hotels to see the archaeological site, that will augment the income for
them as well as the restaurants and tour operators. Of course their continued collaboration will depend on whether we determine there are

enough architectural details to make the site interesting for the public. If there are, then Jaime can probably get the state government to help. On the other hand, if we find that it is not worth restoring, at least we will have a preliminary detailed map of the site."

"Okay. But I need time to finish my commitments with the mining company I have been working for. I can finish my report for the president of the company in about two weeks. When do you think you will start the project?"

"Not before late November or early December."

So it was that on the first of December of 1995, I left a job paying me 1,000 pesos per day plus expenses and began a preliminary survey of the Cañada de la Virgen site for 720 pesos per week.

It was cold that winter and hard to get out of bed. Nevertheless, we left San Miguel each morning at eight o'clock in my old '84 Volkswagen van. Later, Luis Felipe borrowed a pickup truck from the Salvage Department of INAH that we used for several months.

Luis Felipe, Pastor Ojeda, the professional photographer, and I stopped at the intersection of the highways between San Miguel and Celaya and Guanajuato, where we picked up Rene Salinas who was from the village of Orduña de Abajo in the municipality just south of ours.

Rene was a volunteer who had an interest in learning something of archaeology because of the sites located near his village. He saw the opportunity for his community to benefit from a project similar to ours. His enthusiasm eventually stimulated the municipality of Comonfort to take an interest in their national patrimony and they formed a protective association.

Rene always carried the bag that provided the group with his wife's prepared breakfast—delicious egg tacos. It was easy for us to heat them, wrapped neatly in aluminum foil and placed gently over the coals of the fire we built each morning. Less than two feet from the fire, the cold stabbed through our clothing. The only way to keep warm was to get to work. Sometime during the first few weeks of work we were joined by a volunteer, Henry Miller. We mexicanized his first name and began to call him Enrique.

By mid-January, we had freed the main structure from the brush and smaller undergrowth. During the process we noticed that a great number of the huizatche and acebuche trees were dying. Many had been invaded by a parasite that looked something like mistletoe and produced a beautiful orange flower but eventually killed the host. Others were dying due to lack of sunlight, covered entirely by an aerial bromeliad know locally as *paxtte*. We made the commitment to eradicate these elements from the vegetation around the nucleus of the site.

The good news was that the existing vegetation had done very little damage to the structures, indicating to us that many portions of them would be intact. The bad news was that the removal of the vegetation revealed the extent of the damage caused by pot hunters. Every structure in the site had been attacked by looters, but the temple on top of the main structure's pyramidal base had suffered the most. Huge piles of rubble from their looting had poured down the east, north, and south sides of the pyramidal base. Whatever fragments were left of the temple lay waiting under the debris.

During the first winter cattle frequently roamed through the site. As a temporary barrier we deposited all of the cutting and pruning we had accumulated during this phase along the lines of an earlier thorn fence that Luis Felipe had made in 1989. This vegetation fence encircled the main structures of the center, temporarily but effectively fencing off eight hectares.

In March of 1996 we finished the survey and Luis Felipe reported our findings to the mayor and suggested that the site would make a good tourist attraction. Immediately thereafter we mounted a public exhibition in the Allende Museum of photographs, drawings, and maps that we had produced. In addition, Luis Felipe held various public meetings in the Allende Museum to inform the public of the possible project.

In the same month, Guanajuato's governor Vicente Fox and other state and local government representatives came to see what we were doing at the site. During the site tour, Luis Felipe proposed to the governor a plan to excavate and restore a portion of the ceremonial center, present a proposal for tourist services, and prepare a preliminary management plan for the protection and conservation of the cultural remains as well as the surrounding natural environment.

When Governor Fox accepted the proposal and made the public commitment to match peso for peso any funding we received, we were filled with euphoria and it was hard to conceal our excitement. His acceptance and promised state resources virtually gave the next phase of work a green light. We were going to excavate at the Cañada de la Virgen!

With smiling faces the entire entourage gathered for a parting photograph near the governor's helicopter. After the governor flew off in his whirlybird, the grounded reporters began to interview Luis Felipe and the owner of the ranch, Jesús Cobian.

One of the local reporters for an English-language newspaper, *Atención San Miguel*, asked Luis Felipe about the actual area of the site. Luis Felipe explained that the main nucleus where the larger structures were located was about seventeen hectares that did not include a causeway extending to the east for almost a kilometer. And our preliminary survey of the area indicated the existence of other associated structures that extended over an estimated 600 hectares that should at least be protected culturally and environmentally. During this level of euphoria, Cobian advised the reporter from the same paper that he planned to create another ecological area of 1,500 hectares of oak forests on the ranch. Portions of both interviews were published in *Atención*.

Everything looked and smelled rosy, but all too soon we found that the Lords of Xibalba were full of surprising deceits.

THE DYNAMICS OF A VISION

For four and one-half years, forty-eight hours per week, we worked at the site in an unbroken chain of field seasons. Since our funding was to come from a variety of sources we began to number field seasons according to when each new funding began. There were ten funded seasons. They began in December of 1995 and extended through January of 2000. The second field season lasted five months. It began during the dry season in April of 1996 and lasted through the summer wet months until August.

We initiated this period by designing our excavation plans and documentation strategies as well as training a team.

Our excavation purposes were twofold. The bottom line for us, as with all archaeological excavation projects, was to look for evidence under all that dirt and rubble that might provide information that would help us to write a portion of the history of the area. But we also had taken on the responsibility to prepare the site for the public visits.

Our overall excavation strategy for accomplishing these goals was fairly simple. We would excavate only strategically selected portions of four of the architectural complexes of the site, which we had labeled Complex A, B, C, and D. There was a variety of reasons for this, and at least to us, they were obvious.

First of all, there were economic considerations. This was the first time in the state of Guanajuato that an archaeological site was projected to be opened to the public. It was also the first time in the state that the archaeological research was being financed, in large part, by three distinct sectors of society: the local government, the state government, and a nongovernmental organization. INAH, apart from their academic and technical support, kicked in about 10 percent of the total funding for the project. Completely excavating any one of these architectural complexes would have cost well beyond the limited funding these sectors were capable of producing at the time we began. Also, past experience at other sites indicated that the more cubic meters of architectural features exposed to weathering, the higher the protection and maintenance cost would be when opened to the public. But there were more than just economic reasons for our strategy of not excavating the entire structure.

Another important reason for not excavating any structure completely was the professional obligation to preserve as much data as possible for future research. With proper funding and the rapidity with which technology and other sciences like physics, chemistry, biology, and botany were becoming involved in archaeological projects, it was more important than ever to maintain this time-honored ethic.

Simultaneously, we were driven by our vision of what we thought could be an excellent holistic educational center. We wanted to treat both the cultural and environmental resources at the site as an open-air museum. A controlled walk through the cultural remains meant having to walk through the surrounding environment. Excavating portions of these four complexes and leaving most areas unexcavated would enhance the educational experiences and archaeological value for the visitor. The visitor would be encouraged to visit the entire site, not just one structure. Aesthetically, the visual impact of the closeness of the environment to the cultural remains provokes important questions concerning the daily lifestyles of the ancient occupants of the settlement. At the same time, the visitor could compare the revealed architecture with the mounds of dirt and rubble that had originally covered them, hopefully gaining an appreciation for the excavation efforts.

When we started, only two members of the team, Luis Felipe and I, had experience working in archaeological sites. Nevertheless, supported by a crew from San Isidro de la Cañada, a student architect, Abelardo Quero, and a newly trained photographer, Enrique (Henry) Miller, during the first five months we excavated over 200 cubic meters and documented almost 5,000 square meters with drawings and photographs, most of which concentrated in the area we referred to as the North Annex.

THE TEAM

What do you say about people you see six days a week over a four-and-one-half-year period? Sometimes there were as many as nineteen people working on the project, but depending upon the activities and funds, there was usually a crew of eight to ten.

During the project, Federico Tapia and I formed a special bond. Federico, like the rest of the crew, was from the village of San Isidro de la Cañada. They either walked or rode horseback the one-and-one-half-hour journey to work every day, arriving at the site at 8 a.m. They returned home each afternoon the same way. Federico was born on the ex-hacienda, down in the Cañada, in a *choza* (hut) located near the present ruins of the hacienda buildings. The bond we share to this day

Figure 22 Toads from the Same Swamp (photo by Henry Miller)

can best be assigned to our common rural roots. It is best expressed by a saying I picked up in Tenosique years before, "*Somos zapos del mismo pantano*" (We are toads from the same swamp).

Enrique Miller is a gas. His love for the outdoors and anything indigenous has no bounds. Nobody could ask for a better companion. However, sometimes he took himself too seriously. But that changed after a small picnic down in the canyon. I don't remember exactly why we got together that afternoon. The mayor, Jaime Fernandez, was there, as well as Jesús Cobian. While we were cooking carne asada, onions, tortillas, and the rest of a typical local picnic in the region, some of the younger workmen from San Isidro showed off on their horses. Finally, Enrique mounted a young mare and took off like a real cowboy. After the initial admirations for Enrique's display of horsemanship, the rest of the group lost interest after he disappeared into some trees along the banks of the river at the end of a cornfield.

I can't remember whom I was talking with at the time, but over his shoulder I saw Enrique as he burst into the open. As my father would say, Enrique was "hell bent for leather." I don't know what his original intention was as he raced along the edge of the river, but the river turned and he didn't. Obviously the mare's wish, after finding a steep embankment and huge chasm in front of her, was to stop. She did. Unfortunately, Enrique did not. The sound of flying gravel from the quick stop of the mare brought everyone's attention to the scene. They were just in time to see Enrique flying across the river with his hands and feet in the position of a jockey flying down the last few lengths to the finish line. The only difference was that Enrique was riding an imaginary horse. Luckily, the only thing hurt was Enrique's self-esteem as he took a lot of embarrassing comments from the young cowboys.

Abelardo Quero, the young architect student, is one of the most enjoyable characters to be around I have ever met in my life. Part of the enjoyment is his sincere, polite, and honest behavior combined with a gleeful appreciation for a practical joke. In short, he is a nice guy. There are not another twenty like him in my life.

THE NATURAL ENVIRONMENT

Our interest in the natural environment of the Río Laja drainage began back in the 1980s during the pilot project. Canvassing over one thousand square kilometers, mostly by foot, we had firsthand knowledge of the present environmental conditions in most of Allende municipality as well as parts of Comonfort and Dolores. What we did not know was the overall environmental condition in the valley one thousand years ago. Was it more heavily forested than today? If so, what kinds of forests and how much of the valley did they proportionally cover? What species dominated the valley? Would heavily wooded areas help define the location and construction of the pre-Hispanic settlements a thousand years ago?

Previous studies have theorized that dryer climatic conditions beginning around 600 AD caused a southward retreat of Mesoamerican farming communities. Yet, if our calculations were correct the valley reached its densest population nearly four hundred years later, around 1000 AD. Was this caused by the retreat of Mesoamerican settlements migrating south? Or was the increase of sites in the valley caused by the expansion of Mesoamerican civilization north?

Most of the 115 sites in the valley were farming settlements, and could be explained by their location along the lower alluvial soils of the drainage system. A more limited number of sites were located near sources of exploitable natural resources, such as basalt for metates, lime for stucco, and a variety of volcanic ryholetic materials used for construction and tools. But one question we could not answer was the impact the surrounding vegetation had on these settlements. One of our problems was that we did not know for sure what kind of vegetation they had to deal with. I began to play "what if?"

Today the scrub oak forests are found on the slopes of mountains and hilltops. Most of these forests are located at or higher than 2,050 meters above sea level. However, during the pilot project we located a few remaining remnants of scrub oak on the south end of the valley as low as 1,950 meters. What if a thousand years ago these oak forests covered the valley down to at least this lower elevation? During the Cañada project I scanned a topographic map of the valley at 1:50,000 and saved it in Adobe Photoshop. Working on weekends I created a layer and imposed the 115 pre-Hispanic sites located during the Pilot Project on the map. (This number included the sites identified by Dr. Beatriz Braniff, which are now under the water of the Allende Dam.) Then I created another layer staining all of the elevations on the map above 1,950 meters green. The resultant graphic proved interesting, if not conclusive.

First of all it extended the hypothetical oak forest across the surface of the valley for hundreds of square kilometers. It brought the scrub oaks right up to the upper edges of the arroyos and tributaries that fed water into the Río Laja. Sixty-eight percent of the sites were located below this elevation. The majority of the sites located above this elevation were concentrated in the southwestern area of the map near the Cañada de la Virgen. Smaller concentrations of sites above this elevation were located on the western skirts of the mountains on the mideastern portion of the map near the present community of

Las Cabras. The few remaining sites above 1,950 meters were scattered along the northwestern region.

Excavating year-round at the Cañada de la Virgen gave us a chance to observe more closely the ecological niches and their changing conditions during the different seasons. Even as we began the first excavation trench, we also concentrated on the *medio ambiente* (natural environment). With the help and instruction of Jaime Ocampo, who was working for a nongovernmental environmental group in San Miguel called Cante, A.C., the team learned how to prune and remove parasites from the trees. Under Jaime's supervision, that first season we also built seventeen filtration dams down the south side of the site in order to recapture soil that was eroding down the hill and forming an arroyo. In the months that followed, we recycled close to fifty cubic meters of dirt from our excavation behind these filtration dams, and these areas have started to produce vegetation once again.

In reality we dedicated an impressive amount of energy to the care and maintenance of the environment over the next few years, most of which went unnoticed by the casual observer or the one-time visitor to the site. Later, comments made in a national newspaper by an INAH authority clearly indicated that he didn't appreciate or even acknowledge the work.

Three times during the four-year period of constant fieldwork, we pruned, thinned, and sanitized all of the trees and cactus within seventeen hectares surrounding the site. It became apparent, if only to the team, that our interventions had created a green oasis in the middle of the ocher-colored surroundings. We also began the preliminary documentation of the flora and fauna surrounding the site. The majesty of it all was the forest of Palo Dulce trees located on a platform just south of the main structure. Over the years, cattle lying and browsing under the shade of two older trees created an environment in which their descendants propagated. The large roots of these grandparents tightly gripped the walls of an ancient structure. By the time we arrived on the scene, the forest had become so dense in places that it was necessary to thin out a few of the trees. The reward for our efforts was glorious.

At the first sign of rain, the grandparents began to densely blossom in long, white, sweet-smelling bouquets. Their soundtrack was the constant hum of thousands of delighted bees. As if allowing it to be so, the two old trees reached out their gnarled arms over their offspring and they, too, began to bloom.

We took more than one hundred photographs of wildflowers as well as dozens of photographs of birds, insects, reptiles, and amphibians and made a preliminary reference catalog that we hoped would be beneficial to any future botanists or biologists who wanted to study the area. And when the government began to build a fence around a five-hundred-hectare area for an ill-fated reforestation project, we even measured the depth of the soil to the bedrock in the post holes they were digging around the site. This gave us a profile of the soil depth every four meters surrounding the entire nucleus of the site.

At one point, César Arias de la Canal, director of the El Charco del Ingenio botanical garden in San Miguel, came out to the site to help us identify plants and began a list of some of the vegetation in the area. And over a period of two years, Enrique Miller, apart from his responsibilities as photographer, identified and made a list of 150 species of resident and migratory birds that showed up in the area. Only once did the environment sneak up on us and pose a threat to the cultural remains at the site.

A shallow reservoir located on the northeast corner of the site had attracted our admiration and curiosity since the very beginning of the project. It was being utilized, as it had been used by owners in the past, as a stock tank for watering the cattle on the ranch. It was the only nearby water available during a great part of the dry season. As a result, we always had cattle grazing through the site during the months of April and May.

Immediately following the first rains of late May or early June, the stock tank began to morph into dynamic demonstrations of life. Two days of rain and we had tadpoles. Two weeks later you could hear the changes before seeing them. As soon as we arrived and turned off the truck motor, the undulating, throttled croaks of thousands of tiny green frogs greeted us through the window of the truck. Within a twenty-four-hour period they spread out across the length and breadth of the site. This turned into a huge banquet for the snakes.

During our initial survey of the site, we discovered two drainage ditches. One of them ran from the higher elevation of the southwest corner of the site along the edge of what we thought to be the pre-Hispanic platform, and drained into the reservoir. As part of our work on the surrounding environment, we cleaned these drainage ditches so that we could observe their function during the rainy season. The exposed bedrock in both the ditches and reservoir was the same material used to construct the pre-Hispanic structures of the site.

We began to suspect that perhaps the people who had constructed the site had quarried the bedrock in these locations for their building materials while simultaneously preparing themselves a source of nearby water. It explained why the builders could construct a settlement in such a location with all natural sources of water more than a kilometer away. If this reservoir had pre-Hispanic roots, then there might be some evidence of a sealant near the bedrock, which would give us a clue to its origin. In May of 1999, near the end of the dry season, when for the first time the reservoir completely dried up, I took a crew out to the center and sank an exploratory pit. I chose the area where the accumulation of silt was the deepest and where we had last seen traces of moisture. Still, it wasn't very deep, and the bedrock appeared just shy of fifty centimeters below the surface.

In this pit, we found the same materials and methods of sealing the floor of the reservoir as we had found in our excavations of the main pyramid complex. The sealant or agglutinant even contained pottery shards and flakes of tooled stone. With this confirmation of pre-Hispanic origins, and after sending samples of the sealant to the labs of INAH, we forgot about it until three months into the rainy season.

The rain that summer had come down rather excessively during a short period of time, and the reservoir filled and began to seep over the edges and run down the slope of the hill to the southeast. Directly in its path were the remains of the kilometer-long causeway. After examining the area of the seepage and its course down the hill, we came to the conclusion that this had occurred periodically for centuries and was probably the principal cause of the destruction of the causeway below the level of the reservoir.

As a temporary solution, and with the expert advice of Mr. Val Nicholson of the Audubon Society, we built an earthen dam almost forty meters long on the southeast side of the reservoir. A spillway was built in the dam to direct the seepage away from the causeway.

Upon only one occasion did the project personnel become directly involved in the affairs of the ranch and it was over an environmental issue. It happened when we tried to rescue over thirty thousand pine trees that were left abandoned to rot and die alongside the road as a monument to a faulty agreement between the state government and the ranch's owner. About fifteen thousand of these trees were transported and relocated in an effort to save them. Nongovernmental groups like the Audubon Society and private individuals from San Miguel de Allende supported the team in this effort. These citizens and groups, interested in environmental issues, provided free packing and transportation, and some, like Val Nicholson, even promised care for the trees. More than five hundred of these small pines were planted in and around the site by project personnel. They were watered and cared for by the crew from San Isidro de la Cañada for over two years and up until January of 2000 when we were denied access to the site by Regina A. Thomas von Bohlen, the present administrator of the property.

Because of our involvement and concern for the environment, we began to discuss the possibilities for an "archaeological park."

THE BUREAUCRACY AND COMMUNITY INVOLVEMENT

I have never worked on an archaeological project, other than the Templo Mayor, that was as scrutinized by the government as the dig at Cañada de la Virgen. Everything we did, whether academic, technical, physical, or financial, was authorized, inspected, supervised, and administered by a wide variety of governmental agencies. For the first time in any project of INAH where I ever worked, members of the National Council of Archaeology of INAH showed up. But in the area of the administration of funds, the bureaucracy was so thick that I often found myself whistling a few bars of "Alice's Restaurant."

During the four-and-one-half-year-period of our project, we went from throwing notes and invoices into a shoe box in our preliminary phase to eventually filling out exacting computerized forms and demonstrating in our budgets the details of how we arrived at them. By mid-1997 Luis Felipe was spending more time in fundraising and administration efforts and less time at the site. In June of that year he made me field coordinator of the project.

Both the state and municipal governments that provided most of the funding treated us like contractors. They asked detailed questions about costs and tried to define our efforts solely in terms of square and cubic meters. Frankly, some of the details they wanted were difficult to provide. One example of their tight controls was that they wanted to know how many four-inch brushes we consumed in a cubic meter of excavation! They were not used to dealing with archaeologists, and we were not used to dealing with them, but in hindsight it was a good exercise for us and it revealed how efficiently our team operated.

From April of 1996 through September of 1999, we excavated over 2,500 cubic meters of material, restored 760 cubic meters of walls and structures, documented over 75,500 square meters of the cultural and natural resources with drawings and photographs, and consolidated 2,600 square meters of architecture. In the office, we captured close to sixteen gigabytes of data about the site and surrounding environment on computers.

From December of 1995 until September of 1999, we received a total of 1,436,459.66 pesos. It is interesting to note that the monetary funds coming from the municipal government were voted upon by the city councils of two city administrations, and both the PRI and PAN political parties gave their unanimous support and consent to the project. For the first time since the law of 1973 and the tragic suicide of Miguel Malo y Bueno, there was an infectious interest in the pre-Hispanic history of the valley. The residents of San Miguel responded by giving their support to the project.

Figure 23 Cañada de la Virgen (photo by Henry Miller)

Figure 24 Cañada de la Virgen (photo by Henry Miller)

The owners of the gas stations in San Miguel gave us credit, hardware stores gave us discounts, others donated space and use of computer technology, and still others volunteered to work in the field or in the office. In short, it was one of the noblest community efforts where I have had the privilege of working. Much of this can be attributed to the frank and transparent posture of the project's dealings with the government and community. Nowhere was it more open than in dealing with the tourist industry of San Miguel.

From December of 1995 until March of 1996, we never saw anyone at the site but the occasional curious cowboy riding by from a neighboring ranch. But after Fox's visit and the press coverage of the event, we began to get visitors from San Miguel. At first it was a trickle, but one day a busload of forty or fifty small schoolchildren showed up, and we found it necessary to put aside our activities and give them and their teachers a controlled and informed tour of the site. As a result of this experience, Luis Felipe decided upon a policy for dealing with visitors and acted immediately by informing the community by means of the local news media.

His policy was very simple. He explained that although the site was not open for massive tourism, we would try to accommodate any group that would prearrange a visit when it would not interfere with our work. Internally, the director made it clear to all of the members of the team that we could not accept any remuneration. Nearly every member of the team at one time or another gave a tour of the site.

As a consequence of his policy, 90 percent of the visitors to the site were nationals (students and teachers from the regional public schools or from one of the universities). Most of the remaining 10 percent of visitors who "toured" the site were either governmental officials from whom Luis Felipe had been seeking support for our project or state and local inspectors. These inspectors came from a wide variety of governmental departments checking on our progress to determine how we were spending the taxpayers' money. A small number of visitors came directly from the tourist industry (hotels, travel agencies, tourism schools, etc.). Luis Felipe and the team tried to use these visits as an opportunity to "pretrain" their personnel so that when the site was eventually opened to the public they would have the correct cultural information, know the rules, and demonstrate respect for the environment of the area.

We modified our vision of the site to accommodate the needs of both the tourist industry and the concerns expressed by the owner regarding the ranch. For example, because of the views he expressed to the city council and president of the hotel association, we changed the area of parking and tourist facilities. Originally, we envisioned the tourist facilities down in the canyon on the southeast side of the ceremonial center. We argued that it was better for the visual environment hidden from the original context of the site, at the same time encouraging the visitor to walk up the pre-Hispanic causeway for the most dramatic approach to the ceremonial center. In the interest of harmony, Luis Felipe conceded to their request and changed our proposal.

INAH approved the design and placement of the facilities in January of 1999, but it was not until late in 1999 that construction of the tourist facilities was awarded to the young architect Adrian López Islas. Finally, the state agency CODEREG (the state advisory board created by Governor Fox for regional social, environmental, and economic development) approved the project and initiated the funding in October of that year for these facilities.

The government had started work on the seventeen-kilometer access road in August of 1998, and the work continued until December 18 of the same year.

Unfortunately, the approved public state funding was insufficient to complete the road, and at the request of Jesús Cobian and the mayor, the project donated some of its funds for diesel fuel for the heavy machinery used in the construction. The road was never completely surfaced and during the next rainy season the team was forced to spend two weeks repairing a large washout in the road on the ranch. Of course we did this in order to access the site, but at the same time our labors and the use of our funds benefited the ranch and those nearby communities that access their ranches by means of this road.

On June 7, 1999, the Cobian family sold the ranch property to a foreigner. In the late morning before final papers were signed, the president and administrator of the new ownership attended a meeting in the city council room of San Miguel de Allende. This was the first time I met Regina Thomas von Bohlen, the new owner.

The focus of the meeting was the Río Laja Project of Hernan Ferro de la Sota as well as our Central Río Laja project headed by Luis Felipe. Attending the meeting were various officials from CODEREG. Also present were members of the municipal government and the director and field coordinators of the archaeological project at the Cañada de la Virgen.

At that meeting, discussions concerned the time frame for opening the site to the public and necessary preparations for hotels, travel agencies, and guides in San Miguel to have correct information and regulations for visiting the site. Luis Felipe explained that two things were needed in order to open the site to massive tourism. Although we were just finishing a preliminary Cultural Resource and Environment Management Plan for INAH's scrutiny, an authorized plan was step one. Step two would be the construction of the tourist facilities. In his estimation the site could not be opened for massive tourism for at least a year.

Near the end of that meeting, I showed Von Bohlen a preliminary proposal I had made in 1998 for future owners of the ranch property. The proposal was provoked by Jesús Cobian's desire to sell the ranch and the fact that he asked for our help. The three stated objectives of the proposal were (1) to enhance the environmental resources that already exist and reintroduce some of the original flora and fauna of the region; (2) to investigate, protect, and conserve the cultural sites on the property; and (3) to stimulate the local economy by creating jobs for the campesino residents.

Once Cobian made his decision to sell the property, real estate agents and potential buyers began to come out to the ranch. Most of them, curious about the pyramid, came by to chat with us. It soon became apparent from our discussions that the majority of the buyers were interested in speculating on the property by buying the ranch, breaking it up in one form or another, and reselling the pieces for profit. We were of a different opinion.

We felt that since this ranch was the largest single piece of property left in the municipality, by keeping it in one piece there was a better chance to protect the cultural and natural resources. So the proposal offered whatever investor various alternatives and corresponding contacts for comparables. I gave the proposal to one of the real estate offices that appeared most often at the ranch.

Von Bohlen, after quickly scrutinizing the document, mentioned that she had read portions of the proposal and said to herself that she would like to meet the person or persons who had written it. This document, along with a copy of new legislation concerning the national patrimony then in front of the Mexican congress and an aerial photograph of the ruins, was loaned to her that day as she left with Jesús Cobian to formalize the purchase.

The next meeting with Von Bohlen took place in the hotel Mansion Virreyes a few days after her purchase of the ranch and at her request. Present at the meeting were Von Bohlen, Jesús Cobian, Agustín Madrigal of CODEREG, Luis Felipe, and I.

At this meeting Von Bohlen expressed her displeasure at the approved placement of the parking area and the tourist facilities. Her idea was to place the parking twelve kilometers from the site where the dirt road leaves the paved highway between San Miguel and Guanajuato. I had never been happy with the approved location of these facilities and regretted the compromise that we had made. I proposed the project's original location for the tourist facilities, explaining its advantages, but she indicated that this would interfere with the management of her cattle on the ranch. This was the same argument that had been used by the ex-owner and one of the reasons that we had deviated from our original plan. Luis Felipe agreed to take her proposal to the INAH authorities. Von Bohlen left the country the next day and it was late summer before I saw her again. As the state INAH offices in Guanajuato were without a director at this time, it was not until the first week of September that

Luis Felipe was able to take her proposal to his immediate superior.

Late in the summer, Von Bohlen returned to San Miguel and came to the site. She talked to Luis Felipe about hiring a stonemason of the project to work for her on the ranch. I was some distance away from their conversation, taking advantage of Dr. Oscar Carranza's (the paleontologist) presence in order to gain more information about the geology of the area, so I didn't hear what was said. But it was obvious that both Luis Felipe and Von Bohlen were agitated. Later Luis Felipe explained that in an earlier meeting with her it had been agreed that she would not offer the stonemason a job until after the rainy season. Nevertheless, the stonemason went to work for her that day and never returned to the project.

The next day, the crew foreman, Federico Tapia, came to me and said that the foreman of the ranch had informed him that Von Bohlen had given him instructions to not let the workmen cross her ranch to get to work. The foreman also told Federico that he would talk with Jesús Cobian in order to straighten the problem out. Whatever happened, the workmen were not stopped from crossing the property until January of the next year.

The next meeting with Von Bohlen took place at my home, where the project offices were located. She arrived with her daughter, and the three of us went upstairs to sit on the terrace. From the very beginning there appeared to be some misunderstandings.

I thought that the reason for the meeting was to discuss the preliminary plan for investors that I had given to her earlier in the summer, but instead she started the conversation by saying that she had discovered that I was in charge of "tourism" at the site. It occurred to me immediately that there was a perception problem, so I tried to explain to her that this was not true. Still, she continued to insist and requested that I stop all visits to the site until she returned the following January. I informed her that I was employed as field coordinator of the project and did not have the authority to comply with her request. I advised her that this was a bad idea because agreements had been reached by different sectors of the government and the civil society, that is, the tourist industry.

She then questioned the legal authority of these agreements. I recommended that she talk with the local INAH representative for answers to her questions and told her that I would go downstairs and get Luis Felipe for her.

I returned in a few minutes with Luis Felipe and he explained the process by which the project had evolved and the various agreements that had been made between the ex-owner and the federal, state, and local governments. She wanted to have information concerning the visitors to the site in her absence and left us with a notebook to record the names and professions of the visitors. Luis Felipe agreed to do this, and Von Bohlen appeared to leave the meeting in good spirits and gave us her feng shui business card with telephone and fax numbers and e-mail address.

Hoping to stimulate the conversation before she left, I asked her if she was finished reading our proposal and the documents that I had provided her earlier in the summer, and she said that she wanted to show them to her mother. But instead she asked me to make a written proposal for tourism at the ranch and site.

It was apparent after this meeting that we were not reading from the same book. She appeared to think that she owned the archaeological site and controlled the road paid for by public funds. We were of a different opinion. Thinking that perhaps not only was she badly informed but also badly advised, Luis Felipe contacted the ex-owner, Jesús Cobian. Licenciado Cobian's legal opinion was that the new owner had every right to put padlocks on the gates across the road, even if the road was made with public funds. According to Luis Felipe, it was Cobian's opinion that the only way to resolve the matter was for the government to expropriate the site.

A few days later, Luis Felipe presented Von Bohlen's idea for the tourist facilities to the new director of INAH for the state of Guanajuato, the architect José Carlos Lozano, and his legal advisor when they visited the site.

The new state director did not like the idea yet gave us an alternative for placing the tourist facilities closer to the site but just outside the ranch property's main gate. He then advised us to seek the opinion of the National Council of Archaeology concerning her idea as well as his compromise.

A week later, in the offices of the National Council located in the Casa de Moneda in the Federal District, we presented both proposals to the council president, Ing. Joaquin García Barcenas. He negated both ideas. After explaining his reasons, he reminded us that we already had procured the permission for the design and location of the tourist facilities from the National Council and should continue with it.

At the same meeting Luis Felipe expressed his concern for protecting the environmental and cultural context that surrounded the nucleus of the site. After explaining that expropriation at the federal level was not an alternative because of the current political conditions in the country, he gave Luis Felipe two options. One was that the state and/or local governments could (but seldom did) expropriate an archaeological zone. The second was for us to contact the state environmental protection agency to see if the area surrounding the ceremonial center could come under their protection by a state decree. Afterward, INAH could sign an agreement with them for the cultural patrimony.

Later in the week we met with the mayor of San Miguel, C. Salvador Garcia Gonzales, and mentioned the two alternatives given to us by the president of the National Archaeological Council. Everyone present agreed that the second option was the best solution for protecting the area around the site. The mayor gave his initial support and expressed his concern that the new owner of the property had placed padlocks on the gates across the access road to the site that had been paid with public state and municipal funds. The mayor then instructed attorney Luis Manuel Rosas, who was the secretary of the city council, to formalize a meeting with the state environmental protection agency. The meeting took place in the offices of the environmental protection agency in the state capitol the following week in late September.

At this meeting, the director of the state environmental protection agency, biologist Raúl Arriaga, explained the different categories of decrees that the state could make in order to protect the environment. Afterward it was agreed that Lic. Rosas would invite Von Bohlen when she returned to San Miguel to a meeting in the city council room, where the state environmental protection agency could present her with their different programs as well as demonstrate their successes. At the same time, the municipal government could bring up the issue of the access road to the site.

As the time was approaching for Von Bohlen's scheduled return to San Miguel, we tried to send her both an e-mail and a fax. Both were returned without reaching their destination. In our letter we had explained our activities during her absence and included the information concerning the visitors to the site that she had requested.

During the first week of October 1999, the meeting took place in the city council room of San Miguel de Allende. Present for all or part of the meeting were Von Bohlen; Jesús Cobian; Lic. Manuel Rosas, secretary to the city council; legal staff of the municipal government; Luis Felipe and myself of the Cañada project; architect José Carlos Lozano, director of INAH of Guanajuato; and Raúl Arriaga from the state environmental protection agency.

Von Bohlen arrived at the meeting with Cobian. She was distressed because a policeman had delivered the invitation to the meeting, and second she stated, "Luis Felipe and Don Patterson betrayed me."

This "betrayal" was due to the fact that I had seen her early the previous morning and had not informed her of the meeting. In reality, we had not been informed of the meeting until later that evening and did not have the information for her.

What transpired next was incredible. After everyone was seated, Doña Regina Von Bohlen pointed a finger at me and asked, "By whose authority is this person here?" Luis Felipe responded that he had invited "this person" as he was the field and documentation coordinator of the project. It was clear from the manner of her facial response that she was still upset, so I asked her if my presence at the meeting bothered her. She indicated that it did, so I excused myself from the meeting and left the room.

Immediately following this meeting the relationship between the new administrator of the ranch and the project began to deteriorate quickly. What followed was a series of wild public accusations concerning Luis Felipe and me in particular and the project in general. Within a few days after the meeting in the city council room, César Arias called Von Bohlen to ask for permission for a small group of schoolchildren to visit the site. She "reluctantly" agreed but not before a vicious assault on the ethics, morality, and professionalism of the project personnel.

Luckily, there was some respite from the torrent of her wrath and gossip, as she left San Miguel and did not return until late December of 1999.

In the meantime, on December 7, 1999, several governmental officials visited the ceremonial center and a portion of the surrounding area. They had been invited by Ruben Perez, the president of the hotel association of San Miguel de Allende. Among them were the state director of INAH of Guanajuato, the Secretary of Economic Development for the state of Guanajuato, the mayor and former mayor of the Allende municipality, and various representatives from the state and local governments. After touring the ceremonial center, these authorities met over lunch, and Lic. Miguel Mendoza, Secretary of Economic Development for the state of Guanajuato, said that the only solution to protect the taxpayers' investment was an expropriation. As none challenged this solution, he instructed Luis Felipe, Ruben Perez, and Eduardo Saravia to visit the office of the state judicial department for the necessary information in order to proceed with the expropriation.

When Von Bohlen returned to San Miguel, she was bent on driving Luis Felipe and me from the site. She not only continued her verbal assaults but also began writing complaint letters to Luis Felipe's superiors in INAH and seeking an appointment with the general director of INAH, Maria Teresa Franco, to present her Archaeological Project. Then on January 17, 2000, she denied access to the project architect, Carlos Adrian López, who was building the control and information booths for the tourist facilities. The following week, Von Bohlen denied access to the workmen from the community of San Isidro de La Cañada.

During this period, César Arias de la Canal met with Von Bohlen in an effort to establish some harmony between her and the project personnel.

Later the same month, on January 27, Von Bohlen met with the judicial department and members of the National Council of Archaeology in Mexico City. Also present were Luis Felipe Nieto; José Carlos Lozano, director of INAH in Guanajuato; Matilde González, director of the Allende Historical Museum in San Miguel; Ricardo Vázquez, attorney for INAH, Gto.; and Fernando Balderas, attorney for Von Bohlen.

At this meeting Von Bohlen requested that INAH sign a *comodato* (lease) giving INAH access to the site for five years with the proposal that only restoration be affected by the government during this period. Afterward, the site would return to the owners of the property for their exploitation of the site. The representatives of INAH would not agree to this proposal. Finally, Regina von Bohlen and INAH agreed to have their positions regarding the comodato in clear focus by February 15.

On February 9, 2000, two members of the National Council of Archaeology arrived by plane to visit the site and talk with Von Bohlen and her lawyer, Alfredo Zavala and company. During the meeting in her attorney's office, Regina proposed that the maximum time for the comodato be nine years. She also proposed that the foundation that she was forming would pay for any investigations at the site for one year if INAH would change the active personnel of the project. Later the group visited the site where Regina told those present that she was going to fence off the site because she wanted to begin grazing cattle in the area. She also proposed that the government remove the *casetas* (structures) that had been left unfinished after she denied access to the architects.

La Raza vs El Gobierno (February 2000–June 2002)

Ironically, the first public comments about the troubles brewing with the Cañada de la Virgen appeared unnoticed by the majority of the Mexican community in the local press. The first report came in the English-language newspaper *Atención San Miguel* on February 7, 2000.

The reporter was covering a city council meeting where one of its members, Claudio Meyer, mentioned that the new owners of the property had placed padlocks on the gates and had negated access to the site. He brought the matter up to the city council for their consideration. Another councilman, Balthazar Robledo, stated that the new owner was his client and that this was a federal problem (INAH) and not the city council's concern (I penciled in the margin at one side of Robledo's response three words and a question mark: "conflict of interest?").

If there was further discussion of the problem at the city council meeting, it was not reported in the paper.

One week later, on February 14, in the same paper the new owner of the ranch property wrote:

> . . . the Cañada de la Virgen belonged to the company that she represented and that included the archaeological site with all of its responsibilities.

But all of this escaped the nationals. It wasn't until February 21 when the new owner was interviewed by the state newspaper, *Correo de Hoy*, that the shit hit the fan. Once again the new owner of the ranch declared private ownership of the archaeological site.

> La señora von Bohlen afirma en un escrito en poder de Correo de Hoy que el sitio arqueológico es propiedad privada de la asociación y, por lo mismo, responsabilidad de la asociación.

In the same article Von Bohlen made unsubstantiated accusations against Luis Felipe and me.

> En una entrevista con este medio, la señora Bohlen hizo severas acusaciones en contra del arqueólogo Luis Felipe Nieto. Dice que el arqueólogo hace tours guiados a la Pirámide—'sin que ella le haya dado el permiso,' cobrando 70 dólares por persona.

Von Bohlen continued by implying that I was trafficking in pre-Hispanic artifacts. According to the article,

> Aseguró que las piezas excavadas se encuentran en la casa del arqueólogo Don Patterson, y no en el museo de la ciudad, donde en su opinión pertenecen. Además, "Patterson no es contratado por el INAH y no debe de estar ahí."

The next day I received a telephone call from Andrea Alvarez, who had been a volunteer working on the project.

"What is going on? Can this foreign woman own the archaeological site as she declared in the newspaper?" she began, and continued with a series of questions including the personal accusations.

She wanted to host a meeting of the community to discuss the two issues and asked if Luis Felipe and I would attend such a meeting and explain the accusations that had been made against us as well as what was happening with the national patrimony.

"Personally, I would be happy to do this but I can't speak for Luis Felipe. As he is the director of the project at the site, you need to call him," I answered.

While Andrea was organizing a meeting of community members, reporters from national newspapers began to pick up on the story.

The first national paper to pick up the story was *La Jornada*. In a one-paragraph article, the reporter condensed the story for the public mentioning the negation of access and the general accusation of Von Bohlen.

Meanwhile, another local English-language newspaper, *The San Miguel Weekly*, began to report on the situation.

On March 3, a group of community members met for the first time in the home of Andrea Alvarez. Marisela and I attended this meeting, as did Luis Felipe and his wife, Rosa.

At the meeting, Luis Felipe was asked to explain the accusations and implications of Von Bohlen's interview with the reporters as well as his understanding of the Mexican law concerning the national patrimony.

The great concern of the majority of those present was the question, tinted with a nationalistic fever, of how a foreigner could own an archaeological site in Mexico. Others wanted to know how it was possible that the new owner could close an access road built with public funds.

After Luis's presentation, Rudy Fernández, then director of the Instituto Allende and brother of the ex-mayor, expressed to me in private his apparent anguish at the situation by saying, "Unfortunately, we can't count upon the help of the Mexican middle class. They don't give a damn about the national patrimony."

At their second meeting, the community members decided on a course of action. They would support the Secretary of Economic Development's decision to expropriate, and simultaneously try to negotiate with the administrator of the ranch property. They also requested that Luis Felipe and I prepare a written declaration describing the project and the events that led to the negation of access and subsequent public accusations.

In support of the expropriation they prepared a letter for the governor that was signed by more than thirty nongovernmental organizations in San Miguel de Allende. A week after sending the letter to the governor, a meeting with the biologist for the state environmental department took place in San Miguel de Allende. This was the last meeting I attended during this phase of the conflict, as Marisela and I headed for Spain and northeast Africa for a month.

At this meeting the biologist said he would try to arrange a meeting with members of the community and Von Bohlen. He suggested that neither Luis Felipe nor I attend these meetings because of Von Bohlen's antagonism toward the two of us. He also pleaded that the committee members not go public until after the upcoming national elections in order to avoid politicizing the problem. The committee agreed. I was flabbergasted!

By the time Marisela and I returned to San Miguel, the committee had met with Regina Von Bohlen several times. At the first committee gathering that I attended, there was an air of depression hanging over the event. César Arias told us that it was difficult to negotiate with her for

Figure 25 Cañada de la Virgen (photo by Ricardo Vidargas)

two reasons. First, she was always in town for a short time and was leaving again without giving anyone authority to deal with the committee. She would not be back until the coming summer. Second, she had made the problem so personal that it was impossible for the committee to meet her demands. César showed us a fax. In response to the committee's suggestion that the site be administrated by a nongovernmental association with her included, Regina wanted Luis Felipe and me off the project and for Luis Felipe to apologize to her publicly.

Even though the committee was unable to negotiate with Von Bohlen, they kept their promise to the biologist and awaited a response from the governor. When it did not arrive within two weeks after the national election, the committee published their first public statement to the state press. As a result, they entered into a new phase of their protest.

For the next several months the conflict raged in newspapers, television, and radio. The committee collected more than thirty newspaper and magazine articles concerning the Cañada. For the most part I tried to stay out of the massive media battle; however, I was eventually sought out by a reporter and interviewed by National Public Radio from the United States.

In September the committee wrote a letter to President Ernesto Zedillo requesting that the Cañada de la Virgen be decreed a national monument. By the afternoon of October 24, the conflict had reached the chambers of the federal diputados (congressmen).

Obviously aware of the situation, the National Institute of Anthropology and History issued a press bulletin and had held a press conference earlier that morning of October 24. According to INAH authorities, the problem was solved. Finally, Von Bohlen understood the Mexican laws concerning the national patrimony and as a consequence had donated sixteen hectares to the nation. As for the allegations of criminal and unprofessional acts committed by Luis Felipe and me, the INAH authorities told the press that there would be an investigation. Four years have passed and I have never been questioned or even interviewed by these authorities.

There is only one way to describe the end of the committee's involvement: stagnant. The committee was facing the enormous, clumsy, and inefficient bureaucracy and finally folded under the weight of it.

Epilogue

The Nine Lords of the Night

Growing up as a kid in the radio and black-and-white movie era, I had two distinct images of an investigator. One wore a fedora and a trench coat with the collar pulled up around his ears and neck. This investigator's face was nearly invisible, as he stayed in the shadows with only the red glow of a cigarette to give away his presence. The other investigator always wore a white smock. If this investigator had gone off the deep end he would have electric, white fuzzy hair, bushy eyebrows, and intensely dark eyes set into black, sunken sockets. The former excited me and the latter frightened me.

INAH Revisited

The National Institute of Anthropology and History provided most of the opportunity, road, and transportation on my journey to Xibalba. Consequently, I am deeply indebted to both the beast and those who sustain it. And what a beast it was.

Not only did it have under its jurisdiction thousands of pre-Hispanic sites, it was custodian for an even greater number of Colonial Monuments. Apart from administrating the great museums like the National Museum of Anthropology and History and the Chupultepec Castle of Maximilian and Carlota, INAH programmed and maintained cultural events at dozens more throughout the country. During this period they built and oversaw the new construction of their university, the National School of Anthropology and History, and managed the internationally known restoration school of Churrubusco. In few of the above activities did I directly participate.

The highly centralized power of Mexico resides on or near the ruins of the ancient capital of Tenochtitlán. I was extremely lucky that my first paying job for INAH was at the Templo Mayor. Moreover, working at the Templo Mayor was exciting apart from the daily new archaeological discoveries. The whole center of the capital had an irrefutable breeze of optimism blowing through it. The future looked great.

The positivism of the period was prevalent before I arrived to work at the Templo Mayor in 1978, but I was there to watch it grow. And everything I experienced inside the Cordoba walls of INAH spoke of promise. Even the director's secretary's name, Esperanza, meant "hope"! I dubbed her office *La Sala de Esperanza* (the Hall of Hope). I imagine that the legislation of 1973 laid the foundation for the positive air that permeated Professor Gaston García Cantú's direction.

How it must have elated the field archaeologists of INAH. Imagine it! They now had federal legislation in place that gave them decisive power in the determination of the national patrimony. Those who looted and trafficked in the patrimony were subjected to very stringent laws and severe punishments. But more important, it gave INAH a mandate to conserve, protect, investigate, and diffuse the archaeological patrimony of Mexico. The frosting on the cake for the more pragmatic bureaucrat was simply, "if you don't protect and conserve, you can't investigate." The field archaeologists now had the laws that protected their own futures.

And as far as I can see, it worked for several decades. Compared to many other countries in Latin America, Mexico virtually stopped the massive looting that had been taking place for centuries. Moreover, after the initial terror caused by the new laws, the institution settled into a policy of realistic adjustment.

The positivism within INAH during this period was probably the result of many more subtle factors than a technician is capable of imagining. But at least three stand out in my mind.

First, though not an economist, I suspect that it was the oil economy and the recent discoveries of promising new oil fields in the Gulf of Mexico and huge gas deposits located in the lower Gulf States and Chiapas that jump-started the positive atmosphere. With all of the alleged and potential monies coming from these resources, Mexico City began to swell as another generation of the "Children of Sanchez" swarmed into the city. Unfortunately, as the population swelled so did the bureaucracy and this included INAH. In short, Social Democracy and the party of the revolution were given a shot in the arm—with oil. Funds were readily accessible, especially for those who wanted to work.

Second, Professor Gaston García Cantú, apart from being a close personal friend of the president of Mexico, was an incredible executive, politician, and diplomat. He not only promoted INAH, the national patrimony, and research, he even pacified the strong movement of the *syndicatilizados* (unionized members) of the institution. Although some critics believed that he gave in too much to the unions and later blamed him for the bureaucratic chaos that became exposed in later administrations, during Don Gaston's administration even the vehicles of INAH displayed a power heretofore unheard of. The presidential seal accompanied by the words "INAH *Poder Ejecutivo*" (Executive Power) was displayed on the doors of the institution's vehicles.

And third, during this period there was a resurgence of pride in the national patrimony unheard of since the golden epoch of Manuel Gamío, Alfonso Caso, and Jose Vasconcélos, one consequence being the swelling up of nationalistic fervor. Of course, this was augmented within and outside the institution by the discovery of the Coyoloxauqui and the subsequent excavations at the Templo Mayor.

Don Gaston was the first general director of INAH to come from outside the ranks of the institution. Yet, he is remembered fondly as the director during the "good old days" by many of the employees of INAH, especially the archaeologists and obviously at least one technician—me.

Under Don Gaston's direction, the national patrimony was protected vigorously. I remember in 1978 flying out of Pedro Joaquín's small airfield in Tenosique, Tabasco, with Roberto García Moll. Just a few minutes in the air brought us over a cal factory that the Mexican Army was in the process of surrounding. They had instructions to close it down because the owners were using the cut and faced limestone building blocks from a nearby archaeological site as their base material. The National Institute of Anthropology and History protected their patrimony more than any other country in North and South America. Nevertheless, some foreign archaeologists have implied that INAH jealously guarded its patrimony by denying them intellectual access. Along those lines, I was surprised to read Michael Coe implying in his book on Maya hieroglyphic history that Mexico was suffering from xenophobia. I found that not to be the case. Indeed, I found things to be quite the contrary.

It seemed to me there were foreigners everywhere! I stumbled or bumped into them on every project I worked on in INAH, including but not limited to the Mexican states of Yucatán, Chiapas, Tabasco, Oaxaca, Federal District, Guanajuato, and Veracruz. In reality, there were globalizing efforts in Mesoamerica as investigators, documenters, and epigraphers came from all over the world to work in Mexico. From the United States, investigators came from universities such as Harvard, University of Michigan, University of Colorado, Tulane, Peabody, University of Arizona, University of Texas, Stanford, and Purdue. And in less than a decade, there was even a project from Yale.

If the investigators of INAH had a phobia, it was caused by strong social nationalistic fervor added to a dislike of gringo foreign policies in regard to Latin America—in Cuba, Chile, Argentina, Bolivia, and so forth. Mexico became a refuge for many leftists in Latin America and elsewhere during the late sixties and all of the seventies. A large number of young leftist Chileans sought, and were granted, political asylum in Mexico in order to escape the death squads and dictatorship of General Pinochet. A number of them found employment in INAH. One of them in particular, who worked in the administrative secretary's office, used to annoy the hell out of me because I could only understand one phrase of his Spanish, "No hay dinero!" (There is no money!). As

I found out dealing with the ENAH students in Yaxchilan, Templo Mayor, and Monte Alban projects, gringos were suspect, and as far as I know, there were only two who worked for INAH at that time, Dr. Marcus Winters in Oaxaca and me.

In spite of Don Gaston's publication, "North American Interventions in Mexico," and the museum he inaugurated by the same name, if he hated gringos as Dr. Grove suggested, he was without equal as an actor. In reality, he never showed me anything but the utmost respect and consideration. This was certainly not the case on the shelves of bureaucracy below his office.

I will have to admit that there was a widespread antigringo sentiment within the institution. I am sure that some very powerful academic and administrative figures of INAH held similar attitudes. Some of these figures were even members of the National Council of Archaeology, known as the *Consejo*. The Consejo made all of the final decisions about any archaeological projects in Mexico. Yet, for all of the criticism they had (which they probably still get), most of them tried to be "just" if not completely impartial. And the only time it got messy was when there was a battle of funding or something personal between the authority and the investigator. Actually, it was fairly simple.

INAH set the rules and those foreigners and nationals who broke the rules were made persona non grata in INAH. It didn't matter how bright the light of your star shone outside of Mesoamerica; in Mexico you followed their rules. Those who kept the rules were given more chances. Even though many of them returned season after season, they bitched about the bureaucracy. But everyone did that, even the nationals.

I don't know if INAH's bureaucracy was something special or not, but the little contact I have had with other areas of the government leads me to suspect that it was not. I do know one thing for sure: good news traveled a hell of a lot slower that bad news did.

When one hoped for expedience from INAH, displaying arrogance or anger was like throwing wrenches into the machinery. And when you were awaiting a suspected negative to your request, it arrived almost as fast as "Montezuma's Revenge." Late-night telephone calls suggesting proposals and solutions that preceded official notification added more excitement.

Ironically, the bureaucracy became bloated with the best of intentions. What they didn't realize was that the institution's eyes turned out to be "bigger than its stomach." Hiring bodies was a good humanistic approach to spending the oil monies; but as oil prices dropped, dollars flowed outside the country, inflation soared, and the peso devalued, the illusion of positivism began to disappear. In fact, the mixture was so bad that a common joke was that the president was going to receive the Nobel Prize for Chemistry that year because "he had turned the peso into shit."

In hindsight, I realize that I hadn't the faintest idea of the importance of Don Gaston's social and political connections. The funding and power behind his direction in the institution was immense. I was content to keep out of his hair and ignorant of his political affairs. I consciously stayed out of things—as we say in English, I played dumb. However, on many occasions as I waited in the Hall of Hope, I would consider the man in the other room and as a consequence I have come to the conclusion that I have never known another man who loved his patria more than Don Gaston.

Then came the Madrid era and Dr. Enrique Florescano took charge of an institution that was forced into a radical change.

DR. ENRIQUE FLORESCANO

Dr. Enrique Florescano took over the controls of INAH as the entire nation was beginning to morph. Plagued with enormous social and economic problems, the executives within the palaces of power above INAH began to change the focus of their previous cultural policies. During the next six-year period, the institution retreated from an executive posture. In the process of doing so, it revealed some of the weaknesses of the institution.

Without the funding and political power of the prior administration, INAH had changed from having executive power to becoming an administrative arm of the secretary of education. Gone were the impressive and powerful presidential seals, and in their place the small center of the Aztec calendar with the letters "INAH–SEP." Mexicans have a saying that seems to fit the situation: "De árboles caídos hacemos leña" (Out of fallen trees we make firewood). In this decaying environment, and only thirteen months after assuming charge of INAH, Dr. Florescano decided to visit the INAH offices in Guanajuato.

When he arrived unexpectedly in San Miguel in 1983, we made an equally unexpected presentation. In our Pilot Project, we argued for a National Archaeological Atlas. Dr. Florescano was impressed, and as a result the Archaeological Atlas became a national project for INAH.

The National Archaeological Atlas project was never completed. I hate to admit it, but even some of the most important researchers of Mesoamerica protested the concept. More than a decade after proposing to Dr. Florescano the Archaeological Atlas, I ran into Dr. Ian Graham in Yaxchilan and he chided me for promoting the atlas and gave the most often used argument against it.

"It would create a road map for looters," he stated emphatically.

Out of my deep respect, admiration, and even awe of Dr. Graham, I did not answer him.

I had heard this argument so many times before and it just didn't jive with my empirical field experience. In fact, it is an intellectual myth. I would be willing to bet a hundred dollars that Dr. Graham has never visited a Mayan archaeological site that has not been looted prior to his arrival. As Dr. Paul Schmidt recently said when we were discussing the pros and cons of the atlas project, "The looters already know where the sites are. It is the archaeologists who don't know where they are."

ILLUSIONS

Many changes have happened in Mexico since I left INAH nineteen years ago. During that time the institution went through a restructuring. However, mindsets are hard to change and the institute lumbers along with a seeming inability to cope or provide legislative solutions for the problems of the twenty-first century.

For example, the neoliberal economics of globalization, NAFTA, and the Salinas amendment to article 27 of the constitution, allowing the privatization and sale of ejido (communal) lands, have spurred an enormous growth in land speculation within the municipality of San Miguel de Allende and area of the Pilot Project. As a consequence, land values are skyrocketing as people move into the area. With privatization come walls and fences. It remains to be seen what is happening to the archaeological patrimony behind the fences, gates, and padlocks that now surround these properties and the majority of the hundred sites in the valley.

Perhaps more significantly, the movement of the indigenous community that began in Chiapas challenges the very roots of Mexico's search for a national identity and hence INAH's reasons, means, and strategies for protecting the national archaeological patrimony.

According to William Golding's essay "Thinking as a Hobby," merely being critical is grade-two thinking. In an effort to be a grade-one thinker, I suggested the following while having lunch in Eduardo Matos's house with a federal congressman, Dep. Luis Alberto Villarreal, and Dr. David Carrasco from Harvard:

- Finish the National Archaeological Atlas because INAH still needs to know the answer to three things: (1) how many archaeological sites with standing architecture are there in the country? (2) where they are located? and (3) what is their condition? This information is the basic data in order to develop the necessary criteria for how and what archaeological patrimony Mexico can feasibly conserve. The actual fieldwork should be carried out by small but professional technical teams that include specialists like cartographers, photographers, and draftsmen.

- With the data collected in the atlas, decide how and what patrimony Mexico can realistically protect and conserve in each state, municipality, or cultural region. In the Pilot Project, for example, we came to the conclusion that only eighteen of the one hundred archaeological sites we found (with standing architecture) within a thousand square kilometers were worthwhile academically to investigate or economically feasible to protect. And of those eighteen, only two or three had any economic value to the region, that is, tourism. Perhaps the most important criteria for our selection of sites to protect were based upon the overall physical condition of each site. However, this might not be the case in another area. For example, over 80 percent of the sites we located in the Pilot Project were mortally damaged academically and economically by pot hunters.

• Pass the proper legislation. The spirit of the present law governing the archaeological patrimony is good. However, it is full of holes that need to be plugged. Also, legislation should be passed giving the National Consejo absolute power over the academic and technical, as well as judicial, aspects of Mexico's archaeological patrimony.

• A few years ago, Dr. Alejandro Martínez implied in an interview on National Public Radio that INAH would have to negotiate each case individually. It is obvious that la raza wants a "voice" or some self-determination and INAH needs a crisis management team for dealing with these problems.

• Diminish the administrative responsibilities of the federal government by turning them over to a combination of state and municipal (or regional cultural) governments, as well as, and perhaps more importantly, nongovernmental organizations. Why? Because an excessive number of trained archaeologists are employed by INAH as administrators. Most of them are located in the Federal District far away from the regional and local problems. It would be interesting to see the results of meeting INAH's obligations to conserve, protect, investigate, and educate if a greater number of archaeologists (investigators) were working in the field rather than having administrative assignments in INAH.

My friend Mario Perez Campa, the current technical secretary of INAH, argues that turning over the administration of the archaeological patrimony to the state and municipal governments would end in disaster by provoking massive looting and abuses. However, I would argue that INAH has no idea today whether the archaeological patrimony within the one thousand square miles of the Pilot Project is being destroyed anyway. As far as I know, only a few of these sites have been inspected since the Pilot Project.

Also, la raza is much smarter than the government gives them credit for. Establishing an NGO in each municipality or cultural region for the protection of the archaeological patrimony creates a grassroots vehicle for educating the public as well as a watchdog organization for any abuses in the state and municipal government's administration.

Whatever the future holds for the archaeological patrimony, INAH will have to transform itself in order to meet the challenges of tomorrow.

FINAL LETTER TO JESSICA

In this way, the Lords of Xibalba were overcome. Only by the miracle of their own transformation could they (the Hero Twins) have done it.

—*Popol Vuh*

▣ ▣ ▣

It seemed like the first question I was always asked at any social gathering in San Miguel de Allende was, "What is the most important discovery you have ever made?" My frequent reaction was to disappear into my impersonation of James Thurber's Walter Mitty.

I have worked on more than 150 archaeological sites from Honduras to northern Mexico, and when asked this question I would systematically run through the romantic project names in my head.

An overwhelming torrent of images of people, environments, books, and archaeological sites with euphonious names like *Popol Vuh*, *Chilam Balam*, Ococingo, Eugenio May, Victor Ik Tun, Usumacinta, Totonaco, Copan, Quirigua, Tikal, Tatiana Proskouriakoff,

Yaxha, Chincultic, Yaxchilan, Monte Alban, Tenochtitlán, Chichén Itzá, Comalcalco, Río Bec, etc., would flood my mind. It was much like mulling over a shopping list.

By the time I was ready to reply with something like, "That is very difficult to answer," the questioner had usually, and very stealthily, disappeared, perhaps looking for a conversation that better satisfied the need for instant gratification. I stopped getting invited to cocktail parties.

Then a number of years ago I read of the young Mayan epigrapher David Stuart's reply to the same question. "The last one," he responded. I used this response a few years ago but so far I have not got invited to any more cocktail parties. Go figure.

La neta (the bottom line) of my advice is that you should do something with your life that excites you. Once you find out what it is, don't let go of it until you have no other choice, such as an act of God or senility in old age.

The lesson in this story is simple: in order to defeat these archetypal Lords you must either be smarter than those of the Infraworld or at least *menos pendejo* (less dumb). The journey for me has been full of challenges and there were many pitfalls along the way. Some of the pitfalls were provoked by my own mistakes. As time and direction draw me relentlessly closer to Xibalba, I have used this tale to check on myself.

Whatever happens, I would like to be part of it. I understand that the Tibetans have a saying, "The yak is slow but the earth is patient." But as I told you in Mexico City, I am sixty and don't have the time to wait on an administration change, as some friends have suggested, in order to become involved again. The Lords of Xibalba are tricky, right? I don't have very much patience.

▦ ▦ ▦

INDEX

Page numbers in italic text indicate illustrations.